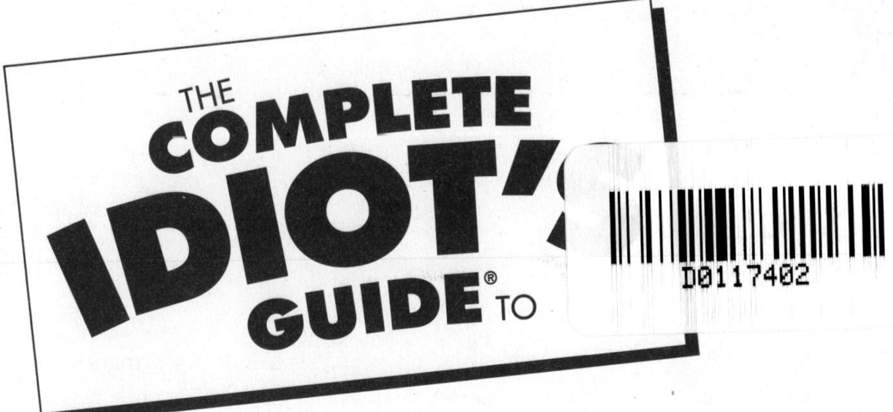

D0117402

Real Estate Investing Basics

by *David J. Decker and George G. Sheldon*

A member of Penguin Group (USA) Inc.

Dave: For Bobbi
George: For June

ALPHA BOOKS

Published by the Penguin Group

Penguin Group (USA) Inc., 375 Hudson Street, New York, New York 10014, U.S.A.

Penguin Group (Canada), 10 Alcorn Avenue, Toronto, Ontario, Canada M4V 3B2 (a division of Pearson Penguin Canada Inc.)

Penguin Books Ltd, 80 Strand, London WC2R 0RL, England

Penguin Ireland, 25 St Stephen's Green, Dublin 2, Ireland (a division of Penguin Books Ltd)

Penguin Group (Australia), 250 Camberwell Road, Camberwell, Victoria 3124, Australia (a division of Pearson Australia Group Pty Ltd)

Penguin Books India Pvt Ltd, 11 Community Centre, Panchsheel Park, New Delhi—110 017, India

Penguin Group (NZ), cnr Airborne and Rosedale Roads, Albany, Auckland 1310, New Zealand (a division of Pearson New Zealand Ltd)

Penguin Books (South Africa) (Pty) Ltd, 24 Sturdee Avenue, Rosebank, Johannesburg 2196, South Africa

Penguin Books Ltd, Registered Offices: 80 Strand, London WC2R 0RL, England

Copyright © 2006 by David J. Decker and George G. Sheldon

All rights reserved. No part of this book shall be reproduced, stored in a retrieval system, or transmitted by any means, electronic, mechanical, photocopying, recording, or otherwise, without written permission from the publisher. No patent liability is assumed with respect to the use of the information contained herein. Although every precaution has been taken in the preparation of this book, the publisher and authors assume no responsibility for errors or omissions. Neither is any liability assumed for damages resulting from the use of information contained herein. For information, address Alpha Books, 800 East 96th Street, Indianapolis, IN 46240.

THE COMPLETE IDIOT'S GUIDE TO and Design are registered trademarks of Penguin Group (USA) Inc.

International Standard Book Number: 1-59257-516-1
Library of Congress Catalog Card Number: 2005938297

08 07 06 8 7 6 5 4 3 2 1

Interpretation of the printing code: The rightmost number of the first series of numbers is the year of the book's printing; the rightmost number of the second series of numbers is the number of the book's printing. For example, a printing code of 06-1 shows that the first printing occurred in 2006.

Printed in the United States of America

Note: This publication contains the opinions and ideas of its authors. It is intended to provide helpful and informative material on the subject matter covered. It is sold with the understanding that the authors and publisher are not engaged in rendering professional services in the book. If the reader requires personal assistance or advice, a competent professional should be consulted.

The authors and publisher specifically disclaim any responsibility for any liability, loss, or risk, personal or otherwise, which is incurred as a consequence, directly or indirectly, of the use and application of any of the contents of this book.

Most Alpha books are available at special quantity discounts for bulk purchases for sales promotions, premiums, fund-raising, or educational use. Special books, or book excerpts, can also be created to fit specific needs.

For details, write: Special Markets, Alpha Books, 375 Hudson Street, New York, NY 10014.

Publisher: *Marie Butler-Knight*
Editorial Director/Acquiring Editor: *Mike Sanders*
Managing Editor: *Billy Fields*
Development Editor: *Nancy D. Lewis*
Senior Production Editor: *Janette Lynn*
Copy Editor: *Emily Garner*
Illustrator: *Chris Eliopoulos*
Cover Designer: *Bill Thomas*
Book Designer: *Trina Wurst*
Indexer: *Julie Bess*
Layout: *Ayanna Lacey*
Proofreading: *Mary Hunt*

Contents at a Glance

Contents

Appendixes

Introduction

Welcome to *The Complete Idiot's Guide to Real Estate Investing Basics*. We are delighted to be your special tour guides as you learn the basics about real estate investing. We realize your goal is to learn more about investing in real estate. While it is not nearly as complicated as brain surgery, sometimes you might think it is. There are many things to learn. Along the road to your first and subsequent purchases of investment property, you will find bumps and pitfalls. We'll do our best to warn you and guide you through to success.

Real estate remains one of the best investment opportunities available to the average person. No advanced education degree, certifications, or licenses are required. There are no glass ceilings here. Anyone and everyone can be successful.

One important thing to always keep in mind is that there are no quick, easy shortcuts to immense fortunes and income. This is not a get rich quick scheme. But you can get rich slowly. Right now, you probably already have a job where you're working hard. If you're an employee, then some business owner or stockholder is already getting rich from your efforts. In real estate, you will still need to work hard, but now the chances of your hard work counting for something are much greater. You can find success through a methodic process of intelligent investing—and that is something we will show you in these pages.

In fact, that's one of the beautiful things about investing in real estate. Anyone can get started doing this. Using real estate as an investment, you can make money. It is one of the best proven methods for ordinary people in America to greatly improve their financial situation.

Over the long term, you should see a return of approximately 20 percent on your real estate investments. You might do even better.

Please understand that if you are sloppy with your real estate investments, you are not going to make as much money. In fact, you could lose money by overpaying for properties. If you are lazy and do not complete your homework, you might invest in properties needing expensive and extensive repairs, or rent to deadbeats who will never pay the rent they owe you. It is up to you as to how much you will—or will not—earn from real estate investing.

There are many different ways to make money by investing in real estate. Some of those methods include deceit or dishonesty. We're not going to advocate any such thing. If you are looking for techniques to trick an aging widow out of her lifelong residence, this is not the book for you.

Real estate investing requires honest work. If you are not willing to do the work, don't expect big returns or even mediocre success. We're going to show you how to make money legitimately, honestly, ethically, legally, and morally. We look at this as a long-term investment strategy. We will show you how to find investments that will provide safe and reasonable returns to you. You will earn your money the old-fashioned way: by working for it.

And we will show you how to do this repeatedly, so you can build your portfolio as large as you desire. You are going to learn how to do this primarily with residential properties, but we will also cover other types of properties that can become successful real estate investments.

While we do not think this is the only book you will ever read about real estate investing, we endeavored to make it the best one to use to get started. We have tried to write a book that will serve as a guide to get you started in the least amount of time, and to help you find and acquire profitable properties.

You will have a lot of work to do and many things to learn on the road to becoming a real estate investor, and as such, we've tried to make the tasks easier for you. This book can help you in many ways, and certainly help you focus on the most important things.

How This Book Is Organized

We have organized this book into five main sections. Here is what you will find in each part:

Part 1, "Getting Started in Real Estate," is where we get started talking about real estate investing. In the chapters in this section, we introduce the basics, and discuss different types of real estate. We cover the concepts of homes, and why someone would want to live in any particular area. We soon delve deeper into real estate investing, as you learn about properties acquired to make money. Finally, we describe the people that you need to help you invest in real estate, and how to make sure you find only the best at what they do.

Part 2, "Finding the Properties," is where we roll up our sleeves and help you find the properties that are good investments. We start off telling you where to buy, and what to avoid. We offer solid advice on those kinds of properties that are sure to be solid investments for you. You will learn how to identify the gems from the marginal properties. You will learn how to educate yourself about the local markets, and what it takes to find properties. Then you learn about foreclosures, checking out the numbers, and finally, how to make offers to purchase.

In **Part 3, "Locating the Money,"** you will learn how to finance your purchases. You will learn the ins and outs of dealing with bankers and others who want to lend you money. You will learn when to seek seller financing. We include information that will help you get your loan approved quickly and easily. You will learn about traditional and nontraditional financing. Just as important, you will learn about the costs associated with purchasing property. And you are going to learn the truth about buying property with no money down.

Part 4, "Managing the Property," provides the information you need to make money with your investment property by managing it correctly. Here you will learn how to find tenants, manage them, and make sure you get the money you are owed. You will learn how to maintain your property. We'll discuss the types of improvements you should make, and how to fix up a property to sell it. We will conclude this part of the book by helping you control your expenses. As you read Part 4, you will learn how to solve the problems associated with owning real estate investment property. From dealing with problem tenants to completing repairs, this part of the book will help you avoid the pitfalls so many investors face. You will also learn when it is time to sell your investment property. Finally, we are going to tell you about the headaches no one ever told you about, and how to deal with them.

Finally, in **Part 5, "Beyond the Basics,"** we conclude by taking you far beyond the basics of real estate investing. We provide you with lots of needed information to take your real estate investing to the next level. We will tell you how to keep acquiring properties so that you can grow as big as you want. We'll show you how you can go from a part-time to a full-time investor and how to refinance and improve your properties. And you'll learn about investing in commercial properties, and how to maintain your positive cash flow.

What to Do First

While you are most likely excited about the prospect of getting started investing in real estate, we recommend that you read this entire book. As we prepared the text, we endeavored to make this book both a learning manual and reference guide. You will be best served if you read the book, and then go back to sections when you need a reference.

Skipping sections in an effort to get started quickly probably will not work. You are likely to miss important or key information. We suggest you take your time, and read the book entirely.

Extras

Be sure to check out the Appendixes for additional information and useful forms that will help you buy, sell, and rent real estate.

This book is packed full of information, tips, explanations, and real estate techniques. Many tips, tools, advice, and specific information are offered to you in sidebar boxes. You will find these useful in understanding the topic.

Here are the tips that are provided in these sidebar boxes:

Author's Advice

These are tips and information that anyone learning about real estate might find useful.

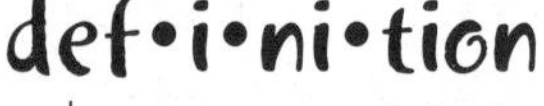

Here you will find useful terms and their definitions.

Buyer Beware

These boxes contain warnings and information that you should carefully consider before going forward.

Real Deal

These boxes contain facts, things you probably don't know, and odd information about the real estate industry—information to pique your interest.

Acknowledgments

The authors especially want to thank Robert (Bob) Diforio for his guidance, help, and direction in bringing this book to life. As our agent, he had the foresight to bring us together as a team to produce this book.

We also want to thank the entire team at *The Complete Idiot's Guide* offices for helping to make this book what it is. We especially want to thank Mike Sanders for his patience and assistance in making this a better book.

Trademarks

All terms mentioned in this book that are known to be or are suspected of being trademarks or service marks have been appropriately capitalized. Alpha Books and Penguin Group (USA) Inc. cannot attest to the accuracy of this information. Use of a term in this book should not be regarded as affecting the validity of any trademark or service mark.

Part 1

Getting Started in Real Estate

Some new investors constantly complain there are few good investment properties to find. When you hear that, you are simply listening to someone who is not looking hard enough or in the right places. There are investment prospects in every community. Each day presents more real estate investing opportunities for the astute investor.

Doing what you are doing now is the best place to begin. Educating yourself about investing in real estate is a smart strategy. As an active investor, you should always be learning as much as you can about buying, holding, and selling real estate.

Chapter 1

Why Real Estate Makes Sense

In This Chapter

- Learning why real estate is a worthy investment
- Understanding different types of residential property
- Defining real estate market cycles
- Learning about other real estate types

Investing in real estate makes sense in many different ways. There are other investments that make money, but real estate has several unique characteristics. Real estate ownership includes emotional bonds.

Real estate investing is not a passive investment. It is not something you can buy and forget. It requires management and constant maintenance. You have to pay attention to the details—from leaks to insurance payments.

Real estate experiences different market cycles in response to changing market conditions. Real estate is not immune from the business cycle. Changes in market conditions can make for buying opportunities in different stages of the business cycle.

In this chapter, you will learn how and why real estate should be part of your investment plans. You will study real estate cycles and the different types of residential real estate investments. The chapter closes with a brief introduction to commercial real estate.

Should Real Estate Be a Part of Your Investment Plan?

There are many investment choices for today's investor. From savings bonds to the stock market, from fine art to baseball card collections, there are many different opportunities to make money by buying and investing. Real estate is just one choice of many.

Real estate is unique compared to most other investments. By investing in real estate, you can:

- Achieve a positive monthly cash flow.
- Use a small amount of money to buy the investment.
- Use other people's money to buy your investment.
- Take advantage of appreciation—the value of the property is likely to be worth more in the future than it is now.

Consider the differences between real estate investing and other possible places to invest your money. Walk into a bank, and ask to borrow $100,000 to invest in the stock market. You will soon be leaving without a free coffee mug. But walk into the same bank and ask to borrow the same amount of money to buy real estate, and watch the reaction. Not only will you receive royal treatment, your application will cheerfully be taken and accepted. You will receive free pens, coffee mugs, and who knows what other gadgets with the bank's name on them just for asking for the money.

You have to ask yourself why a banker would want to lend money to you against real estate, but would give you the cold shoulder to borrow the same amount for many other investments. The answer is simple: bankers know that real estate holds its value. Sure, they're going to put you through the wringer to protect their loan. Nevertheless, you can be assured that if they can make the loan, they will.

Real estate is a thing. You can see it, touch it, live in it, change it, and enjoy it. Try to do that with a futures option. Few people understand complicated financial documents, but they sure understand what a two-story, three-bedroom, two-and-a-half bath, two-car garage home on a half-acre lot means. They know you can enjoy living in it and it can become their special sanctuary in the world.

They understand if you want to own it, you have to pay $200,000 (or whatever the current price is). They understand over the years, if it is maintained, it will be an asset worth at least $200,000, or more.

Real estate investing allows you to build *equity*. This quickly reflects in your net worth. Almost without exception, the longer you own the real estate, the higher your equity and the higher your net worth.

def•i•ni•tion

Equity is the cash value of your real estate minus any debt owed on the property. For example, if you could sell your property for $250,000, and you owed $160,000, your equity in the property would be $90,000. ($250,000 – $160,000 = $90,000)

Comparing Real Estate to Other Possible Investments

There are many other types of investments available today. You can invest in the stock market, coins, or collectables. You can also invest by placing your money in a certificate of deposit (CD) or a simple bank savings account.

Real estate does have some drawbacks. As an investment, understand that your real estate has special characteristics:

- **It is not liquid.** If you want your money out of your real estate, it could take some time to sell it. It could take you months before you have any cash in your hands.
- **It is expensive to buy.** Real estate is not available for just a few dollars.
- **It is costly to buy and sell.** There are specific costs associated with buying and selling. The buyer and seller pay fees such as transfer taxes, title insurance, and brokerage commissions associated with each purchase.
- **It will complicate your tax return.** You might need professional help rather than preparing it yourself. You will also need to keep an accurate bookkeeping system.
- **It requires you to remain actively involved in the management and supervision of your property.** This means you must collect rent, manage tenants, pay expenses, arrange for repairs, complete inspections, and more—or pay a property management company to perform these services for you.

Other financial investments are far less labor-intensive than real estate. If you put your money in a certificate of deposit, there is nothing more to do than to keep the document in a safe place. Periodically, you receive your interest income and that's about it. Of course, your return is likely paltry compared with what you could have earned from investing in real estate.

Investing in the stock market is more risky—and needs your constant attention. When the market drops, you have to decide how much you are willing to lose before selling. When the market rises, you have to decide if it is time to sell, or keep holding. The market can turn volatile on the day's news, which is one reason you have to watch your investment.

Real Deal

There is an emotional attachment to real estate. No one has fond memories of growing up with shares of stock in a company, but people love to recall their childhood days growing up with a backyard, or eating Thanksgiving dinner at Grandma's house. No other investment tugs at the heartstrings more than real estate.

Collectables are fun. There are plenty of stories about someone who has collected something in their basement that is worth money. Stories make the news about someone finding something in an attic that was sold for thousands of dollars, dramatically higher than its original worth. What the news does not report is that most collectibles are risky investments. They are difficult to sell and can be expensive to liquidate. You have to be an expert in the area you are collecting to make money. You should invest in collectables only because you would enjoy owning and keeping them, without concern about what they might be worth in the future.

In good or bad times, people always need a place to live. In hard times, people will sell all their other investments, turning them into cash, just so they can keep their home. These circumstances make real estate a safer investment opportunity than most alternatives.

Risks and Rewards

There is a risk associated with all investments. Some risks are greater than others are. For example, investing in certificates of deposit is much less risky than investing in common stocks. As for the risk associated with investing in real estate, there is always a chance the property could prove to be worth less than its purchase price (especially if you paid too much when you bought it). For example, without proper maintenance, your property could rapidly decrease in value.

No matter how much or how little money you have to get started, real estate investing offers specific advantages:

- **Tax benefits.** As a real estate investor, the Internal Revenue Service is on your side. You can lessen your tax obligations by claiming legal deductions available to you.
- **Quick and easy start-up.** You can start investing in real estate quickly. You do not need to set up an expensive office or buy much business equipment. There is little reason to set up a company or corporation—which saves money.
- **Financing.** You can borrow money to buy real estate much easier than you would be able to borrow to buy competing investments.
- **Status.** Enjoy the prestige of being a landlord. As a real estate investor, your status in the world changes the moment you become the person in charge of a property that others rent.
- **Other people's money.** Allow others to pay for your property for you. Other people's money is known as OPM. By collecting rent each month, you use that money to pay for your investment. Others will pay for your investment for you over time.

Real estate holds its value. People will always need a place to live. Our nation's population has always had a steady track record of growth. Immigration will continue to swell the ranks of the nation's population. Our fellow citizens will remain mobile—moving from one location to another. Children will grow up, go to schools, marry, and look for homes. The economy—despite up and down cycles—is usually creating more jobs.

New jobs translate to a need for new housing. Individuals, as they become successful in life, will move to what they consider better housing. They too will have children, need more space, and seek more housing. Historically, there has always been steady demand for real estate over the long-term.

It does not make sense to wait to start investing in real estate. Opportunities are available to the astute investor. There is no better time to start than now.

Don't fall into the trap of waiting for the real estate market to go down, or a so-called bubble to burst. The United States has not experienced price reversals on a nationwide basis since such records were kept. There have been and probably always will be regional bubbles. We will show you how to assess your local conditions to determine whether your area is at risk of a bubble popping.

When you find a property that meets all the criteria for being a good investment, make an offer to buy it. There is never a better time than now to get started as a real estate investor.

Good Real Estate vs. Bad Real Estate for Investment

As a real estate investor, you must realize that not all real estate is good for investment. As you will learn throughout this book, there are many reasons that make a property good—or bad—for investment purposes.

Author's Advice

Remember that you have to look for the right property. If you were buying a house to live in, you might look at five or ten before finding one you want. With investing, you may have to look at even more before you find the property that makes sense to buy.

You want property that will provide positive cash flow. Of course, problems can arise throughout your ownership. Buy and hold only those properties that are producing income each month. Never invest in a property because you think it might become profitable someday.

You might find a property that is beautiful and in excellent condition. The owner is offering it below fair market value, with favorable terms. There is no reason not to buy it, except for one: when you do your analysis, it produces a negative cash flow. It is not a good investment. Pass on it and look for another.

Understanding Real Estate Cycles

Real estate is a cyclical business. The Federal Deposit Insurance Corporation (FDIC) recently reported, "A widespread decline in home prices appears unlikely." Nevertheless, it does not mean prices or values will not rise and fall. The FDIC added, "Because home prices are chiefly influenced by local economic and demographic causes, significant price declines have occurred historically only in markets experiencing serious economic distress."

Real estate markets in various places throughout the country will always experience pressures caused by changing events. One region could be experiencing brisk economic expansion, while another region is suffering job losses. For example, suppose a small community relies heavily on one employer to provide jobs. If that employer suddenly closes its doors, real estate prices may drop. It only makes sense. If the people who are living in the community cannot produce an income to pay for their housing expense, they will have to sell. Many houses for sale and low demand translate into a lower price. Several years later, another company may buy that old, closed factory and start hiring hundreds of people. Suddenly, the housing market improves, because people want to live closer to their new employer, or move to the area for the new jobs that are available. This cyclical market always exists in real estate.

Author's Advice

As a real estate investor, you must remain knowledgeable about the market in the geographical area where you want to invest.

Buyer's and Seller's Markets

Sometimes the local real estate market is known as a buyer's market. This occurs when there is too much supply and too little demand for real estate. At this point, sellers have to do all kinds of things to sell their properties. They might offer help paying for closing costs, or offer seller financing, or offer reduced prices. A buyer's market develops when the local economy is weakened, demand for housing is off, and buyers can choose to buy whatever they want.

A seller's market occurs when the local real estate market is hot and demand for housing is high. There is too little supply and many people want to buy property. At this point, the price of houses becomes higher, and sellers can ask more for their property. Sellers are not inclined to offer any aid to buyers. Many times, properties can sell within days, if not hours.

The Real Estate Bubble

You may often hear talk about the real estate bubble. This term is often used during a hot real estate market where prices are rapidly rising. The idea is that the bubble will eventually burst, sending prices plummeting. Usually something happens to make the bubble burst, such as mass unemployment. When the real estate market becomes ridiculously overinflated, prices can suddenly fall.

The danger is you might buy a property at the higher price, and when the bubble bursts, you'll still own the property that is now worth far less than what you paid for it. In effect, you have lost money.

Real Deal

Today's prices always seem high, yesterday's prices a bargain, and tomorrow's prices beyond our comprehension.

Types of Residential Real Estate

Throughout this book, our main topic is residential real estate investing. These are real estate units used mostly for people to live in and use as their homes.

Residential properties come in different sizes and styles. A single-family residence can be a tiny home, about 750 square feet in size, or a large 7,500 square foot mansion. Single-family houses can be ranch style, one-, two- or three-level homes. They can be townhouses. Their architectural styles can vary, including colonials, bungalows, saltboxes, and more. The one common element is that they are designed to allow one family to live on the property.

Duplexes offer two separate living spaces for two families. These include homes that have separate kitchens, separate baths, separate living spaces, and access to the outside without going through the other unit.

Triplexes are much like duplexes, except they have three separate living units. A four-unit building offers four separate living spaces for four different families.

Residential property that has more than four separate living units is referred to as commercial property.

There is a special type of real estate known as condominiums. Ownership of a condominium allows a person to own an apartment or house in a complex of similar units. The condominium owner receives a deed to the property. The owner also holds a common or joint ownership in all the common areas, such as hallways, entrances, grounds, and elevators. Condominiums are known as condos.

Owners of condominiums obtain their own mortgage on their individual unit. Condominiums are available in all sizes and shapes. Some offer luxurious amenities, like pools, hot tubs, and golf courses. The styles of condominium units include row houses, townhouses, apartments, and even single-family home condominium developments.

Author's Advice

It is essential that you thoroughly review and understand the condominium association bylaws before you buy a condo. For example, some bylaws prohibit renting the dwelling to a non-owner occupant.

With a condominium, each unit owner pays a fee to the homeowners' association. The fee covers expenses for maintenance, management, insurance, and occasionally, utilities for the common areas of the property. This fee, usually paid monthly, is often called a condo fee or condo association dues. The condominium association is likely to have its own set of rules or bylaws. These rules govern the condominium, and may determine whether or not and what kind of pets are allowed, or whether an owner can rent his or her unit to a tenant.

In some regions of the country, instead of condominiums, there are cooperatives. Cooperatives are often called co-ops. In practice, they are similar to condominiums. Technically, the title for a cooperative is held by a trust or corporation. The trust or corporation is owned and managed by the individuals living in the building. Sometimes being able to agree on a purchase price with the seller of a cooperative is not all that is required to buy a co-op unit. The co-op board may also need to approve the sale.

Like condominiums, cooperatives also include a monthly fee for the maintenance and upkeep of the common areas of the building.

Types of Available Residential Real Estate Ownership

	What You Own	Your Rights	What You Pay For
House	The building and the land where it is located.	You can rent or sell as you desire.	Your mortgage; your homeowner's insurance; real estate taxes assessed on the value of the land and improvements. All maintenance, utilities, and all repairs.
Condo	Your own living space. (The association owns the land and the building.)	You can rent if the association rules permit. Sell as you desire.	Your mortgage; insurance on your unit. Real estate taxes assessed on the value of your unit. All maintenance, utilities, and all repairs in your condo unit. Monthly fee to the association to a pay for building maintenance, real estate taxes on land, and any common amenities.

continues

Types of Available Residential Real Estate Ownership (continued)

	What You Own	Your Rights	What You Pay For
Co-op	Shares in a corporation that owns the building and land, which entitles you to live in an apartment in the building.	You can select a buyer, subject to board approval. Renting the unit may be prohibited.	Loan payment to pay for the shares of the corporation. All repairs inside your unit. Monthly maintenance fee, which covers real estate taxes, mortgage on the building, maintenance, costs of operating the building (water, heat, sewerage insurance). Repairs paid by co-op.

Non-Real Estate Residences

Not all places where people live can be considered real estate, at least within the scope of this book. Some people might live on an 80 foot yacht, and it might cost millions, but the yacht is not considered real estate.

Mobile Homes

Mobile homes are available in all sizes and shapes. They are 12 or 14 feet wide, and many are "double-wides"—designed to fit together, making a much larger living space. They offer all kinds of amenities, from working fireplaces to luxurious whirlpool bathtubs.

Mobile homes are not real estate. They offer affordable living to many Americans. Most mobile homes are designed to be used within a mobile home park. Each month, the owner of the mobile home pays rent to the mobile home park owner.

Mobile homes are personal property, and considered to be much like an automobile. Therefore, they depreciate, rather than appreciate. Mobile homes are issued a title by each state's Department of Motor Vehicles. For more information about personal property, see Chapter 9.

Timeshares

In America, timeshares are as much of the vacation experience as silly hats and sillier pictures of the family. In the early days, obnoxious salespeople sold one-week vacation contracts carved out of a developer's complex of tawdry construction.

The timeshare industry has changed over the years. The properties have vastly improved, even if the sales pitches have not. Reputable world-class companies now offer them at major vacation destinations. The shoddy construction is gone. Yes, you can have a great vacation if you own a timeshare.

But timeshares are lousy investments. If you buy one new, and decide to sell it, you can expect a return of about 50 to 70 cents on the dollar. If you want to buy one—for the fun of it—consider buying a used one and enjoy your vacation. But do not look at timeshares as a real estate investment opportunity.

With timeshares, there are two types: Right to Use (often called RTU) and Deeded Property. With a deeded property, this is a true property ownership with a deed recorded in the county where the property actually exists. This type of timeshare property has the same rights of ownership accorded to it as any other deeded real estate. The property owner may sell, rent, give away, or bequeath the property.

With a Right to Use, perhaps the more familiar timeshare, a lease, or right to use ownership grants the lessor the right to occupy the property for a specified period of time, usually from 20 to 99 years, and often only for one or two weeks each year. During the right-to-use period, the owner may rent, transfer, or bequeath the remaining years of their right to use property. With a RTU timeshare, you do not hold the title to the deeded property. Deeded timeshares afford the owner greater rights and thereby help these timeshares hold greater value over time.

Commercial Properties

One other property that must be discussed is commercial property. Simply stated, any real estate that is not residential is commercial property. Of course, there are other types, such as municipal or government-owned real estate like parks or roads, rivers or lakes; and nonprofit property, such as churches or camps, etc. These property types do not matter for our discussion in this book, as they are not available for investment.

Commercial properties include such properties as:

- Land leased for a commercial building (restaurant, convenience store, etc.)
- Factories

- Mobile home parks
- Apartment complexes larger than four units
- Malls and shopping centers
- Stores
- Office buildings
- Land used for mining, oil drilling, or quarries

Commercial property is often valued for its future cash flow stream. Investing in commercial property is discussed further in Chapter 23.

The Least You Need to Know

- Real estate makes sense as an investment.
- Residential real estate is available in many different styles, types, and sizes.
- Real estate markets have different cycles: buyer's market, seller's market, hot, cold, bubbles, etc.
- Mobiles homes—without land—are not real estate.
- Nonresidential real estate or apartment buildings bigger than four units are commercial property.

Chapter 2

Investing in Residential Real Estate

In This Chapter

- Reasons to Invest in Residential Real Estate
- Buying to Hold and Rent
- Buying to Resell for Quick Profits
- Understanding the Perils of Flipping

The most common form of real estate investing is buying a home. The house you buy is a fundamental real estate investment. It provides a place to live, and for most, offers a hedge against inflation. But remember, the house you live in is also your home. The degree to which you treat your home as an investment is a personal decision. You should not justify a larger home than you can afford, lavish upgrades, or expensive improvements to your home based on the premise that such spending is an "investment."

Although you have to live somewhere, your home will not provide you with an income stream. In fact, your home will instead require monthly payments for a mortgage, property taxes, utilities, and repairs.

One characteristic of many assets is that they provide an income stream. A characteristic of a liability is that it requires a monthly financial commitment or payment. Your home is one part asset, one part liability. Exercise prudence in buying a home that fits within your family budget and entire financial plan.

There are two other main reasons for investing in residential real estate: (1) to buy and hold while collecting rent and (2) to buy for resale later for a profit. In this chapter, we look at all the ways, reasons, and strategies for investing in residential real estate.

Buying Residential Property to Live In

One reason to buy residential property is to provide you with living space and a home. With home ownership comes the intangible benefit of being in charge, and doing with the property what you want. You do not need permission to change the color of the walls, buy new appliances, remodel a room, or plant shrubbery. You are in control. You can later sell your real estate investment.

Buying Residential Property to Hold and Rent

Another reason to buy residential real estate is to own it as a rental property. Each month, a tenant will pay you rent for the right to remain on the property and to use it for their home.

As you learned in Chapter 1, residential real estate is available in all sizes and shapes. When you are considering buying property to be used only to produce rental income, you need to be acutely aware of two important numbers as well as the purchase price:

- The rent the property is likely to produce each month.
- The total cost of operating the property.

Determining the Amount of Rental Income

If the property is already producing rent, it is easy to determine what the rental income is. All you need to do is ask the seller what the current tenant(s) are paying for rent.

Your knowledge of the local real estate market will also tell you what a specific-size residential property is likely to produce in rent. This varies from area to area. What a one-bedroom apartment produces in rent in New York City compared with Dubuque, Iowa will always be different.

Author's Advice

Learn your local market by reading your local newspaper's classified "for rent" section. Do your own rental survey. In performing the survey, visit and analyze several similar rental properties the same way that a tenant would as he or she goes about shopping for rental housing. See Chapter 6 for more information.

To better understanding your local rental market, perform a rent survey. Shop competing rentals. However, when viewing other rental properties, do not pretend to be a tenant. You can ask the landlord far more questions about his or her experience in the marketplace by being upfront about being a landlord doing market research. Offer to share the results of your survey so other landlords are more likely to be cooperative. In a short time, you will have an excellent review of the competition in your rental market.

The larger the space, the more amenities, the more rent you can charge and collect. When considering properties to buy for rental income, always think about inexpensive, practical ways you might be able to increase the rental income.

For example, co-author David J. Decker owns an apartment building where some of the units had a den. The den had its own door and closet, but only a temporary accordion wall separated the living room from the den. The accordion wall could be deployed to divide the den from the living room, or it could be left open to make one big room. These accordion walls were a dingy brown color and showing their age. Dave decided to frame in the accordion wall with drywall to make the den a permanent room. He no longer calls this room a den, but instead refers to it as a bedroom and charges more rent.

You'll learn more about developing your own vision for improving property values in Chapter 10.

Looking at Cash Flow

When considering the purchase of residential real estate for rental income, the costs of buying and maintaining the property are important. As a typical example, let's assume you found a well-maintained property in a great neighborhood. There is no reason to assume that you could not rent it for $850 a month. Your knowledge of the local real estate market tells you that other similar units within a short distance are producing about this amount of rent.

Through negotiation, you believe you could buy this property for $100,000. You are planning to put $10,000 down, so you would have a mortgage for $90,000. Further, let's assume your mortgage would be for 30 years at 6.5% interest. Your monthly principal and interest payment would be $568.86.

Insurance costs $360 per year and the property taxes are $1,800 per year. Here's a summary of this example:

Example 1

Income	
Rent Received Each Month	$850.00
Expenses	
Monthly Payment	$568.86
Insurance	$ 30.00
Property Taxes	$150.00
Total Expenses	$748.86
Net Monthly Income	$101.14

From this example, the property would produce a positive cash flow of $101.14 a month, or about $1,213 a year.

In this example, this would be a possible property to buy. But there are still several other factors to consider.

You, as the landlord-to-be, have not considered any of the "freebies" for your tenant. If you proposed to include water, sewer, and trash removal for the tenant, those expenses need to be added. If these three items cost $50 a month, you have reduced your annual income from the property by $600. You can see how little you have left for repairs, maintenance, and other necessary expenses.

Beginning landlords often underestimate the entire costs of operating a rental property. There will likely be advertising costs, yard maintenance, waste hauling, painting, carpet cleaning, and credit reports. Additionally, you may also need to pay for pool maintenance, association dues, snow removal, water softening, and more. Even this list isn't comprehensive. Hidden costs can really add up. Make sure you understand the true cost of operating any property before you buy.

This could now be a marginal property for producing cash flow. There is nothing wrong with it, and it would make a wonderful home. However, from an investor's viewpoint, this is a property that it would be better to pass on than to pursue.

In another example, using the same property and buying and financing details, suppose the maximum amount of rent you could collect is $650. This deal would clearly not work as a rental income property. Each month you own the property, it would be costing you money just to meet your monthly obligations. This is not a good investment strategy. This real estate would be a negative cash flow property.

Buyer Beware

Never invest in any property that produces a negative cash flow unless you have a concrete plan for restoring profitability soon. Move on to search for another property that can produce a positive cash flow for you.

As your search for investment properties continues, we will assume you found a two-unit property for the same costs. However, each unit produces a rental income of $700. Now the deal will look different. Consider this example:

Example 2

Income	
Rent for Unit #1	$ 700.00
Rent for Unit #2	$ 700.00
Total Rent Received Each Month	$1,400.00
Expenses	
Monthly Payment	$ 568.86
Insurance	$ 30.00
Property Taxes	$ 150.00
Total Expenses	$ 748.86
Net Monthly Income	$ 651.14

The $651.14 in positive cash flow on this property would create plenty of income to cover monthly expenses and maintenance. With over $7,800 of annual positive cash flow, you can see how profitable this example could be for you.

Forgetting for a moment your ability to afford different amounts of down payment, when looking for residential real estate property for investment to produce monthly rental income, the price range of the property may not be important. Obviously, what you pay is important, based on the rental income produced. But it does not matter if you invest in a property that costs $50,000 or $300,000. What matters is the positive cash flow. As long as you are able to receive a reasonable cash flow, it makes sense to buy the property as an investment property.

Author's Advice

As a beginning real estate investor, it makes sense for you to look for a multifamily property (two units or larger) as your first investment property, if you can afford the down payment.

Let your ability to afford a down payment be the only limit on the price range you will consider. A property that costs $250,000, and produces $4,000 of positive cash flow a year is a far better property to buy than one that only costs $50,000 and produces only $500 in annual cash flow. Of course, even a property such as this—producing only $500 of positive cash flow—is far better than any property producing a negative cash flow.

Another consideration often neglected by first-time landlords is vacancy and collection loss. No matter how careful and diligent you are, you will not collect every month of rent from every occupied unit and sometimes a unit will be vacant. Quiz other landlords about their collection and vacancy experience when completing your rent survey.

Advantages of Holding Properties

There are several advantages of buying and holding residential properties as investments. As a real estate investor, you will …

- Enjoy tax benefits (see Chapter 21 for more information).
- Build a positive cash flow. Each month, you receive cash and income because you own real estate.
- Develop wealth by increasing equity (explained in more detail later in this chapter).
- Benefit from your tenants paying for your real estate investment through their rent payments.

Buying to Resell

Another real estate investment strategy is to buy the property to resell at a higher price. While you always hope that whatever real estate you buy will later sell for more than you paid, there are some properties that you may buy solely for reselling and making an immediate profit. Unlike buying for cash flow, where the goal is to buy and hold, the goal of reselling is to move the property as soon as possible.

For this strategy to work, you must buy the property below its current market value, or below its potential market value. This sometimes means the current owner, for whatever reason, no longer wants the property and is willing to reduce the price for a quick sale. In other words, you need to find a motivated seller.

The reasons for selling a property below the current fair market value could vary from financial distress to the need to move somewhere else as soon as possible. Other reasons include a new employment opportunity or the wish to be with a loved one. Never forget that some motivated sellers are trying to dump properties that have serious structural or mechanical defects.

Advantages of Buying for Resale

Many times, the reason a property owner offers a property for sale below market value is its condition. If the owner did not maintain the property, or the property is in dire need of major repairs, the property owner may be willing to sell for less rather than bother with getting the required work done.

A fixer-upper property can come in any size, and any condition. Usually they have the three "D's"—Dirt, Disarray, and Damage—often with a strong dose of obsolescence to boot.

A dirty property that just needs cleaned up and trash removed, fresh paint, and some nice decorations—like window treatments—is a great candidate for a bargain purchase.

Often, filthy properties are also in a state of disarray. The same neglect that allowed dirt to accumulate has probably also led to poor tenant selection, sloppy rent collection practices, poor maintenance standards, utility waste, and other problems.

Then there are other fixer-uppers, the ones that need major renovations. The third "D"—damage—is everywhere. From misuse by previous tenants to water damage caused by a leaky roof or defective plumbing, these properties suffered abuse, neglect, or both.

You can sometimes repair damage easily and inexpensively. For example, you can fix a hole in a wall with a few dollars' worth of spackling, a scraper, and some sandpaper. On the other hand, a roof that constantly leaked water into the ceiling and walls might need a repair that costs a small fortune.

Do not assume that a dirty property with some minor faults is without larger problems. A professional inspection might save you from buying a money pit. If you suspect any significant problems, get professional advice—and repair estimates.

Learn there is a real difference between a fixer-upper and a rehab. The fixer-upper is a property that is in need of mostly cosmetic repairs—from fresh paint to replacing gaudy wallpaper. Minor repairs—like a loose doorknob or replacing a missing lamp cover—are also a part of working with a fixer-upper. Scrubbing and cleaning, replacing a cracked window, tidying up and landscaping the yard, and other minor repairs that most homeowners can do are within the scope of the fixer-upper.

A rehab, on the other hand, needs extensive work. This is not just repair, but improvements. Rehab, short for the word rehabilitation, means that you will not just restore the house's appearance, but you will probably also update and improve the *working systems*. This is covered in more detail in Chapter 10.

def•i•ni•tion

Working systems or *mechanical systems* mean everything added to the structure of the residence to make the home habitable and comfortable. This includes such items as the plumbing, the electrical systems, the roof, and the heating and cooling systems.

You will likely need to make major renovations during the rehab. Many of the improvements are probably going to require professional tradespeople to finish the work.

After the rehab is complete, the property should be desirable and easily sold. When you sell the property, you deduct the acquisition costs plus the costs of the rehab from the sale price to determine your final profit.

Advantages of Property Flipping

One particularly enticing buy and resell strategy is property flipping. Real estate investors refer to buying a property and selling it as soon as possible as flipping. It is a wonderful idea—buy a property at a steep discount, resell it, and make a quick, huge profit.

One flipping strategy is to enter into a contract to buy a piece of real estate and then sell your contract before ever taking title to the real estate. For example, many such investors have entered into contracts to buy condominiums that were under construction. All that is needed from the buyer is a minimal deposit of a few thousand dollars. Actual construction can take six months before the buyer has to close on the deal and take title to the condominium. Therefore, the investor has up to six months to flip his contract to another buyer. In regions of the country experiencing rapid appreciation, this strategy has worked well. Forgetting any ethical considerations, if the flipper is unable to resell the contract, all he or she loses is the deposit placed on the condominium if he or she fails to close. How to flip properties is covered in more detail in Chapter 10.

Foreclosures sometimes present an additional property-flipping opportunity. Some properties wind up in foreclosure because there is more debt against the property than what the property is worth. Sometimes a savvy investor can persuade these creditors to discount the amount they are owed. If the discounts are generous enough, an equity position in the property can be restored, producing a potential profit for the investor. You will learn more about foreclosure opportunities like this one in Chapter 7.

Problems of Flipping Properties

In reality, it's not so easy. First, where do you find the properties at such a discount? Some property-flipping strategies press the limits of ethical business practices. Taking advantage of someone's financial situation—because of a death or illness—and offering to pay them far less than their property is worth—is, at best, sneaky. There are plenty of opportunities in the real estate business that will not trouble your conscience. One real estate investor said it best. He said that any deal has to allow him to sleep at night.

Remember the condo flip strategy? The loser in this equation is the condominium developer. The developer cannot break ground on the project until a certain number of units are "presold." Presold is a bit of a misnomer because all the "buyer" has done is put down a small deposit, often only a few thousand dollars. The developer may think he has a sufficient number of buyers in hand to begin construction. But if many of these "buyers" are flippers, and if the flippers cannot resell their contracts, the flippers may just back out of their contracts, sacrificing their deposit. The developer is then stuck with potentially dozens of completed but unsold units where the "buyers" have disappeared. Not surprisingly, developers have begun to take steps to protect themselves. Many developers will no longer allow a buyer to assign or sell their contract. Further, even if the buyer goes through with the deal and takes title to the property, the developer may retain the right to buy the condominium back at the same price for up to a year—or longer—after the first purchase.

Flipping can also be problematic for you and your potential buyer. Because of illegal activities, some banks and lenders have been badly burned on properties that were flipped. As part of the process to approve a loan, they will order a title search to check the history of the property. If it sold three months ago for $25,000 and now it is being sold for $100,000, the lender is going to be asking many questions. Unless there is some compelling, tangible reason for such an extraordinary increase in value, such as a major rehab, the lender is likely to deny the loan. The lender wants to protect their money with stable collateral. Overinflating the market value of a property is a sure way for a lender to lose their money. An astute lender would not make the loan.

One more problem with engaging in property flipping is that you have to keep flipping to continue making money. Owning properties with positive cash flow provides a continuous income stream for as long as you own them.

Property flipping may be a strategy that makes the most sense for an investor starting out with no money available for investment.

Flipping strategies usually have a time pressure element to them. The flipper may need to sell quickly before being required to buy a property he or she cannot afford. Selling real estate under time pressure is inconsistent with the goal of achieving full fair market value for real estate. In fact, the real estate definition of fair market value assumes enough marketing time to achieve a fair market price. In other words, often a flipper may have to discount the property to move it quickly.

Real Deal

Many flippers eventually become owners, buying property to hold for rent.

An investor who buys properties with positive cash flow is always going to win at the real estate investment game.

Buying to Sell as a Rent-to-Own

One problem you may run into with single-family rental homes is that it is difficult to make the cash flow. One solution may be to achieve a higher rent by offering to rent with an option for your tenant to buy the property. It is not uncommon to purchase a single-family property, update it, and then offer it for sale to a tenant.

With a rent-to-own opportunity, the tenant may be obligated to pay a higher rent for the extra value of having the opportunity to buy the property in the future at a price determined today. Alternatively, the tenant could be given the opportunity to improve the property at his or her own time and expense and build "sweat equity" in the home. Either way, by charging extra rent or by avoiding some extra remodeling costs, you reduce the cash flow pressure on your investment.

Often this special renting arrangement creates a better situation for the real estate investor. If the tenant is buying the property, the tenant is likely to take better care of it.

Rent-to-own options can be structured many ways. For example, a part of the rent can be used to reduce the preset price or a nonrefundable deposit can be collected. For more information on this investment strategy, see Chapter 12.

Understanding Equity

Home ownership offers a form of "forced savings" for most buyers. Each month, a small portion of your loan payment becomes part of your equity that you have in the property. When you first buy your home, your equity position is small. With a small down payment, you have only a tiny piece of equity in the property. Each month as you make your payments, you are amortizing your loan. Amortization is the process of repaying a loan in installments of principal and interest. In the beginning, most of your payment will be interest on the loan. But with each payment, the interest portion gets smaller and the principal portion gets bigger. Your equity not only grows with time, but it also grows faster with time.

If you enter into a 30-year fixed-rate mortgage, your payment on your loan will be the same throughout the entire length of the mortgage. For example, if you agree to pay $750 a month for 360 months (30 years), your first payment will be the same as the last: $750. Rent, unlike a mortgage payment, can be raised by a landlord. As a tenant, you have little control over your rent. If you don't like the amount being charged, all you can really do is move.

Most residential properties appreciate (or increase) in value over time. As long as you reasonably maintain the property and do not allow it to decline into a state of disrepair, it is likely to be worth more in the future than it is now. As the owner of the property, the increased value is yours, and becomes part of your equity. While there is never any guarantee of appreciation your property might experience, it is most likely that it will be worth more than you paid for it.

As you can see from the table that follows, as the loan matures and as the value appreciates, your equity in the property continues to grow. Financial experts call this building equity.

How Equity Grows

Property Value when purchased: $200,000
Appreciation of 2% each year on purchase price
Loan $180,000 at 7% interest, 30 year mortgage

	Amount of Appreciation	Loan Balance	Equity*
5 years	$16,486	$169,436	$47,050
10 years	$39,018	$154,462	$84,556
15 years	$63,896	$133,234	$130,662
20 years	$91,362	$103,140	$188,222
25 years	$121,687	$60,478	$261,209
30 years	$155,169	$0	$355,169

**Calculation of Equity includes $20,000 down payment (10%).*

Should you choose to sell the property, the equity is yours. You can use it to buy another residential property, perhaps a larger or nicer one.

Author's Advice

Remember that appreciation is never a guarantee. Many outside reasons beyond your control affect the value of your home. The local economy, nearby land use, noisy and obnoxious neighbors, and the national economy are just some of the causes that can affect the value of your property. While most homes do appreciate, yours may not.

The Least You Need to Know

- There are three types of residential real estate investment strategies—property to own to live in, property to produce rental income, and property to sell at a higher price.
- Buying real estate for investment purposes requires a close look at the numbers to assure profitability.

- Multifamily properties are more likely to produce profitable cash flow for the real estate investor.
- There is a huge difference between a fixer-upper and a rehab property.
- Flipping may be a good strategy for the short-term for the cash-strapped investor.
- Real estate is a great way to acquire wealth through building equity.

Chapter 3

Who Can Help with Investing Complexities

In This Chapter

- Learning the complexities of real estate investing
- Understanding who can help you
- Finding out what real estate agents can do
- Understanding lenders
- Others who can help you

In the good old days, if you had a bucket full of money, buying real estate was rather easy. You simply looked for the property you wanted, gave the owner the right amount of money, received a deed, and the transaction was over.

That was the good old days. Today, a real estate transaction is a bit more complicated. Finding the property you want to buy is a major hurdle. Once you locate a property and decide to purchase it, you put your offer in writing. Once you and the seller agree to the terms of the sale, you move toward the date of the settlement—the day that both of you agreed the property would transfer from the seller to you.

Based on your sales agreement, you may need to arrange financing, get the title of the property searched, and arrange to have funds available for the settlement, among other tasks. Lenders will require you to produce certain documents as part of their loan approval process. Questions could come up about your financial status, and therefore, you must provide proper answers to the lender if you want the loan to be approved.

Financing always adds layers of complexities to a real estate transaction. The lender will order an appraisal of the property, and the property must appraise for the value equal to or greater than the sales price. If the appraiser finds significant problems with the property, the loan might be denied.

Along the path to successful real estate investing, there are people who can help you. Understanding what they can—and cannot—do for you is an important step to becoming successful. The list is long—from realtors to bankers, mortgage brokers to contractors. In this chapter, we will discuss how each has their own place in the overall plan of helping you achieve success.

Although real estate investing can be complicated, with the right team of advisers, you can move forward with confidence. You should know and realize that not everyone will have your best interests in mind. While most of the people you deal with will be honest, hardworking, and professional individuals, you may come across a few bad apples now and then.

Real Estate Agents

You may often hear the term real estate agent. This is the person who handles the buying and selling of homes. Real estate agents are required to be ethical in the transactions they conduct with buyers and sellers. They also are required to comply with appropriate regulations and laws where they work and engage in business.

Sometimes, a real estate agent might be called a sales associate, salesperson, Realtor®, or broker. While the general public sometimes uses these terms interchangeably, there are differences between them that will be identified in this section.

As well as being designated as professionals, Realtors also sponsor and operate the Multiple Listing Service (MLS). This computerized system is used to list houses and other real estate offered for sale.

Buying real estate is complex, and you do not want any mistakes in the transaction. A smooth transfer of the title at settlement is the ultimate goal. As you will see, you can do much to assure that happens. At times, you might think the entire process of buying real estate is one big convoluted mess. Other times, everything will run smoothly. At least 90 percent of the issues can be solved before they become problems. The simple question of whom you choose to work with can solve many problems or prevent them altogether.

A listing offers a piece of real estate for sale. The agent who meets with the seller of the property and obtains the listing is called the listing agent.

Real Deal

The term Realtor is a service mark of the National Association of Realtors (NAR). The term is used to designate a real estate agent who is a member of the Association. Over a century ago, NAR registered the word, so only members of their association could use it. The idea was to enforce responsible and professional conduct of its members.

What Is a Real Estate Broker?

A real estate broker is an agent who has met the additional educational and experiential requirements to obtain a broker's license in the state where he or she is doing business. These requirements vary by state. The broker is in charge of the agency, and is responsible for the conduct of the real estate agents that work for him or her.

The terms real estate agent, sales associate, or salesperson can be used interchangeably to describe a real estate agent who is working for a real estate broker. All agents must work for a broker. Brokers supervise their agents. A broker can also act as an agent. Not all brokers open their own office, preferring instead to work as an agent under the authority of another broker. Brokers acting in this capacity can handle both sales and management.

Real Estate Agent Pros and Cons

As you consider working with a real estate agent, there are some things you should keep in mind:

Not all agents are ethical or honest. There are many wonderful agents working today. Most are ethical in their dealings. Others stretch the limits, and have been known to get involved in questionable practices. Agents who are members of the National Association of Realtors (NAR) are held to a higher ethical standard.

However, even NAR cannot guarantee their agents will be without fault or blemish in their business dealings.

Not all agents are good negotiators. Becoming licensed as a real estate agent does require a certain amount of work and education. However, the focus of the education is on the technical aspects of real estate transactions. For example, the course work will often underline the handling of earnest money, the study of real estate law, preparing contracts, real estate terms, and other related details. While understanding these facts is important, the mastery of them does not make the agent an accomplished negotiator. While the required courses and testing vary from state–to–state, no one requires the new agent to prove proficiency in negotiations. Some agents are just lousy at it; they are ill-equipped to help buyer and seller come to a meeting of the minds.

Some of the most successful agents have terrible blind spots for the technical details of a real estate transaction. This is the opposite condition of the agent with deficient negotiating ability. This agent may be a born salesperson. He or she may seem like your best friend from the moment you meet them. Your agent can sell ice to Eskimos. But these agents may not always be the best students and they may have just barely passed their licensing examination. Be forewarned that the person who cuts your hair has probably received more training than the person selling you real estate. And you don't want to get a haircut in the real estate business.

Agents often use what you say against you. Because agents always want to make a sale, they will use what you have told them—even in confidence—to make the sale move forward. Some states have prohibitions against the agent revealing information disclosed in confidence. As a practical matter, the strength of those prohibitions is dependent on the ethical standards of the individual agent. Telling an agent that you will pay $5,000 more for the property is information you might not want to reveal, even if that information could supposedly be kept confidential. During the negotiation period, the agent may let it slip or not work as hard for a deal in your best interests, because the agent knows you will pay more.

Real Deal

Commissions earned by real estate agents are usually computed on a percentage of the sale price of the property.

Sometimes agents will tell you almost anything or almost nothing. Agents give their greatest loyalty to the deal. Agents do not make any money unless the property gets sold. Therefore, sometimes all of these wonderful ethical standards and loyalties go right out the window. Further, many agents may shy away from giving you the advice you need. Most agents are prohibited by their licensing requirements from giving legal or accounting advice. Similarly, while an agent has a duty to disclose known defects in a property, they may not be able to refer you directly to contractors to help you fix the problem. This limitation may stem from local licensing requirements or it could just be company policy for a brokerage that is trying to absolve itself from liability on any repairs that go wrong. Finally, for the same reasons, if there are potential unknown defects, the agent may encourage you to seek counsel from expensive experts rather than trying to help you him or herself. To a great degree, this situation has evolved because of the litigious nature of our society and is not the fault of the agents themselves. But you get left out in the cold, regardless.

You can—and should—fire a bad agent. All agents are not created equal. Many excellent real estate agents are worth the money they earn from commissions. Unfortunately, there are agents who provide poor service for any number of reasons. Real estate investing is business. And when in business, you have to make decisions that are best for you. When you find that an agent is not working for you—not doing everything possible to help you reach your goals—then you need to move on from that agent.

Everything is negotiable. Again, real estate investing is business, and in business, everything is negotiable. When a real estate agent says their listing fee is always 7 percent, know that the fee is indeed negotiable. From the date of settlement to whether you get possession of the property five days before settlement, everything is negotiable. The more details you are trying to negotiate, the harder the agent has to work. Of course, that is the agent's problem, not yours.

Agents may have a conflict of interest with referrals they make. Agents may align themselves with a lender or title company that gives great service to the agent but does not necessarily have the best rates for a borrower or the lowest premiums for the insured. Further, your agent might gravitate toward inspection companies that never find anything wrong with the property—just so the sale can be completed.

Agents can become lazy. Working in real estate requires long and irregular hours. Unfortunately, some agents become lazy and do not work as hard as they once did.

A real estate agent should constantly earn your business. An agent can help you find the right property and help you navigate your way through the financial steps to purchase the property.

Real Deal

A good agent can help negotiate and close the deal for you. Property sellers may take buyers working with a real estate agent more seriously because they realize the agent has most likely prequalified the buyer. (More on prequalification in Chapter 11.)

A good agent will play the role of matchmaker by listening to what you want and then helping you find the right property. Using the Multiple Listing System and a network of contacts, the agent will keep an eye out for possible properties that meet your criteria. The agent you work with should be an expert in the community and the property type you want to invest in.

FSBO Fiction

Properties being sold directly by the owner without an agent are called for-sale-by-owner properties, or FSBOs, pronounced "fizz-bo." Some buyers have the preconceived notion that FSBO deals are more likely to be better deals because no real estate agent is involved and therefore no real estate commission has to be paid. This preconception is usually not true.

Keep in mind that the seller usually pays the commission. Additionally, a fire-sale FISBO might really be an attempt by an unscrupulous property owner to dump a problem property that no respectable real estate agent will touch.

First, a disclosure is in order. David is a member of the Commercial Association of Realtors and has held a real estate broker's license for nearly two decades. Regardless, if you think that a seller is going to go to the time, trouble, and expense of selling a piece of real estate to save you the commission, then you may be a little naïve. Most often, FSBO properties are way overpriced. However, every once and a while, a poorly informed owner will let a property go at a substantial discount. But if you are looking for motivated sellers, David believes that a seller willing to pay a professional a substantial fee to sell a piece of real estate reflects greater motivation than a typical FSBO seller.

Understanding Agency

A person authorized to act for and under the direction of another person when dealing with third parties is an agent. An agency is legally created when the owner of a property engages a real estate agent to sell their property.

In most areas, the person who appoints an agent is called the principal. By definition, an agent must be working on behalf of a principal, either the buyer or the seller in the transaction. While the agent owes a duty of fairness to all parties, the agent's first loyalty is supposed to be to the seller if the agent has a listing agreement with the seller of a property, or the buyer if the agent has a buyer's agency agreement with the buyer.

What Is a Seller's Agent?

The agency arrangement just described is a handy arrangement in that unless you have entered into any agreements otherwise, every agent you meet is supposed to be working for the seller. However, in practice, these loyalties don't always work out the way they were intended. Often, there are two agents involved in a real estate transaction—the agent who listed the property for sale and the agent who sold the property. Theoretically, unless the agent selling the property entered into a buyer's agency, then the selling agent also is supposed to work for the seller.

However, the selling agent may never have met the seller, or only have met the seller while showing the property. For the selling agent to contact the owner directly is a violation of real estate licensing ethics in most states. Usually, only the listing agent has ongoing contact with the seller. Therefore, sometimes the selling agent acts in the best interests of the buyer, even though the agent's first loyalties are supposed to be to the seller. While this might be to your advantage when you are buying, it can also lull you into a false sense of security. No matter how the selling agent is behaving, he or she is supposed to have first loyalty to the seller.

Your agent may wake up to this fact or be reminded of it by the listing agent in the middle of a transaction. The result could be your agent revealing something to the seller about your transaction that you didn't want the seller to know.

What Is a Buyer's Agent?

As you meet and become associated with different agents, you may be asked to sign a document that defines the agent's relationship with you, or you may want to approach a well-qualified agent about representing you as a buyer. The buyer's agency form varies from state–to–state, but it will delineate how the buyer's agent will be compensated, and how the agent will represent you.

Most agreements specify that you must pay a fee for the buyer's agent service. Sometimes you will be asked for a retainer that may or may not be applied to the total buyer's agent fee. Some agreements specify that the buyer's agent will receive a commission based on the purchase price.

A buyer's agent has a potential conflict of interest. It is in the buyer's best interest to buy at the lowest price possible, but if the commission is based on the purchase price, the agent's commission will be reduced as he or she is more successful in assisting the buyer in negotiating a lower price! In practice, this is rarely a concern, but for reassurance, negotiate a buyer's agency agreement where the commission increases as the price goes down.

Buyer Beware

When a buyer's agency agreement calls for a commission or other compensation to be paid, find out who pays this fee. Be sure you understand this *before* you sign the agreement. The commission can be paid out of the proceeds of the sale of the real estate that you buy. Be sure to include the mechanism for paying the commission in your offer.

If the buyer's agent shows you a property that is listed with the agent's office, a situation known as dual agency is created. Since the same real estate company represents both the buyer and seller, there is potential for a conflict of interest. Ask the agent how the agency will resolve any issues or conflicts.

Most agreements also include an exclusivity agreement that says you will only work with that agent for the time specified. The agent may ask for a longer period than is actually needed. Think hard before agreeing to a period of longer than 60 days. If the agent is performing well, you can always extend the agreement.

It is easy to find a real estate agent. Their ads are all over the place—from billboards to shopping carts. You see their names and faces everywhere. But it may not be easy to find a good real estate agent. You want an agent who specializes in your area of investment, both the geographical location and the type of property. You want an agent who can spot the potential in a deal that other agents might miss. And you want an agent who can get you to the best deals first. Fancy ads do not guarantee a great agent.

If you visit an open house, the agent on duty is often there not only to sell that particular home, but also to find new clients. The agent might quickly show more interest in soliciting your business than selling that property. You might soon find yourself getting hooked up with an agent that you had no intention of doing business with before entering the property.

How to Find a Good Agent

Some of the best ways to find a good agent include:

- Ask your friends and family for recommendations. Some of the best sources for agents are people you know—from your co-workers to your neighbors.
- Ask a broker for recommendations. The broker knows all of the agents working in the office. Tell the broker what you want (and don't want) from an agent, and ask for recommendations from the staff.

- Watch the real estate section of the local newspaper. Agents that win awards and acclaim from their peers are not the ones sitting on their hands. They are working, and have proven experience.
- Talk to other landlords. There are plenty of landlords who have achieved their success due in part to the efforts of a sharp agent. Find out who other successful landlords are using, and that agent might be able to help you too.

Real Deal

A good agent can help you become wealthy. The best agents are likely to be busy.

Before agreeing to be represented by an agent, conduct an interview. Here are some of things you should ask:

- Are you a full-time or part-time agent?
- Are you easily accessible by telephone, e-mail, and fax?
- How busy are you? Do you have time now for another client?
- How long have you been licensed?
- How long have you lived in this area?
- How many other clients do you have who are real estate investors?
- Do you see any conflicts arising from serving your other investor clients?
- In the past year, how many transactions did you complete? How many of those were for real estate investors?

Listen carefully to the agent's answers. An agent who is only in the business part-time and relies on income from another source is probably not the best agent for you. Agents who do not know the area, or are too busy, should be avoided. You do not want an agent you cannot contact when you are ready to make an offer, or who is too busy to draw up a sales agreement. Perhaps most importantly, you want an agent who specializes in your area of investment.

Dealing With Agent Problems

Obviously, you want to fire your sales agent before a major problem occurs. Almost always, you can tell when things are not going right and it's time to fire your real estate agent.

Some sure signs of problems ahead are:

- The agent is not easy to contact by telephone, e-mail, or fax.
- The agent shows you houses or properties that are nothing like you have said you wanted to see.
- The agent is too busy to work with you.
- There is a personality conflict developing.
- The agent is always disorganized.
- The agent always blames someone else for any problem.
- The agent does not know the area well.
- The agent is unable to answer basic real estate questions for you.
- The agent does not show houses listed with other agencies, dramatically limiting your choices.

Saying good-bye to an agent may not be easy, but sometimes you have no other choice. Tell the agent you are not happy with their service, and you want to move on. Be up front and forthright. Tell the agent that it would be a waste of your time—as well as the agent's—to continue the relationship.

Nobody likes being fired, but agents know when they are doing a good job or bad. If they don't return calls, they know it. If they are too busy or do not have the time for you, they know it. While they may ask for a second chance or respond negatively to your criticism, remember: this is only business. And it's your business that they are affecting.

Author's Advice

It is not easy to find good help these days. Your success is more likely when you surround yourself with good people.

If you have entered into a buyer agency agreement, then leaving your agent is trickier. The agent may be entitled to compensation or reimbursement of expenses if exiting the relationship could be deemed a breach of a contract. Be mindful of this problem before entering into buyer agency agreements.

If things are going terribly wrong, the decision to leave is the best decision.

Initially, you may need to work hard to gain the attention of the best real estate agents. The best investment-oriented agents usually already have a stable of repeat customers who are easy to work with. These repeat customers have fewer questions and require less hand-holding than a beginning investor.

However, good agents are also always on the lookout for that next great client—you. You can prove that you are serious about working only with the best by being up front about your financial qualifications and ability, and by promptly returning calls and quickly scouting out property leads the agent might find for you.

Lenders

For the real estate investor, lenders will be among your best friends. Borrowed money is essential to real estate.

As an active real estate investor, you need to have various ways of borrowing money for your purchases. Some of your real estate investments will work well with traditional financing, while others may require nontraditional or creative financing to make the deal work.

Working With Bankers

You should cultivate a business relationship with a number of different banks that routinely lend on properties similar to those that you are trying to buy. Money may be a commodity, but not all banks are the same. Many banks will shy away from lending against nonowner occupied single-family rental houses. But some banks will make those loans.

One great way to find a loan is to approach the bank that already carries the financing on the property that you are trying to buy. Obviously, this lender is already acquainted with the building and they must like the location or they would not have made the loan to your seller. Another source for finding lenders is your fellow landlords. When you are talking to or meeting with other landlords, be sure to ask them about potential lending contacts.

There are some things you should realize about banks:

Banks must reveal all the fees they plan to charge you. Banks are required to give you a good faith estimate of your closing costs. Pay attention to these details so that there will be no unpleasant surprises later.

> **Buyer Beware**
>
> Property tax estimates are often based on last year's taxes. Insurance estimates can also be low, or assume minimum policy features that you won't ultimately find acceptable. The result is that these estimates are often lower than reality.

Some banks pay their loan officers on commission. Borrowers sometimes anticipate that their banker will always be a conservative, prudent businessperson. Usually, this is a safe assumption. But sometimes your banker may be a wild man hungry for a commission. Do not be lulled into thinking that your deal must be a great one because you were able to convince the lender to make you a loan.

The bank may sell your loan. Banks make money from two sources—fees for making a loan and the interest on the loan itself. Banks often sell the loan immediately after making it, keeping the fees but selling the interest benefit. The corporations that buy these loans, such as FannieMae or FreddieMac, make up the secondary market for loans. Lenders who routinely keep their loans are called portfolio lenders. There are all different kinds of lenders. One way to differentiate them is to divide them into two groups, portfolio lenders and everyone else. Portfolio lenders are in the minority. Portfolio lenders usually have a little more flexibility because they do not necessarily have to comply with every requirement necessary to sell the mortgage on the secondary market. However, any lender willing to make you a loan at a reasonable rate and terms is a lender whom you would do well to cultivate a relationship with.

The bank may not drop the mortgage insurance. Private Mortgage Insurance is often called PMI. Banks require mortgage insurance when you borrow more than 80 percent of the purchase price from the bank. Mortgage insurance protects the bank—not you—if the loan defaults. Each month, you pay for this private mortgage insurance in addition to your loan payment. The bank is only going to drop the insurance once your loan balance is paid down to 80 percent of the original purchase price. Long before that date, you may have gained a 20 percent or more equity position in the property through appreciation, but you may have to pay to get a new appraisal of the property in order to convince your bank. Your loan documents should spell out when and under what circumstances the mortgage insurance can be retired. Make sure you understand the requirements.

The bank charges you to prepare the documents for your loan. Sometimes called the doc fee or document preparation fee, this charge is for the bank to prepare the loan documents. Often, they charge hundreds of dollars for this service. You can try to negotiate a lower fee or even the elimination of this fee. However, remember that every negotiation is a give–and–take. You should not expect to win on every point.

If interest rates decrease, your bank may not pass along a lower rate to you. From the time that you apply for a loan until it closes (is funded), the interest rate could change to your benefit. But if you applied for a higher rate loan, your bank may not be required to reduce the loan to the lower rate. The bank's obligation in this circumstance can be spelled out at the time you make application.

The time to start talking to your banker is long before you ever intend to apply for a loan. Make an appointment to visit with the bank's loan officer, and find out what types of programs they offer to real estate investors. You need to learn what types of properties they will lend on and what kinds they will not accept as collateral. Be prepared for your meeting. Be sure to bring with you a copy of your personal financial statement and copies of your last two years of tax returns. A personal financial statement is an accounting of all of your assets and liabilities. Assets minus liabilities equals your net worth.

Real Deal

One banking bonus is that mortgage payments are typically not subject to a late fee until the 15th of the month. Therefore, you can "float" your monthly payment for up to two weeks every month.

Find out about down payment requirements, and how the bank calculates projected income and expenses so you can qualify for the loan. The more they can educate you before you actually apply, the easier the loan process will be. The knowledge you gain will certainly be useful. Finally, try to get preapproved for financing. That way, you will have more negotiating leverage when you go to actually buy.

Every bank has a set of parameters for evaluating a loan. Applying these parameters to a credit application is called underwriting a loan. Each bank is likely to have slightly different underwriting parameters. Thoroughly learn any particular bank's underwriting parameters, and you can know before you apply for the loan whether or not they are likely to give you the money.

Understanding Mortgage Brokers

A mortgage broker provides a matchmaking service similar to that of the real estate agent. They bring lenders and borrowers together, earning a commission for originating a loan. Good mortgage brokers will have contacts with numerous lenders, and will know who is likely to accept the loan.

Local banks often do not want properties with more than four family units, but a mortgage broker might have lenders who would lend against this kind of property. Mortgage brokers can be particularly helpful for borrowers with blemished or damaged credit.

Should You Deal With a Mortgage Broker or a Banker?

An important difference between a banker and a broker is that with the mortgage broker, you are not speaking to the final decision maker. So long as the mortgage broker knows his lender well, this does not have to be a problem. However, you should ask your mortgage broker how many loans of the type you need he or she has placed. Loans for investment properties can be sufficiently different from the owner-occupied loans that make up the bulk of the mortgages most brokers place, so seeking a specialist in your area may be warranted.

The final answer to deciding between a mortgage broker and a banker is that you should deal with both. This is business, and whoever can give you the best deal is who should earn your business. If you are borrowing $100,000, what is it going to cost you to get the loan? What are the terms of the loan? The answers to these questions should determine who earns your business.

There is nothing wrong with being straightforward with the banker and broker. Tell them you are searching for the best deal. Allow them to compete for your business.

David has a preference for dealing directly with bankers. Having been in the business for several years, he has already solidified a number of banking relationships. He no longer needs the matchmaking service provided by a mortgage broker. But for a property plagued by unusual circumstances, even David might need to approach a mortgage broker to find a specialist to make the appropriate loan.

While some bankers also work under a commission structure, nearly every mortgage broker is compensated by earning a commission from the lender. The mortgage broker has the same obligation as a banker to disclose to you in writing all of the fees required to obtain a loan.

Buyer Beware

Some of the protections and restrictions imposed upon bankers and mortgage brokers apply only to residential one- to four-unit dwellings. Buildings with five residential units or larger are regarded as commercial real estate and are not subject to all of the same protections. In short, the legislature is saying that by the time you are sophisticated enough to afford these larger properties, you should know better.

Mortgage brokers should know what loans can and cannot get approved. No one can work miracles. If you just declared bankruptcy last week, have a total of $200 in cash, and no job, there is no legitimate lender that will lend you $200,000 to buy a home. The system just doesn't work that way.

Never deal with a mortgage broker who wants nonrefundable money or a retainer up front to look for a loan for you. See Chapter 11 for more information about mortgage brokers.

Private Lenders

There are legitimate private lenders who will provide funds to purchase real estate. They are not easy to find. The rates and terms and kinds of financing are as varied as the individuals willing to make these loans. Some lenders will lend money for properties when regular lenders will not. For example, a rehab property—one without working mechanical systems or a roof—might be ripe for a private investor. If the plan is to purchase the property for ⅓ of the potential fair market value, rehab it, and sell it, and conventional financing cannot be found, a private lender might be interested in the investment. Expect to pay higher than market rates for the private lender's money. There is more at risk, and a greater chance for loss. For more information about private lenders, see Chapter 12.

Accountants

As you progress in real estate investing, an accountant will become an important ally in handling your business operation. The accountant will provide advice on how to document your expenses properly and can provide expert assistance in filing required tax returns.

Accountants know the legitimate deductions. A good accountant will make sure you are not overpaying your taxes. The accountant will also be certain you are claiming proper depreciation.

Lawyers

Although we love to laugh at lawyer jokes, an attorney who knows your state's real estate laws is a great ally. A good attorney can give you advice that could save you thousands of dollars in legal fees.

Always use your attorney to settle any real estate transaction whenever possible. And always use your attorney to approve any documents if you are purchasing real estate without a real estate agent involved in the transaction.

Real Deal

It always costs less money to *stay out* of legal trouble than it does to get yourself *out* of legal trouble. Use your lawyer to avoid costly mistakes.

Title Companies

Title companies offer *title* insurance and in some areas, complete settlement or closing services.

Never buy real estate without obtaining title insurance. The insurance protects you against various liens that may be unknown to you. Sometimes the buyer has to pay and sometimes the seller pays for the title insurance—it varies by state.

def•i•ni•tion

In real estate, the word **title** is used to describe ownership. Title insurance is issued by a title insurance company to protect an owner of real estate against defects in the title.

There are policies written to protect the lender, as well as the buyer. Title insurance that benefits the lender, often called the mortgage policy, is nearly always paid for by the party taking out the loan, typically the buyer. Fees for title insurance vary from company to company. Be sure to get competitive quotes if you have to pay for any title insurance.

It's a good idea to develop a relationship with a sharp title agent. The agent can help save money on your title work by using any prior title insurance issued on the property. By going to one title rep with all of your needs (purchase, refinance, sale), you are more likely to get a discount.

You can learn more about title insurance by contacting the American Land Title Association (ALTA), 18128 L. Street, NW, Suite 705, Washington, D.C. 20036; Phone: 202-296-3671; www.alta.org.

Contractors

A good contractor—someone who can provide repairs or improvement services to your real estate at a reasonable price—is a valuable asset. As you look at properties—and find ones that had work recently done—inquire about who the contractor was. Keep notes, especially about work that was done well.

Also keep notes on bad or shoddy workmanship. You not only want to know who does good work—but also who does work that you want to avoid. Keep in touch with other landlords as well. These referrals from your peers are your best bet for finding a qualified contractor.

Property Managers

One unique feature of real estate investing is the need to watch it and maintain it. When the property is used to generate rental income, the management of the property becomes more complex. Not only must you find and qualify tenants, you must respond to their problems and issues. Collecting rent, resolving problems, and scheduling routine maintenance takes time. As a real estate investor, you can do this yourself, or you can hire a property manager.

Property managers handle the day-to-day issues involved with real estate. For the most part, real estate investors handle the property management themselves. When investors own many properties, or as a matter of personal preference, it may become necessary to hire an employee to manage the properties, or, alternatively, the investor might consider hiring an outside property management company to serve as their property manager. For more information about property managers, see Chapter 17.

Finding Help

Nothing seems to have grown faster than the World Wide Web. You can find nearly anything on it. You can find people and companies online, but be sure to check them out before you decide to do business with them.

Government websites can also provide valuable information for the real estate investor. Check out www.hud.gov for thousands of pages of useful information. Also check Appendix C for additional resources available online.

There are likely some local resources that could help your real estate investing career. In many parts of the country, there are real estate investing clubs or apartment associations that meet once a month. If there is not one in your city, there could be one in a nearby city. Many times their meetings include a speaker and time to mingle and talk with other investors. Check your phone book and ask around—and don't give up until you find one.

The Least You Need to Know

- Investing in real estate becomes more complex if you borrow money to purchase property.
- Real estate agents can provide valuable service to a real estate investor.

- Bankers and mortgage brokers offer access to funds to purchase real estate. Brokers can match lenders and borrowers to make more difficult or nontraditional loans.
- An accountant and a lawyer can keep you out of trouble.
- Title insurance should always be obtained for any real estate purchase.

Chapter 4

Buying Homes for Investments

In This Chapter

- Learning about your customers
- Understanding minimum property requirements
- Reviewing how important knowledge is
- Discovering different needs and wants of tenants

Residential investment real estate comes in all kinds of styles, shapes, and sizes. What at first may not seem like a good investment may turn out to be an excellent one.

The more you know about real estate, including its uses, the more likely you are to be a successful investor. Getting started requires basic knowledge about what you are buying: a property that someone is going to call their home.

In this chapter, you'll read about how to get started in real estate investing, including minimum requirements you should look for in any investment property. Then you'll learn about the wants and needs of your customers—your tenants.

Fast Starts for Investors

Congratulations! You're going to be a real estate investor!

The big question is, where do you start? Now that you have made the decision to invest in real estate, there is overwhelming temptation to start right away. You may want to phone that number on the "For Sale" sign, or look in the real estate section of the Sunday newspaper, read some ads, and start calling.

But is this the best way to start?

Anyone who knows anything about real estate has probably heard the first three rules of real estate—location, location, location. This is good advice for both beginners and seasoned pros.

There's more simple advice for investors. Perhaps you've heard that in the stock market, the key is to buy low and sell high. That's wise counsel. Many times, implementing such strategies is easier said than done, and difficult to put into practice.

When it comes to getting started with investing in real estate, the first three rules are knowledge, knowledge, knowledge.

You are already on the right track. Reading this book is expanding your knowledge of real estate investing.

What All Residences Must Have

Any home must have the basics. A roof and a sound foundation are basics. The mechanical systems—plumbing, electricity, heating/cooling—are also essential basics. All homes need an area to prepare and keep food (the kitchen), and a bathroom with a toilet, tub/shower, and sink. There needs to be some living space, as well as a bedroom.

When considering properties for investments, these basics must be considered. You will need to provide them to your tenants. Generally speaking, these items include …

- **Security.** The home you are providing needs to be secured reasonably with locks on the doors and windows.
- **Plumbing.** You need to supply safe drinking water in sufficient quantity. The plumbing that disposes of waste water needs to work properly with the sewage system. Water pressure should be adequate to every faucet. Low water pressure can be a sign of plumbing pipes constricted by years of mineral deposit accumulation. Expensive plumbing repairs could be required.

- **Electricity.** The home needs a safe supply of electricity. Many municipalities require electrical systems to be inspected and certified. The electrical system must be sufficient to provide power for household appliances and entertainment electronics. Much older housing is plagued by obsolete electrical systems that would require expensive repairs to update. Electrical systems with fuses or with less than 100-amp services are obsolete.
- **Heating/Cooling systems.** A home must have a sufficient heating or cooling system, or both. Depending on the region where the home is located, you may need to provide only a heating system or cooling system. The climate in your part of the country will govern what is needed. Heating systems that are not mechanically sound may threaten the health of your tenant with possible carbon monoxide poisoning.

Buyer Beware

Notice that the basics you must provide could all be classified under the category of safety. Don't buy an investment property that may not be able to provide a safe living environment.

Almost any property you consider as an investment is likely to need something fixed, replaced, or added. That's part of the real estate business. Some small items can easily be added or taken care of with minimal effort.

For example, every rental unit should have working smoke detectors. If it does not (or the number of detectors is insufficient), you can easily add one for just a few dollars and a few minutes of your time.

Some things are indeed minor repairs. A loose doorknob or kitchen drawer with a handle missing takes little time to repair. For some reason, people will live with these annoying problems rather than fix them. Realize what is minor and what you can fix with minimal cost or time.

The Rooms in a Home

As an active real estate investor, you look at many properties. You only make offers to purchase those that make sense to buy. As you inspect the properties, ask yourself questions about the rooms in the property:

- **Living room.** How large is the room? Where would a television/entertainment center be placed? Will it be easy to place furniture? Does this look like space where people would want to live and spend their time?

- **Kitchen.** Does the kitchen have a stove/oven? What about the counter/workspace? Are there sufficient cabinets to hold food, glasses, tables, and other kitchen utensils? Where would the refrigerator or microwave be placed? Are appliances included or will the tenant be required to furnish them? Does the sink work (both water supply and drain)? What is the condition and quality of the cabinets, countertops, and flooring?
- **Bathroom.** Does the bathroom have the three essential items: shower over tub, toilet, and sink? Do they all work? Are they in good condition?
- **Bedroom.** Are the bedrooms large enough to place at least a conventional-size double bed and furniture? Are there sufficient electrical outlets? What about the closet space? Sometimes a three-bedroom dwelling is easier to rent than a two-bedroom. Know the market in your area.

There will be other rooms in some residential units. These could include dining rooms, dens, recreation rooms, and powder rooms, also called half baths.

What's Important to the Tenant

If you always keep in mind that you are investing in a property for someone to live in, it becomes easier to realize what you need in your units. Much is easy to overlook, but will be important to your tenant.

Some of those items are …

- **Closets.** Does the unit offer sufficient closet space for storage?
- **Bath space.** Does the bath include a shower? Are towel holders available?
- **Lighting.** Is there sufficient lighting in the kitchen and the bathroom?
- **Kitchen extras.** Does the kitchen offer any extra amenities, such as a dishwasher, microwave, or garbage disposal?
- **Cleanliness.** The battle for customers, be they buyers or tenants, is won and lost over the quality and cleanliness of the kitchen and bath.
- **Basement.** Is the basement always dry or is it prone to leaking?
- **Other hazards.** Your tenants don't want to have anything to do with asbestos, in-ground oil tanks, radon gas, or other property hazards. These problems are discussed further in Chapter 17.

Another important tenant concern is laundry equipment. Can your residents do their laundry at your rental home, or must they go to a laundromat?

You will have to decide what appliances to provide for your customer. There are two schools of thought in regard to providing appliances. One school says to allow the tenants to provide their own appliances. Tenants who provide their own appliances tend to be more stable and the landlord is relieved of the responsibility of maintaining the equipment.

The second school of thought notes damage can be done to the rental unit while moving in and out large bulky items like appliances. Further, an old leaky washing machine or dishwasher can ruin the flooring. Finally, not every customer has their own appliances, so the pool of potential tenants is smaller.

Properly providing the right amenities and removing any defects or hazards will increase the likelihood that someone will want to become your tenant and live in your investment property.

Trying to figure out what looks nice is never an easy task. Potential investment properties that have not been freshened or updated exist in every town throughout the country. Sometimes, old-fashioned hard work and soap is all it takes to bring a shine to dingy housing. A good cleaning can do wonders.

Removal of trash or junk is also a certain way to improve the appearance of any property. Other simple items are improved lighting, professional carpet-cleaning, and clean windows. A well-maintained lawn and attractive landscaping are a must. It doesn't matter how great your property looks on the inside if your prospective tenant is turned off by what he or she sees on the outside. The outside appearance of a property is often referred to as the property's curb appeal.

A good first impression in the only impression you want to make. When a potential tenant walks into the property, what will they think? One certain turn-off is offensive odors. Try to prohibit smoking indoors if you can. Sometimes, removing odors from negligent pet owners is a real challenge. If the property you are considering has such a problem, make sure you can remove the odor for your tenant.

> **Real Deal**
>
> Paint is cheap, but don't buy cheap paint. The greater cost associated with painting is the labor to apply the paint, not the cost of the paint itself. Never underestimate how a fresh coat of paint can vastly improve any property. Be prepared to spend a few dollars on quality paint.

Pet odor can penetrate deeply into porous building materials. An animal urine stain can sometimes require removal of carpet, pad, and even portions of a wood subfloor or the drywall. Sometimes hard surfaces like wood and concrete can be sealed to eliminate the odor without removing the affected building materials. The appropriate sealers will be in the paint department of any hardware store.

Cosmetic Appearances

Many potential properties you will consider for investment will have serious cosmetic appearance problems. Cosmetics are those things that can easily be changed. For example, a bedroom painted in a drab olive color could be revitalized with a fresh coat of white paint. A kitchen floor might appear worn, but a fresh vinyl floor would bring new life to it.

> **Author's Advice**
>
> Learn what the expense of specific cosmetic updates will cost you. You need to have a general idea as you are considering properties. If you are willing to do it yourself, you can save a lot of money. Painting is always a good do-it-yourself project.

Some things are not as easily changed. You might have a bathroom from the 1960s where the toilet, sink, and tub are yellow. Now out of style, it would take a major renovation to change all three to white.

While it will cost you money to correct cosmetic items to improve the appearance of the property, do not discard a potential investment because it does not show well or it needs an update.

Who Would Want to Live Here?

There is always a fundamental question that you must ask yourself before investing in any property. Because you are buying residential property, the goal is for someone to live in it. As you consider investment properties, always ask yourself, "who would want to live here?" The answer to that question might determine whether or not you even consider the property.

For example, consider a simple two-story, 3 bedroom, 1 bath modest house. It's about 50 years old, and is a typical find anywhere in the country. Every community has this property. Let's think about this home in three different locations.

Our first location for this home is on a quiet, tree-lined street. Within three blocks, there is a park. In the opposite direction, there is an elementary school. Public transportation is available only a short distance away. There's a small shopping area within easy walking distance, which includes a drug store and convenience store. All the properties on the block where this house is located appear well maintained.

Our second location is a predominately industrial area. The air is permeated with a sour odor. Train tracks are located immediately to the rear of the property. When the long freight trains pass, the house seems to rattle and shake. Heavy truck traffic rumbles in front of the property all hours of the day and night. A questionable bar with a history of problems is just down the street.

The third location for our sample property is at a crossroads in the middle of nowhere. The nearest town is about twenty miles away, on a two-lane road. It takes a good 30 minutes to get there. The location is so rural there is no cable for television. The only thing nearby is woods and farmland.

Remember we are talking about the same house, just in three different locations. Who would want to live in the house at each location?

At location one, the rent would be the highest, because most people would want to live there. It would be easier to attract a good tenant and to rent the property. At location two, the rent would need to be less, only because it would be harder to find a tenant. At location three, the rent would be somewhere in the middle, since some people would love to live in the country, while others would hate being miles away from others. What determines the rent for each location is the type of person who would want to live there.

Let us assume the rent for location one is $800, location two is $400, and location three is $600. Some people would prefer location two over the other locations. Why? The rent is less. Some people could not afford $800 a month, or would simply prefer to pay less. This does not necessarily make them bad or suggest that anything is wrong, it is just a matter of reality.

However, be careful of the location-two type properties. There are plenty of good tenants on tight budgets who are seeking affordable housing, but if the location is truly problematic, no respectable tenant on any budget will want to live there.

Some people would prefer location three and pay $600 a month and travel to work—even if their transportation costs and rent would be more each month than a closer location. Some people prefer to live in a rural location. It may not make logical sense to some, while others think this makes perfect sense. There is no right or wrong here, just the way people are different.

Who My Customer Might Be

The property will determine who your customer might be. As a real estate investor, your tenants are your customers. Each month, your customer will pay rent for the privilege of staying in your property.

As you evaluate properties for purchase as investments, constantly consider your future customers. What the property offers—and does not offer—will determine who your eventual customers will be.

Author's Advice

Always think of your tenants as your customers.

In real estate, the spectrum of your potential customers can be divided by income into three categories: low-income, medium- or middle-income, and high-income. Each customer group has unique characteristics and concerns.

One thing common to each group—regardless of income level—is the desire for cleanliness. It is amazing how often landlords fail to provide this simple and basic requirement. It is nearly impossible to attract good customers with dirty housing.

Working with Low-Income Tenants

Low-income tenants can include young people just starting out in their first home to elderly folks on fixed incomes. In between are other customers that for whatever reason just do not earn a lot of money. Your experience as a landlord renting to these customers will depend on the demographic characteristics of your low-income tenants.

For example, low-income elderly tenants tend to be stable customers who pay their rent reliably and rarely move. On the other hand, they can be quite sensitive to rent increases. Younger tenants tend to be transient, subject to moving more frequently. Younger customers are often living hand-to-mouth, without any cushion of savings or health insurance. Therefore, if there is an illness, an inability to work, or a job loss, this customer may immediately become unable to pay the rent.

The median household income in the United States is $44,473 in 2004 dollars according to the U.S. Census Bureau. The Federal Government defines low income in at least some of its housing programs as those households earning 60 percent or less of the median income.

Providing clean, mechanically sound housing will probably be enough to satisfy lower income customers. Accessibility to grocery stores, other service retail outlets, and public transportation is a greater concern for this customer group. Security features may also be important.

You should not fall into the trap of associating lower income customers with being less desirable. When interest rates are low, many rental units suffer vacancy loss because customers are buying homes. However, lower income customers may not be able to afford their own home. If you carefully screen your customers, you should be able to find plenty of good, reliable, low-income tenants.

Buyer Beware

All tenants must be carefully screened. It does not matter whether they are low-, middle-, or high-income.

Working With Middle-Income Tenants

Middle-income tenants will have the same expectations as low-income tenants, but will also expect more amenities and a larger unit. These customers will often view dishwashers, garages, and private laundry equipment provided by the landlord as standard equipment. If the kitchen cabinets have a worn or outdated finish, you may be able to get away with painting the cabinets with an off-white, durable paint in a low-income unit. However, this idea is not going to work for a middle-income unit. New cabinets may be required. Similarly, this customer may be expecting self-cleaning ranges and an automatic defrost refrigerator.

Middle-income customers come from all occupations. They can include younger families and older empty-nesters. They can be lifelong tenants or candidates for future home ownership.

Working With High-Income Tenants

High-income customers again have all the expectations of their less affluent peers but have still greater expectations, both in size and available amenities. There is no room for any kind of obsolescence in any part of the housing unit. The customer may expect a premium location such as those locations with a golf course or water view. Expectations may include access to a fitness center or swimming pool and even concierge services. The customer may expect two covered garage spaces attached to the dwelling.

Pet policies excluding pets may be accepted by the rest of the tenant population, but high-income customers are more likely to have less patience with such rules and may expect to bring their cats, dogs, and other pets with them.

Usually, only larger apartment communities of 150 units or more can provide amenities such as fitness centers, swimming pools, and concierge services. A recent trend in luxury real estate is to provide various concierge services for tenants. This can include making dinner and ticket reservations, taking in package deliveries, watering plants and tending to pets during an absence, and other services.

High-income customers are looking for housing that is unique, and they are willing to pay for it. Sometimes middle- or even low-income units can be repositioned as high-income units by making the right improvements and upgrades. Such repositioning represents a terrific profit opportunity for the investor.

David bought a dilapidated apartment building for less than half of its tax-assessed value! This building was designated by the Federal Government as low-income housing. However, behind all the dirt and grime, he envisioned a gem. The apartments had unique architectural features such as lofts and enormous bay windows. The property was structurally and mechanically sound. Little more than upgrading carpets, painting, and cleaning repositioned this building as a middle-income offering, with increased rent to reflect its new status.

Why Would Someone Want to Live Here?

The location of the property will greatly influence who your customer will be. As you learned earlier, different people will prefer different locations. Some will not be concerned about a location if it offers a less expensive place to live. Others will pay more for what they perceive to be a better location.

Buyer Beware

Good schools are important, but being located directly adjacent to a school may not be the best thing. Monitor the property at the hour when the school dismisses before you buy.

Many times, people choose their residences based upon the quality of the public schools. A strong public school system is one of the most important aspects of infrastructure that any community can provide. Infrastructure describes the road, bridges, rail lines, schools, and other public works found in a modern economy. Good tenants may flee or avoid a declining school system. Realize the availability of good schools will often determine who will want to live in your investment property.

There is always a demand for properties near colleges or universities. If your property is near such an institution, your customer could be a student or a teacher. Many times, creative people—artists, writers, musicians—have a desire to live near these types of schools because of the culture and learning opportunities they offer. Be advised that student housing can be one of the more management-intensive landlord opportunities.

While you are searching for investment properties, you may not know who your future customer will be. You should still ask yourself, "why would they want to live here?"

There must be logical reasons why someone would want to reside in the property. Many times, with a little imagination and small amount of money, you can greatly improve a property, making it look nicer and more desirable. Always consider the extras you can do—the easy things—that can add value, quality of life, and improve the appearance of the property.

You can see how your expanding knowledge—from neighborhoods to living space to fix-ups—can help you in real estate investing. The more knowledge you have about all aspects of real estate, the better off you'll be.

A property that is appealing to as many customers as possible is always best. The more appealing you can make the property, the easier it will be for you to maintain a profitable return on your investment. It has to be a place that someone is going to want to call home sweet home.

Lead Paint and Other Hazards

When buying properties for real estate investment, the investor must realize the potential for hazards. Over recent years, government policies and regulations have been established that require the elimination or abatement of specific hazardous conditions. As a landlord and under the law, you are held responsible for any hazards on your property.

Before buying a property for investment, you should realize the possible hazards, and understand what you might need to do to eliminate them and make your property safe for your tenants.

Lead Paint

Older residential properties could have lead paint in them. Lead was a common ingredient added to paint for several decades prior to 1974. Many homes with this paint still exist.

Because of the danger to your customers—especially children—a property with lead paint is a particular problem. Lead-based paint cannot simply be scraped off and the surface repainted. Strict environmental regulations must be followed.

Make sure you realize the problems associated with any property that has the potential of having lead paint. Lead-based paint is a critical issue in housing today. Lead-based paint can be toxic, particularly for children. The Federal Government banned lead as an ingredient in paint in 1974. However, owing to the existing stock of paint

Buyer Beware

Never disturb lead-based paint. The legal liability and health issues are real.

that may have already been in existence, the government has determined that any housing built prior to 1978 may contain lead-based paint. If the real estate was built before 1978, the government requires sellers of real estate and landlords to furnish buyers and tenants with a copy of a booklet called "Protect Your Family From Lead In Your Home." It is available online at www.hud.gov.

Never scrape or sand a painted surface unless you are sure there is no lead in the painted surface you are working on. Paint test kits are available in most hardware stores. If a contractor (or anyone else) is disturbing more than two square feet of painted surface, the pamphlet "Protect Your Family From Lead In Your Home" must be again provided to anyone who might touch the work area.

Mold Problems

There are no established standards for acceptable or unacceptable concentrations of mold. Levels of airborne mold fluctuate rapidly, rendering mold testing of little value. Mold is a risk that few insurance companies cover. There are cases where mold contamination has resulted in condemnation of the real estate. Overlooking a potential mold problem could have devastating financial impact. Mold requires water and a food source to grow. Most building materials are suitable for hosting a mold bloom if they get wet. The only practical way of combating mold is to keep water out of where it does not belong. Any building materials that get wet from a sewer backup, roof leak, or other calamity should be removed if possible.

Buyer Beware

Mold is a hot-button issue in real estate today. Mold can be toxic in sufficient concentrations. Some people are allergic to mold. Mold is always around us in varying degrees of concentration.

Beware of musty odors or visible signs of mold. Any property that has had roof repairs, basement leaks, or any extensive plumbing problem should be further investigated to make certain there is not a related mold problem. A good home inspector should be able to help you assess any property for the potential presence of mold.

Other Hazards

There are a multitude of additional hazards that you might encounter. Many of these perils were hot-button hazards a few years ago. Asbestos is one example. Other lasting hazards include radon gas, termite infestation, and in-ground storage tanks.

Asbestos is a fire-resistant material that has been known to man since nearly the beginning of time. It can be found in floor and ceiling tile and in insulating materials like boiler pipe wrap. It can also be often found sprayed on the ceilings and support structures of underground parking garages.

Asbestos can be carcinogenic, causing lung cancer. Asbestos is most dangerous when it becomes friable. This means when the asbestos product starts to deteriorate it begins to crumble or turn to dust, creating greatest potential for harm.

In its heyday as a hazard, the standard response to asbestos was to remove it using specialized contractors. The flaw to this approach is that the removal process can pose the greater risk of disturbing the asbestos and releasing toxic particles into the air. Today the approach is most often to either encapsulate the asbestos in place or to even to just leave it alone if the asbestos material is in good condition. If you suspect asbestos is in a dwelling you are considering buying, the best approach is to rely on a home inspector to identify whether asbestos is present and if so, what should be done about it. More information about asbestos is available from the Environmental Protection Agency (EPA) at www.epa.gov/asbestos.

Similar to asbestos, radon gas is another carcinogenic associated with lung cancer. Radon is a colorless, odorless, radioactive gas. The only way to be certain of its presence or absence is to test for it. Radon levels vary according to location. Local geology, construction materials, and how the home was built are among the factors that can affect radon levels in homes. Radon comes from the ground underneath a home, well water, or building materials. Newer or more tightly insulated homes may be more prone to higher radon concentrations, because the gas is less likely to escape. The EPA believes radon remains a serious hazard. Other studies and experts contest this position. Test kits are inexpensive and can be purchased at home improvement centers and hardware stores. Remediation is typically inexpensive, averaging about $1,200 nationally per dwelling unit abated. More radon information is available from the EPA at www.epa.gov/radon.

Termite infestations can have a devastating impact on real estate. Since termites will bore into the insides of wood building products, the damage can be invisible. For those areas of the country, primarily in the south and west, where termite infestations are an issue, a termite inspection by an experienced, trained contractor is a must.

Preventative termite measures include keeping any wood products in the dwelling from being in contact with the ground. Make sure that perimeter grading drains water away from the foundation to deprive termites of needed water. No standing water or firewood should be allowed near the foundation. Even cardboard boxes in a garage should be elevated off the floor.

Underground storage tanks (USTs) as a real estate hazard usually relate to heating oil that was stored for use in fueling an oil furnace. These old tanks may have been abandoned years ago when natural gas became available to the dwelling. But the tank may still be in the ground and it may have begun to leak because of its age.

Until the mid-1980s, most USTs were made of bare steel prone to corrosion and leaking. Soil and groundwater contamination can result and remediation costs can be punitive. The key is to determine whether a UST may be present and to then act prudently if one is discovered.

Abandoned USTs may leave telltale signs. The old oil furnace may be long gone, but the fill pipe for the UST may still be in the yard. Be on the lookout for fuel lines coming through the basement walls near the basement floor. All that may be left of the fuel line is the portion still stuck in the wall. The rest will probably have been long ago cut away.

Seller condition reports that are a part of most real estate offers usually require the seller to make a representation about whether the seller has knowledge about any UST. However, do not rely on the seller's representations alone. A good home inspector can again be of help.

If you find an UST, having an appropriate contractor remove the tank is the only remedy. The seller should undertake this project, never you as the buyer. The reason is simple. You cannot know until the tank is out whether it leaked. If there was a leak, the soil around it will probably be contaminated and require expensive remediation. You don't want to take a chance on getting stuck with this cost. More information about USTs is available at the EPA website at www.epa.gov/swerust1/overview.htm.

Buyer Beware

If you discover an UST, always make the seller responsible for its removal.

One universal remedy to concerns over USTs, petroleum spills, or other environmental contamination is to hire a consultant to perform what is called a Phase One Environmental Study. The parameters of this study do not include taking any soil borings. Instead, the approach is to study the history of how the site was used to determine whether it would be likely that petroleum or other contaminates may have been disposed of on the site. The surrounding area is also studied to assess whether an adjacent contaminated site may have impacted the site. The review typically includes the study of building permits, aerial photographs, historical municipal directories, governmental environmental databases, and a physical inspection of the site. A Phase One study is not cheap and may cost $1,000 or more. However, this expense pales in comparison to the cost of an unanticipated environmental cleanup.

While the preceding discussion should leave you well equipped to handle most property hazards experienced in real estate investing, this list is by no means comprehensive. Until you gain greater experience, you should rely upon a qualified home inspector to uncover every potential problem that might exist in any property you are considering buying.

Best Properties to Buy and Rent

You will wonder what are the best properties to buy, hold, and rent. Any property has the potential of producing rental income. Even bare land could be rented to a farmer for crop production.

Commercial properties—which are covered further in Chapter 23—are legitimate investment opportunities, but for our discussion here, we are looking at either single-family or multi-family properties.

Single-Family Homes

Single-family properties come in all sizes, shapes, and styles. They are saltboxes, colonials, bungalows, in one, two, or three stories, designed to accommodate a single family living on the property.

Single-family properties are the most common availability in most areas of the country. The best for rental income are …

- Maintained in reasonably good condition.
- Homes that provide a basic residence.
- Clean, secure, and safe.

You do not need to have expensive and potentially fragile features in your rental home. In fact, such features can be a detriment. For example, a property with an expensive carpet throughout may not generate more income than one with less expensive carpet. Yet if the carpet is damaged by a tenant, the loss is less when the carpet is not as expensive.

Consider properties that offer rental income more than 1⁄100 of the acquisition price. For example, a property that costs $100,000 should generate a $1000 a month in rental income. If the property would only generate $750 per month in income, the property may not be desirable from a real estate investor's viewpoint.

A property that generates more than the 1/100 formula is an appealing property for the real estate investor. For example, a property that produces $1000 a month in rent but only costs $75,000 to acquire would be a lucrative investment for an investor.

Multifamily Homes

Properties designed for more than one family to live in are called multifamily. These properties are commonly called apartment houses, and the units where people live are referred to as apartments. Even duplexes and triplexes could be accurately referred to as multifamily properties.

Multifamily homes are appealing to real estate investors because they usually generate greater rental income at a lower cost per unit. Often, multifamily units are good real estate investments. It is easier to generate positive cash flow in a multifamily property than with single-family homes.

Best Properties to Buy and Resell

Properties that you purchase to resell require one thing: a below fair market value price. The only way to make money is to buy below fair market value, or to buy below potential fair market value. These discounted properties may be available because, for whatever reasons, the owner wants rid of the property quickly—perhaps because the property has not been maintained or because of a personal calamity. The better the discount from the market value, the more money you will make when you resell the property.

Distressed and Ugly Homes

Properties that are distressed can occasionally be purchased for less than the fair market value. Sometimes owners of properties do not maintain them, and allow them to become run-down. Sometimes, the repairs that need to be made are cosmetic in nature, while others could be extensive and expensive.

Distressed and ugly homes are just that: these are the properties that no one wants—in the condition they are in at the moment. They may need paint, landscaping, cleanup, and more.

Real estate investors may purchase these properties for the sole purpose of flipping them. Sometimes it is after repairs are made. Other times, it is without any work being completed. This occurs most often when these properties are sold to another real estate investor. You will learn more about property flipping in Chapter 10.

Homes Owned by Motivated Sellers

Another way to buy properties below fair market value is to acquire them from motivated sellers. These are owners who want to sell the property immediately, and are willing to take less to get rid of the responsibility of owning the property. These owners are often under financial pressure, perhaps from an illness, death, job loss, or divorce. For more information about buying properties from motivated sellers, see Chapter 12.

The Least You Need to Know

- Knowledge is your best tool when considering any real estate property for investment.
- Properties that at first seem undesirable might actually be good investments.
- Your eventual customer is one of the most important considerations when investing in real estate.
- Some properties can be easily improved with cleaning and minor repairs.
- You should be on the alert for mold, lead paint, and other hazards in every property that you consider.
- Real estate investing presents opportunities for profit by either buying and holding for cash flow, or buying and reselling.

Part 2 Finding the Properties

There is an old saying in the real estate business that goes like this: you make money when you buy. There is much that can go wrong in real estate. The furnace may fail, the roof shingles may blow off, or the basement may leak, and as a result, your cash flow may be impacted. For a while.

If you buy the wrong property, your days of misery may be without end. But when you buy the right property, broken furnaces and leaky basements are just speed bumps on the road to prosperity.

Chapter 5

Before You Start Looking

In This Chapter

- Finding the right investment properties
- Recognizing good and bad deals
- Learning when to buy or pass on a property
- Knowing the best locations for investment properties

Once having made the decision to get into the real estate investment business, there can be an overwhelming temptation to start quickly and buy any property that looks tempting. Before jumping in, ask yourself a question. How did you go about buying your last car? Were you just tooling down the street one day when you spied that gleaming new model in the showroom window and you just had to have it? Maybe you pulled right off the road and thirty minutes later that beautiful new car was yours. Most people would say you did nothing wrong if this was your experience. Just understand that you made an impulsive, emotional decision as a consumer. Impulsive, emotional decisions have no place in the arena of investment decisions.

The better car-buying example would be the shopper who first reads a few respected consumer's guide magazines to get a feel for which cars are best. The car buyer considers mechanical reliability and crashworthiness. Then our savvy car buyer consults a pricing guide to learn something about the dealer's cost and typical sale prices. Then our buyer goes on a few test drives. He or she does not even begin to start negotiating a purchase price before getting the financing lined up. Does this sound like a good way to get a good deal on a car? The same thinking applies to real estate—do your homework.

In this chapter, you will discover that real estate investing is a business just like any other, which is to say that competition is keen. The wise conquer and the foolish perish on the real estate battlefield. But don't be alarmed—the information in this book will be your sword and your shield.

Comparison Shopping for Real Estate

How can you know if any particular real estate deal is a good deal? By comparing your potential deal to the done deals, you can begin to determine values. You need to keep an eye on the properties that have already sold. Many times, real estate sections of Sunday newspapers list the recently completed real estate transactions. Better yet, just about any real estate agent can do a search of closed transactions in the multiple listing service.

As an active real estate investor, you should constantly be looking at the market prices of real estate. You should visit open houses, and keep yourself aware of what properties are being purchased for what amount in your area.

Valuing the Property

To determine your own value on a property, you'll need to learn something about operating statements and comparable sales. The operating statement summarizes the income-producing capacity of the real estate. Comparable sales are the done deals, the similar recently sold properties that you just read about. This discussion has a particular name in the real estate industry. It's called *appraisal theory.*

Appraisal theory is the process by which three value yardsticks are applied to measuring the fair market value of any particular piece of real estate. The three yardsticks are called the income approach, the market approach, and the cost approach. All are easy to understand.

Using the Income Approach

The income approach involves analyzing a property's operating statement. The operating statement is a summary that contains important information for the real estate investor. Operating statements are typically a one-page synopsis of the income and expenses the property produces. See the table that follows.

A Typical Property Operating Statement

Rent Income	Monthly	Annual	% of Gross
Unit 1	675	$8,100	31%
Unit 2	455	$5,460	21%
Unit 3	480	$5,760	22%
Unit 4	595	$7,140	27%
Gross Income	2,205	$26,460	100%
Vacancies		–$1,323	–5%
Adjusted Gross Income		$25,137	95%
Operating Expenses			
Taxes		$4,516	17%
Insurance		$582	2%
Electric		$420	2%
Natural Gas		$360	1%
Water & Sewer		$1,115	4%
Repairs/Maintenance		$1,200	5%
Lawn Service		$655	2%
Snow Removal		$550	2%
Supplies		$275	1%
Advertising		$300	1%
Accounting		$125	0%
Appliances		$800	3%
Trash Removal		$950	4%
Total Expenses		$11,848	45%
Net Operating Income		$13,289	50%

Author's Advice

Operating statements are sometimes called **Liar's Statements** because many times the operating statement is the seller's dream about how his property might operate if reality was not getting in the way!

These statements go by several names, including P&L (as in profit and loss) Sheet, Spec Sheet, and Write-Up, but a favorite name for these sheets is the *Liar's Statement.*

You need to develop your expertise to the point where you can breathe some truth into these statements. Your growing knowledge of the local market will soon allow you to spot numbers that do not make sense on an operating statement. For example, in at least some regions of the country, a good budget for annual repairs would be an amount equal to 5 percent of gross income. Some of the numbers on an operating statement can be directly verified because they are public information.

Property taxes and utilities (electricity, natural gas, and sewer and water) are public information that can be confirmed by calling the taxing authority and the utility companies in your area. You can and should get an estimate for insurance on the property from an insurance agent. Waste removal should also be checked and quoted.

Find out where rental homes are advertised in your area. They are probably advertised in the largest local daily newspaper, but sometimes the dominant source for rental advertising is the shopper's guides that are published weekly or biweekly and distributed to readers for free. Find out what advertising costs and make an estimate of the number of *turnovers* you are likely to experience so you can estimate an advertising budget.

def•i•ni•tion

When one customer-tenant moves out and a new one moves in, that is called a **turnover**.

Every turnover will require painting and cleaning at a minimum, and these costs should also be reflected in the operating statement.

Do not neglect the income side of the operating statement. You should perform a rent survey to determine whether the quoted rents are high, low, or just right. Tips on completing a rent survey will be included in Chapter 14.

Does this sound like a lot of work? It is. Fortunately, as you put forth the effort to research each particular property that may interest you, you will get better at making your own estimates and it will take less time. Additionally, the exercise will help make you a real estate expert!

Using the Market Approach

The market approach is the process of accumulating and evaluating recent comparable sales of similar real estate. You know if you got a good deal not based on anecdotal fishing stories from braggart real estate investors, but from good, hard verifiable data. You'll learn where to find that data in Chapter 8.

Comparable sales data of similar properties nearby is a great way to estimate the value of the property.

Using the Cost Approach

The cost approach is the third yardstick of value. This approach tries to discover how much it would cost to find a piece of land just like the one you have and build the same building all over again. A depreciation adjustment is made to reflect that the building being evaluated is not new. The cost approach is most effective for those properties that do not have information readily available for the other two yardsticks, the market approach or the income approach. For example, schools and churches do not produce income. Likewise, often there are not enough recent sales of church and school buildings to make an accurate determination.

Therefore, when good income and sales data *are* available, the cost approach becomes less valuable. Another limitation of the cost approach is that it is less useful for evaluating older properties. Older properties may have characteristics that would not be duplicated today (for example, smaller closets, wall-hung kitchen sinks, and 30 AMP electric service with fuses). In this book, the income approach and market approach will be the emphasis for your value judgments.

Real Deal

Property and casualty insurance agents are an excellent source for obtaining replacement cost estimates for most real estate.

Determining the Best Locations

As you learned earlier in this book, there are many different types of properties, and all kinds of renters and buyers. That means, as an investor, you should consider many different kinds of properties.

When you gain experience and more knowledge, you may begin to focus on one property over another. But that does not mean you should dismiss anything until you analyze each opportunity. As an active real estate investor, do not put your head in the sand. Keeping an open mind—and analyzing each property correctly—is the best way to determine if any particular property would make a good investment.

Your analysis should include the hard numbers already discussed, as well as several other factors:

- Whether the property has visual appeal. It looks good from the street, and looks good inside, or it has the potential to look good, inside and out.
- Whether the property is in an acceptable location. It is not beside a landfill or some other detrimental site that is likely to make it decrease in value, rather than increase.
- Whether the property can be acquired at or below a price comparable with other similar properties that recently sold.

The cost of the property, based on square footage, should be similar to other properties within the area. For example, if a property recently sold that has 1,000 square feet of space and the price was $50,000, the value was $50 per square foot. ($50,000 divided by 1,000 = $50). If a similar property is available at $100 a square foot, should you pay that much more per square foot? At the least, you should question the cost. If nothing more, it makes a strong negotiation point for you.

The smaller the dwelling, the higher the cost per square foot may be. For example, a 4,000-square foot home might sell for $80 per square foot ($320,000) that is right next door to a 2,200-square foot home that is selling for $95 per square foot ($209,000). They might have all the same exact amenities and upgrades in the home, but the larger home might have 5 bedrooms instead of 3 bedrooms. This is not unusual.

Minimally, every home must have at least one kitchen and one bath. Typically, kitchens and baths are the most expensive rooms in the house. Consider two three-bedroom one-bath homes. One is 1,200 square feet, the other 1,500 square feet. If the kitchen and bath in both homes cost about the same to duplicate, the cost of these relatively expensive rooms will be spread over a greater number of square feet in the larger dwelling, resulting in a lower cost per square foot.

Knowing When to Say No

In the beginning, the excitement and determination to get started in real estate investing may cloud your thinking. Lose the emotion. Look at each potential property and deal as a hard, cold business decision. If the numbers make sense, proceed to purchase the property. If there is any doubt, pass on the property and look for another.

Do not second-guess your decision when you decide not to purchase a property. Instead of focusing on what you should have done, use your energy to search for another property. You should not worry about what you could have done. Look instead at what you can do.

There are properties you should always pass on. Some examples of properties to pass on include properties that …

- Generate negative cash flow.
- Are likely to decrease, rather than increase, in value.
- Have uncorrectable obsolescence.
- Are overpriced.

Bad Deals, No Matter What

Some properties are bad real estate investments. They are not necessarily bad properties, but they will not provide a good return on the investment. Consider this example …

Property 1: Price $200,000

Rental Income: $1,000 per month ($12,000 per year)

To purchase, you must make a 20% down payment ($40,000). Your mortgage is $160,000 at 7% for 30 years. The payment is $1,064.48 (principal and interest only).

The property is nice, looks wonderful, and likely to appreciate. But you will be losing far more than $64 per month. Don't forget the taxes, insurance, and other expenses. Each month you own and operate this property, you will be going deeper into the hole. Your losses could be $5,000 or more per year. This is not a smart way to be a real estate investor.

Author's Advice

Avoid any property that does not have the potential for positive cash flow.

Now let's look at a similar property that is available for the same price …

Property 2: Price $200,000

Rental Income: $2,000 per month ($24,000 per year)

As in the first example, to purchase this property, you must make a 20% down payment ($40,000). Your mortgage is $160,000 at 7% for 30 years. The payment is $1,064.48 (principal and interest only).

If the cost for insurance, taxes, and other expenses is $400 per month, you will still see a profit of approximately $500 per month, or $6,000 per year. This example makes far more sense as an investment than the first.

Another factor is what it costs you to earn the $500 per month property. From these two examples, you can see that you would need to invest $40,000 (the down payment) before you can begin earning the $500 per month. Suppose you could buy another property that would require only $20,000 to earn the same $500 per month. That would likely make more sense to buy than the second example. As you can see, while property 2 might at first look like a good deal, it might make more sense to move on to another property. Your knowledge of the local market will tell you how likely it is that you can find other properties that have greater profit potential at a lower cost.

Let us do one more comparison at a different property. Here are the details …

Property 3: Price $100,000

Rental Income: $1,200 per month (2 units, $600 rent per month)

Financing: 20% down, $80,000 mortgage at 7% for 30 years: monthly payment $532.24 (principal and interest only).

Other Expenses: $250 per month

From an income approach, the property looks good. It produces about $400 positive cash flow per month.

From a market approach, the property also looks good. Other duplexes with the same square footage have sold for roughly $10,000 more in the past three months. These comparable sales have $78 per square foot to $86 per square foot with an average cost per square foot of $83. You can buy your building for $77 per square foot.

Quantity Versus Quality

As a new real estate investor, your zeal to move forward with multiple deals may again cloud your thinking. One of the mistakes many new investors make is falling into the trap that you must make many deals or at least one deal. Nothing is further from the truth.

Your success as a real estate investor should be measured by the quality of the real estate deals you participate in, not by the number. The quality should be based on several factors:

- **Profitability.** Whether it is a buy and resell deal, or a buy and hold, your deals should always be a moneymaking opportunity for you.
- **Meets Your Overall Goals**. Any real estate deal should fit into your overall investing goals and plans.
- **Ethical and Honest.** The transaction is above reproach—it is a fair deal where you have not taken an unfair advantage of a seller (or buyer).

Buyer Beware

Forget quantity, and stick to quality, in all of your real estate transactions. Do not fall into the trap of many new investors to buy something, just to get in on the action.

It is always best to complete quality deals. Just because you can do a deal is not a reason to do it. You may have to sort through dogs by the dozen before finding one good investment.

Local Versus Nonlocal Property

You learned earlier in this book that as a real estate investor, you should be involved with your property. Unlike opening a CD in a bank, where there is not much to do after signing the appropriate forms, real estate requires your attention. From handling a problem tenant to doing minor maintenance, it helps to be close to your investment properties.

Problems of Distant Rental Property

Let's look at the issue of renting a typical property. Most likely, you will erect a "for rent" sign with your telephone number on it. If your property is 15 minutes from your home, it will take about 45 minutes at the most to do this work. Assuming you work at a regular job during the day, you could do this easily in the evening. But if your rental property is two hours away, it will take all day. You might not be able to do this within a week because of your inability to leave your job during the day.

The problem becomes worse for a distant property: once you have the sign up, you need to show the property to potential renters. With a long distance property, that's another four-hour driving trip (two hours each direction). And if the person you show the property to does not take it (or you decide not to rent it to that person), it means additional trips.

Keep in mind that you might be more willing to take a marginal tenant, just to avoid the trips. This, of course, could cause you more potential headaches in the future.

Author's Advice

As a beginning investor, do not acquire any properties that are more than 30 minutes from your home.

It is always best, at least in the beginning, to invest in properties that are closer to your home. Minor maintenance—such as replacing a filter in the furnace—can cost next to nothing to do yourself. But this item will cost more if you request a service call from the local plumbing and heating contractor because you do not want to hassle with it.

Solutions for Distant Rentals

Some investors deliberately seek properties not close to their homes for various reasons. Sometimes the property is in a prime resort location where the goal is to retire there eventually, or the property was just too good of a deal to pass up, despite the distance. David owns properties as much as an hour from his office.

There are two ways to overcome the distance management problem. You can employ a nosy neighbor or obtain professional property management. These solutions are just the extremes of the cost spectrum of using someone else to manage your property.

The nosy neighbor is someone living nearby who clearly takes pride in his or her own property. This neighbor's concern even extends beyond his or her property to the entire neighborhood. Retirees or block watch captains are often excellent leads for being or finding a nosy neighbor to help you. Simply put, you want the nosy neighbor to help you keep an eye on your property. Mr. or Ms. Nosy can tell you if your tenant is failing to cut the grass or if there is litter in the yard. Maybe Nosy can even help you rent the property or make a minor repair. Obviously, you will need to pay them for their help, but the cost will be much less than calling contractors or using professional management.

If you have more than one unit in your building, then maybe you can get a nosy-neighbor type to move into your property. Now the nosy neighbor becomes an on-site manager or caretaker. The on-site manager is the one responsible for cutting the lawn, showing the apartments for rent, and making minor repairs. Sometimes it's a good idea to find a nosy neighbor to keep an eye on the on-site manager. Further, if you are going to use a nosy neighbor or an on-site manager to help you rent your housing units, you had better spend some time with this individual to make sure they understand all the applicable fair housing regulations in your area.

However, if you cannot find the appropriate nosy neighbor or if you just want the additional support that would be available from professional property management, the answer to owning a distant property is to turn over managing the property to a local property management company. This is the surest and easiest way to handle distant rental properties.

Property Management Companies

For a fee, property management companies will take care of all the details—from routine maintenance, handling rentals, issuing rental contracts, collecting deposits, dealing with the tenants, etc. The fees charged by management firms vary, but are usually based on a percentage of the gross income. There may be additional fees or leasing commissions.

The management fee for a medium-size apartment building (16 units or larger), might be 5 to 6 percent of the gross income. Expect the fee to be higher on a percentage basis for smaller properties. There may be a flat minimum fee.

The fees paid to the management company are in exchange for property supervision only. Repairs and supplies are extra. After-hours or weekend service calls may be subject to a premium charge.

The quality and ability of these firms can vary widely. Select a firm in proximity to your property that is already managing real estate similar to yours. Get a list of the firm's current clients, talk to some of these owners, and make some unscheduled visits to these properties to assess the quality of care exhibited.

> **Buyer Beware**
>
> Even with a property management company handling a distant piece of investment property, you still can't just forget about your investment.

You will still need to keep an eye on your property management firm with a few surprise visits to your property and scrutinize the monthly statement to make sure that your management company is doing its job.

The Least You Need to Know

- Comparison-shopping is the best way to search for investment real estate.
- Study the operating statement in order to ensure cash flow in the property you purchase.
- Of the three methods to determine if the property makes sense as an investment, the income approach and market approach are the most important.
- The best investments are properties that are close to your home.

Chapter 6

Getting to Know the Local Market

In This Chapter

- Learning the local market area
- Gathering information
- Becoming an investor now
- Finding bargain properties
- Investing in neglected properties

It is time to take what you have learned and start applying it to the area where you are going to invest. Now you must learn everything you can about your local market. The more you know, the better your investments can and will be.

Each community has prime, and not so prime, investment opportunities waiting for you. It is up to you to find each, and invest in only those that make the most sense for you and your plans.

Do not overlook the information in this chapter. Your knowledge of your local area will be one of the most important keys to your success as a real estate investor.

Learning Everything About a Community

One of the biggest advantages you can create is learning everything you can about your local market area. By now, from reading this book, you should be forming a good idea of where you are going to invest in real estate. In the beginning, the properties should ideally be within a half hour or less of your home. As you learned in the last chapter, you should not be focusing on distant properties, at least while getting started.

Depending on where you live, that probably means you should only be considering properties that are in about a 25-mile radius from your home unless you live in a sparse location. Using a map, draw a circle, and highlight it. This is your investment circle, where you will be focusing your efforts. The smaller the circle the better, and the easier it will be for you.

Gathering Your Own Information

As you closely look at your investment circle, start identifying the following:

- Daily, weekly, and Sunday newspaper(s) published and distributed in this area.
- Real estate magazines and booklets distributed in the area (at grocery stores, real estate agent's offices, convenience store racks, etc.).
- Television and radio stations that cover your investment circle area.
- Major real estate offices that serve the area.
- Counties that make up any part of the investment circle (get the locations of the county courthouses).
- School districts that are located within your investment area.
- Which municipalities are included within the designated area.

After gathering this information, it is time to start taking action. For the beginning investor, here is a list of actions you should check off within the next 90 days:

- ❑ Start reading the local news and all of any real estate sections of the major daily newspaper that covers the largest part of your investment circle.
- ❑ Determine which school districts are the most desirable in your investment circle.
- ❑ Go to several open houses (always try to meet a different real estate agent).
- ❑ Perform a rent survey within one neighborhood of your investment circle.
- ❑ Read several issues of any real estate magazine published in your designated investment area.
- ❑ Read the Sunday real estate classified advertising section and display advertisements in major Sunday newspapers published in your investment area.
- ❑ Listen to radio stations (their news programs) that are located within your investment circle.
- ❑ Watch the television news that covers your designated area.

It is critical that you stay informed about the community where you are going to invest. Newspapers routinely cover school board meetings, town meetings, and county commissioner meetings. Many people pay little attention to what occurs at these local government meetings, yet what the local officials decide can affect your real estate investing business. It is here where local tax rates are set and levied. It is here where plans for new schools, new roads, developments, expansions, land use, and so much more are decided. Any one of these factors can affect your business.

For example, the local school board might have approved construction of a 400 million dollar high school in an adjoining town. Property taxes for that school district may be increasing as a result. Properties in that area might become cheaper as homeowners or other investors decide to get out now. Alternatively, once the better school is built, people may want to live in that district so they can send their children to a new and better school. This is the knowledge you must always be gathering as an active real estate investor.

Meeting working real estate agents in your investment area is good for the active real estate investor. Be sure to tell the agent that you are an investor. Be prepared to tell the agent what properties you prefer. Always be courteous and polite. Take the opportunity to look at the property when visiting at an open house. You are gaining important knowledge just by browsing at a property offered for sale.

Local news is often presented with huge fanfare. Do not act impulsively when the local media announces a tax increase or other "shattering" news. Take time to absorb the full story before acting. A tax increase, for example, might mean a $40 a year increase for you. But the media may make the local increase sound much bigger—they have to sell advertising in their newspapers, or on their airwaves.

Becoming an Investor Now

Real estate is a competitive business. Once you make the decision to begin searching for an investment property, you are pitting your wits and experience against other real estate investors with years or even decades of experience. How can you expect to win? First, understand your competition and second, apply the experience you already have.

Your competitors come from two areas—buyers looking for homes for themselves to live in and buyers who are buying for investment (in other words, other real estate investors). The buyer looking for a home to live in will most likely have a different mind-set than an investor. Despite all that has been written about how to profit from fixer-uppers, most buyers looking for their own home are looking for something that is already in move-in condition.

> **Author's Advice**
>
> Most of your direct competition will come from other real estate investors.

The good news is that your real estate investing competitors were once beginners too. It should make you feel good knowing that because they were successful, you can be also. The chances are that many real estate investors with extensive experience have probably moved on from the beginning investments to other opportunities.

There are some quick ways you can start now as a real estate investor.

Buy Your Own Home

One way to get started is to buy your own home, especially if you do not have one already. The best financing rates and terms in residential real estate are reserved for the owner-occupant. You will have access to these favorable terms so long as the property you are buying has no more than four residential units. A four-unit property is still treated as owner-occupied property as long as you live in one of the units.

You can start today as an investor by buying a four-unit with an FHA Loan, a loan guaranteed by the Federal Housing Administration, which is administered by HUD. An FHA loan is obtained from a local bank or mortgage broker. You only need a 3 percent down payment to qualify. Closing costs (up to 6 percent) can be paid by the seller. Best of all, the down payment can be from a gift from a blood relative, government entity, or nonprofit association. You do need to plan to live in the property to qualify for the loan.

Living In Your Investment Property

There are a number of strategies that involve living in your own investment property. You could move into a fixer-upper, make any needed repairs, improve the appearance, then move out and rent out the home, or sell it for a profit. This works for either a single-family home or multifamily property. However, there are many pitfalls to this strategy:

- **Living in a construction site.** You and your family may get sick of the inconvenience, dust, and noise from living in what may be a construction site.
- **Living next door to tenants.** When you live next door to your tenants, count on them to take advantage of your accessibility. From the most minor repair to making change to use a coin-operated laundry appliance, your neighbors may not hesitate to knock on your door at all hours.
- **Frequent moves.** Moving is an expensive hassle. It may mean uprooting your family often.
- **Lifestyle considerations.** Sometimes the best housing for an investment does not have all the amenities that you would like to have for your home.

In general, only you can decide how investing in real estate fits into the lifestyle you and your family would like to have. If you are thinking of embarking on a strategy that will require your family to live in a construction site, live next to tenants, or move more frequently, get your family's support. They need to understand the benefits to come and not just the sacrifices to be experienced now.

Being able to live in your own investment property is a great way to start, but it is an avenue that is often not available for every beginning investor. Regardless, there will come a time when you will want to begin acquiring properties for investment that you will never live in. For many, if not most new real estate investors, that time will be when they buy the first investment property.

Finding Properties

Happily, many of the strategies for finding a property to invest in are the same whether you intend to live in the property or not. In fact, there will be more properties that you will be able to consider for investment if you do not have to meet the restrictions you may impose on yourself for a property that you would be willing to live in. For example, if you want your children to be able to stay within the same school system, then you are restricted by where you can move and the properties that you can consider buying as a real estate investor.

Some of the most logical ways to look for properties include the following:

- Search the local real estate advertisements in the classified section of the newspaper. Sunday newspapers are usually the best.
- Look through local real estate books and magazines, distributed free from racks at local grocery stores, convenience stores, etc.
- Contact a realtor and ask for listings.
- Search online at popular sites. (See Appendix C for a list of websites that offer properties for sale.)
- Place a small advertisement in the classified section that says, "I buy real estate."
- Let people know that you are actively seeking real estate as an investment. Tell your friends, relatives, and business associates that you are interested in acquiring real estate as an investor. Ask them to keep you in mind for any properties they hear might be available.
- Put up bandit signs—these are the signs you see placed at busy intersections. Erect a sign (if local ordinances allow) that matches your classified advertisement.
- Advertise in church bulletins.
- Place free flyers on bulletin boards in places like laundromats, supermarkets, etc.

Use your imagination to get the word out that you are an active real estate investor.

Your search for real estate investment properties is going to take time. You might get lucky and locate a property immediately. But most likely, you will need to look at many different properties before finding one that meets all the criteria that make it a great investment property for you.

Remember there are other investors out there. Everyone wants the easy deal—the one you can buy with little down payment, bought far below market value, with exceptional cash flow. You have to search extensively to find such deals—and they only come along now and then. Most deals will require work on your part—searching and analyzing to determine if the property would make a good investment.

To be successful as a real estate investor, you need to market yourself, and let others know that you buy and sell real estate. Just like any other business, you need to get the word out about what you do. This is especially true if you are going to acquire preforeclosure properties. This is because you want potential foreclosure property owners to call you before the property begins the foreclosure process and becomes public knowledge. At that point, you will be competing with other investors.

Real Estate Advertising

When searching the real estate ads looking for properties, there are certain key words that will often indicate that the seller may be looking for a fast transaction. Often, these types of sellers are those who might be willing to take less, or agree to pay additional closing costs, or perhaps offer partial seller financing to make a deal work.

Some of the key words you might see in advertisements are:

- Motivated Seller
- Great for Investors
- Price Reduced
- Must Sell
- Owner Transferred
- Asking $xxxx
- Immediate Possession
- Rent-to-Own
- Owner Financing

Author's Advice

When reading the real estate ads, always keep a highlighter nearby so you can mark specific ads you have located that look interesting.

All of these words suggest the current owner might be willing to sell the property quickly and is looking for a deal now.

As you continue to review the real estate ads, you will soon discover properties that are being advertised for sale week after week. You will see other properties that move quickly. A property that is constantly advertised and not sold is property that may be overpriced.

Read not just the advertisements for properties for sale, but also for properties for rent. It is important to learn what a one-, two-, or three-bedroom apartment in any specific area is renting for now.

Look at the business property and investment property sections of the advertisements, too. Do not overlook any listing in the real estate section of the newspaper.

You have already learned a great deal about how to find properties to buy. So far you've learned about the conventional methods investors have applied and been successful with for decades. If you likewise work hard and apply these methods, you should be able to acquire investment properties at a fair price.

However, there will be those investors who demand more. Some investors are willing to go the extra mile to catapult their investments forward by ferreting out true real estate bargains. If you see yourself in this description and you are ready for the additional challenge, this next section is for you.

Finding Bargain Properties

Earlier, you read about how knowledge was key to getting started in real estate. In fact, the first three rules for getting started are knowledge, knowledge, knowledge! To stay ahead of your competition, you want to leverage the knowledge you already have. This is why you will want to draw your investment circle close to home.

Chances are, if you have been living in your current community for any reasonable amount of time, you already know which communities have the great schools, the better shopping, lower crime, and faster appreciation than surrounding areas. Whether you realize it or not, you already are an expert on your home turf. You just need to start paying closer attention.

Start with your drive to work or your typical route when you are running errands. Start taking note of the properties that you drive by each day, and not just the ones that have a sign indicating that they are for sale. Look at everything. What you are looking for are properties that are not improved to their full potential. This could be something as simple as the property with the peeling paint and the unkempt landscaping, or it could be something subtler. For example, make note of the property that underutilizes the land it was built on. Consider a small home on a large lot in a desirable neighborhood. The lot may be worth more with the small home removed from the property. Or maybe the lot can be subdivided into two lots, creating additional value.

If a property has potential, but it does not appear to be for sale, research the ownership and contact the owner anyway. Often, the owner will have no interest in selling, but once in a while, you will hit on a great deal.

Once you have exhausted the properties on your work commute or on your errand route, start deliberately taking a new route to work or on your errands. Yes, this may be more time-consuming. However, if you make a few good deals, you may never need to drive to work again by any route.

Truthfully, while taking note of the properties that you come in contact with through your daily commute or chores is a good start, you probably will need to apply a more deliberate effort to finding the right investment property.

Selecting the Neighborhood

The first step is to decide on a neighborhood to invest in. Within the 25-mile radius of your investment circle there are probably some neighborhoods that are appreciating more rapidly than others. Some neighborhoods may be stagnant, and some areas in decline. The obvious solution may be to gravitate toward the appreciating neighborhoods. However, future expected appreciation is almost always going to be factored into the present prices. The result is higher prices. You may even be priced out of some of the best areas.

An alternative strategy is to target the neighborhoods that you think are poised to take off and experience a rebirth. In essence, you are applying the same thinking that you used to identify individual properties that are not at their full potential to identifying entire neighborhoods that are not realizing their full potential.

Before you embark on a strategy of trying to predict the future for a neighborhood, you should understand some fundamentals of the risks associated with real estate. Every investment in real estate assumes certain predictions about the future. For example, you may be assuming that there will not be massive layoffs or that a neighborhood that is desirable now will be desirable in the future. As you begin to assume that circumstances in a particular area will be dramatically different from how they are now, you are beginning to make bolder predictions about the future and are therefore taking on more risk. Perhaps this is not a risk that you should be taking. You do not have to make wild gambles to be successful in real estate investing. But if you want to get on the real estate fast-track, you may need to be more aggressive about finding those sleeper neighborhoods and investments that are waiting to be rediscovered.

Any conclusion about a neighborhood experiencing a renaissance must be based on something more than wishful thinking. You do not want to be a pioneer with your first real estate investment. If the neighborhood you are considering is legitimately poised for growth, there will be signs of that potential even before the growth takes off and everyone becomes aware of this new great location.

Gentrification

Gentrification is the process of reclaiming old deteriorated neighborhoods. Signs of growth include the wonderfully remodeled home in among the derelict houses that are ready to fall down. On further investigation, you may find that by driving around other parts of the community, there may be a few more of these freshly minted diamonds in the rough. If there are too many of them, maybe your discovery has come too late.

Whether you are considering an individual property or an entire neighborhood for investment, you should be asking yourself how this property or neighborhood could dramatically increase in value, commanding higher rent and making available higher cash flow. Most of the time you will not know the answer to how a particular neighborhood or property could be improved. This is because most properties and neighborhoods are already at their maximum value, or at their highest and best use. If you cannot determine how a property or neighborhood can be improved, perhaps you should just keep looking at other opportunities.

There is no requirement that you get involved in gentrification to be successful in real estate investing. This is just one proven strategy that has worked for many real estate investors in the past. The key is to find and develop your own niche or strategy that you can employ over and over on your way to success.

For example, David knows of an investor who routinely buys single-family rental homes that do not have a garage. He then adds a two-car detached garage to the property. This investor finds the whole is greater than the parts. By adding a garage, he expands the number of potential customers that would be interested in renting the property. With increased demand comes a higher price, both in rent and resale value.

Whatever investment strategy you may develop, knowledge will always be the foundation of your investment approach. Become an expert in the neighborhood where you intend to invest. Before you buy, you should have a good handle on what the sale prices have been on the properties in your area. You should know the rental market equally well. You should be able to walk into an open house in your area and know immediately whether the home is priced within reason. Similarly, if you visit a property for rent you should be able to discern quickly whether the rent asked is above, below, or at the market price. If you are not confident about your opinions in these areas, you are not ready to buy investment property yet. Keep doing your homework.

Buyer Beware

Before making a major change to a dwelling such as adding a garage, you will need a building permit and may need additional variances or other permissions from the local municipality before you build.

Good Properties to Avoid

There will always be properties to avoid. There are some deals that no matter how good they sound, you want someone else to buy rather than you.

One of the first questions you should always ask yourself is, "why is this property for sale?" The answer is important. Understand that sometimes there are two reasons the seller has for selling—the reason that he or she tells you and the real reason.

Most of the time, real estate properties are offered for sale for good and valid reasons. It could be the simple desire to move on. There could have been a death, birth, marriage, divorce, job change, or some other legitimate reason.

Often, you may never be able to discern the true reason someone is selling their property. Sometimes, however, the property is being sold because there are major problems with it.

The property may be offered for sale because of a foreclosure. Many times, foreclosure properties can be problematic because the people living in them did not have the money to maintain the unit, or deliberately caused damage when they realized they were going to lose the property.

Be leery of any property being offered for sale by another investor. Investors do not get rid of properties that are producing a positive cash flow unless they are moving on to some other investment. Or perhaps the investor is retiring. Otherwise, if the seller cannot make money from the property, ask yourself why you think you can.

What Are the Best Investment Properties?

Investment properties come in all sizes, shapes, and styles. You could invest in multimillion-dollar properties, or smaller, $30,000 units.

The price point is not a factor in determining what makes a good real estate investment. Would you be better off buying a property for 2 million dollars that brings in gross revenue of $300,000 a month, but costs $400,000 a month to operate? Or would you be better off buying a property for $100,000 that brings in $1000 month and costs only $500 a month to manage? Bigger dollars do not make a property a better investment.

The best properties to produce rental income are …

- Close to where you live.
- Generating monthly income greater than the total cost of operations.

- Easily obtained through financing.
- In a good state of repair.
- Easily rented.

The best properties to buy and resell immediately are …

- Close to where you live.
- Purchased well below current or potential market value (at least 20 percent less than potential market value).
- Easily obtained through financing.
- Able to be quickly resold.

The best properties to buy and rehab are …

- Close to where you live.
- Purchased far below market value.
- Resold for a profit quickly after the purchase price and rehab costs are combined, or will produce sufficient rental income.
- Easily obtained through financing.

Of the three types of properties to acquire for real estate investing, notice that each has two similar characteristics. They should be close to your home and easily obtained through financing. Finding properties that meet your criteria is what most of the work of being a real estate investor is all about.

Where Are the Bargains?

The bargain properties—the ones you want to buy—are in your investment circle. You just need to locate them. Some will be great bargains, while others will just be reasonably priced. What follows is a list of still more ways to look for properties at discounted prices:

- Have a real estate agent search them for you.
- Find them yourself in the For Rent section of the newspaper. (Many times, people tire of being a property owner, and are willing to sell their rental property quickly and for below market value).

- Look for them online at the government-operated website: www.homesales.gov.
- Locate them by spotting For Sale signs on properties.
- Target foreclosure properties, as you will learn in Chapter 7.

How to Value the Property

In Chapter 5, you learned about how the appraisal theory applies three value yardsticks determining the value of a real estate property. These yardsticks are:

- Income Approach
- Market Approach
- Cost Approach

This is how lenders, real estate agents, and insurers will determine the value of real estate. As an investor, you need to look at each property a bit more critically. We will call this the Investor Approach.

> **Real Deal**
>
> There is no such thing as an investor approach except to the readers of this book. But it is an important concept.

The investor approach is where you apply the appraisal theory, but you also include other factors before moving to purchase a real estate investment property.

The additional factors are the answers to these questions …

Question #1: Does it make sense to buy this property now?

Only you can decide if it makes sense for you to buy the property now. Sometimes, it just feels right, and other times it does not. Some properties look good, but something tells you no. If you have any doubts, do not buy. Pass and move to the next possibility. Your self-doubts are there to protect you. Trust your instincts.

Question #2: How much will it cost me to purchase this property?

Real estate always costs more than the asking price. Even if you had the cash to buy the property, costs associated with the transaction will increase the price. Those costs include things such as title insurance, transfer taxes, recording fees, and so on. Look at the true bottom line, not just the purchase price.

> **Author's Advice**
>
> The expenses of a transaction may not end after the acquisition. There may be an immediate need to make repairs, replace appliance, or redecorate.

Question #3: How much of my cash will it take me to buy the property?

A property that uses much or all of your cash may not be a good investment. You can be rich in real estate, but cash poor with your investments. When you give up your cash to make a purchase, you are at a disadvantage to buy anything else you may need. Always consider how much cash it will take to complete the transaction.

Question #4: What degree of management intensity will be associated with owning this property?

Some properties just require more of your time and attention to own and operate. One property owner had a property with 2 separate living units and 15 garages. The garages rented for $60 a month. The property was located in a town with limited parking and no nearby storage units. The $900 a month from the garage rentals was great additional income. In addition, the garages were always rented. The problem: collecting the money for the rent. Each month, the owner spent hours chasing the money. It was nearly impossible to catch people at home who rented the garages. Some people simply disappeared. What on paper looked like a great deal was, in reality, a hassle to own and operate. This is not to say that garage rentals are always difficult to collect, just that each deal has its own nuances.

Question #5: Do I want to own this property?

It has to be one that you would be proud to own. After all, your name will be on the deed. Is it a property that you want to call your own?

Buying Neglected Properties

These properties are the ugly ducklings—the ones that have been neglected and need plenty of tender loving care. Or they may simply be an underuse or a misuse of the land.

The ugly ducklings are easy to spot—their yards and lawns are poorly maintained. Landscaping is shoddy or overgrown. There is no mulch. They have been neglected so long that they may have even become eyesores. The property is in need of paint. Debris, clutter, litter, and junk may be everywhere. There could be an abandoned car or other large items on the property. Windows may be boarded up.

These are properties that need someone like you to get in there, throw stuff away, and clean. You update the yard and exterior, fix broken doors and windows, add some fresh paint, and turn an old dog into a winning breed of property. It's amazing what some old fashioned elbow grease, a dumpster, and a little imagination can do.

Properties that fall into disrepair and are in need of basic maintenance can be great investment opportunities. Many times these properties are not listed for sale. They may have been rented, and now sit empty when the last renter vanished, perhaps having skipped out in the middle of the night to avoid paying rent. Because the owner has let the property fall into its current ugly state, there is little chance of renting or selling it.

Every real estate agent's office has at least one neglected property for sale. If you let them know you might be interested in such properties, you can be certain they will show them to you.

The underutilized or misused properties are easier to miss. The property may look just fine, or even be in a pristine condition. But the property is not all that it could be. As you learned before, maybe a tiny home is wasting a beautiful large lot that could either accommodate two or more homes or one larger, more luxurious home. Perhaps the property is a four-unit apartment on a busy street that has trouble staying rented because of the traffic noise. This property may command higher rent and be more likely to stay full if converted to office use.

Another example is an apartment building with a waiting list of renters waiting to get into the building. Any building with a waiting list is a building with rents that are too low. Maybe the building can be purchased based on a price that reflects those current low rents.

Look for properties with unusual architectural features. David has purchased at least two buildings that would fit this description. The drawback to these buildings is that it will be difficult to discern the potential for rent because no rent comparables will be available owing to the unique nature of the real estate. However, if the property in question has a waiting list or an exceptional history of strong occupancy, you may be able to conclude the property is under-rented. You may never know just how much the property can command in rent until you own the property and start testing new and higher rents in the marketplace. But you may be pleasantly surprised by the answers.

Finding the Owners

When researching these underutilized, poorly maintained ducklings, it may take some work to find out who the owner is. When you spot such a property, one that has some investment potential, and has no "for rent" or "for sale" sign, ask a neighbor who owns the property. You can also find out who the owner is by visiting the county courthouse. Property ownership is a matter of public record. You might find the information at the Recorder or Register of Deeds office, tax assessor's office, or some other office—it all depends on your jurisdiction. But the ownership information is easily determined somewhere within the courthouse or municipal government. Many of these agencies even offer this information online.

Making friends with a title agent will pay dividends here. Title companies are researching properties all the time. Today, many jurisdictions have put real estate records on computer files. Some of those files are available to the public, but if they are not, it is a safe bet your title company is accessing them somehow. Your title agent may be able to coach you on how to access public records.

Author's Advice

Sometimes owners do not want to be found. They may have an unpublished phone number or merely a post office mailing address. The more difficult it is to find an owner, the more valuable it is to find them. You will be more likely to be the only investor speaking to them.

Once you know the owner, call them and ask if they might be interested in selling. Many times, you will not be able to persuade the owner to sell. Do not be discouraged. Keep a record of the conversation and check back with the owner in a few months. They may change their mind. David has purchased properties from individuals who he kept in contact with for five years or longer before they decided to sell. But it was worth the wait. While you are waiting, keep looking for other properties and other owners to call on. You will not have to wait five years to find a good deal.

Determine what the property would be worth if it were cleaned up and well-maintained. Also figure out what it would cost the owner to pay someone to do all the work that is needed (not necessarily what it will cost you). With those two numbers in mind, you can start with an offer below the potential market value.

For example, suppose the property would be worth $100,000 if it were cleaned up and in good repair. And let's assume it would cost $10,000 to clean it up. Here is how you might structure your offer: $100,000 less 20% discount = $80,000 minus $10,000 in repairs = an offer of $70,000. (Of course, the owner may want more, but this may be a good place to begin negotiations.)

Let's say the owner agrees to a $70,000 price. You take possession and start the cleanup. Because you are able to do cleanup without the need of professionals, you can turn the property around for $6,000 (rather than $10,000). You then sell the property for the $100,000, what it is worth.

Roughly speaking, your work netted this profit:

Property Cost: $70,000

Repairs/Cleanup: $6,000

Total: $76,000

Sale Price: $100,000

Gross Profit: $24,000

Of course, there are probably other expenses (such as transfer taxes, closing costs, etc.). Nevertheless, you can see there is still some substantial profit available by investing in neglected properties. Even if you paid $75,000 or $77,500 for the property, you could still make a reasonable profit in just a few months with some wise improvements. These kinds of deals are not easy to find, but they are out there.

The Least You Need To Know

- You need to learn your local market area to maximize your profit potential.
- Start an action plan to gain knowledge of your local investment area.
- Create your own investment circle and look for investment properties in that area.
- Evaluate any potential real estate investment using additional factors beyond the appraisal theory.
- You can make money investing in neglected or underutilized properties.

Chapter 7

Opportunities in Foreclosures

In This Chapter

- Learning about foreclosures
- Problems with foreclosures
- Bidding for properties at real estate auctions
- Bank-owned properties for sale

As a real estate investor, you are always looking for properties—whether to buy and hold, or buy and resell. And you are always looking for properties that are being offered for sale at reasonable prices and terms.

One type of property that you will want to consider for potential deals is a foreclosure. Foreclosure is the legal process by which the mortgagor's (borrower's) rights to his or her property are terminated. This most often occurs when the lender does not receive the monthly payments from the borrower, but could also occur for other violations of the mortgage agreement.

Properties where the owners could not manage to pay their monthly payments are often of interest to investors because they might be priced for less or offer advantageous financing. These types of properties are the focus of this chapter.

In this chapter, you will learn about the various stages of foreclosure and the advantages and disadvantages of buying at each state.

Understanding the Four Stages of Foreclosure

Foreclosures offer unique opportunities for real estate investors. You need to understand the process. For our discussion, we are going to identify four stages of foreclosure:

Stage 1—Owner In Trouble

Stage 2—Preforeclosure

Stage 3—The Auction

Stage 4—Postforeclosure Bank-Owned Properties

Owner in Trouble

When the owner falls behind on the monthly loan payments, the lender hopes to get their borrower current again. The lender serves notice, usually through an attorney, that they will foreclose on the property unless all amounts due are paid immediately. The borrower is usually at least two months overdue on their monthly payments. There has been no public notice yet of the pending foreclosure.

Preforeclosure

If the owner is still in trouble, and there is no sign the loan will be brought current, the lender sets the account for extra collection effort. Often, an inspection is ordered to check on the collateral. The account is referred to the lender's collection department. After a review, a decision may be made to proceed with a foreclosure.

If the decision is made to start the foreclosure, the lender files a lawsuit in a court having jurisdiction. By now, the property owner is three or four months behind in monthly payments, or more.

When the lawsuit is filed, it has become a public record in the courthouse. The legal action is reported in some local newspapers, and almost always in the local legal newspaper.

The Auction

If the owner has not been able to refinance or sell the property or otherwise stop the foreclosure, then the sheriff for the county where the property is located will conduct an auction, selling the property to the highest bidder. The auction terminates the borrower's rights to the property.

Most often, the lender buys the property and takes possession of it. Oddly enough, the owner could still be living there. The owner either voluntarily vacates the property, or the owner may have to be evicted by the sheriff, executing a court order.

Finally, depending on the jurisdiction, the auction may be subject to confirmation, a process whereby a judge reviews the circumstances of the sale to make sure the foreclosure was executed properly and the auction obtained as high a price as possible under the circumstances.

Buyer Beware

While the general process of foreclosure is similar from state to state, the legal procedures vary. As an active investor, you need to learn the standard procedure in the state where you intend to invest.

Postforeclosure Bank-Owned Properties (REOs)

REO is short for real estate owned. It is a term used by lenders to describe properties the bank owns most often as the result of foreclosure. REO properties owned by a lender offer special opportunities to real estate investors. Lenders are not in the business of owning properties. Once they have them, they want to get rid of them. And they will often sell them at a discount.

When a lender receives a property through foreclosure, they will probably send a local representative to check on the property. This individual will make sure the building is secure. They may hire contractors, if necessary, to make any emergency repairs or to secure the property. They will usually also winterize the property—getting it ready to survive cold weather by draining pipes, making sure heat works, etc. This is their collateral—and they want to do what is necessary to protect it.

Somewhere in the process, the lender may send a local broker to the property and request an analysis of the probable market value. In addition, the lender may also obtain repair estimates.

Real Deal

Lenders also receive property without foreclosing. This is called *Deed in lieu of foreclosure*. The property owner simply turns the property over to the lender and vacates the property.

Finally, the lender will offer their REO for sale to the public. Some real estate agents specialize in selling foreclosures. Some investors specialize in buying them, repairing them, and selling them (or holding them for rental income).

A lender will not always have the same mind-set as any other property seller. Theoretically, any owner of real estate should be trying to sell the property for as much as possible. If at first the desired price cannot be achieved, the property owner may hold out for months trying to get his or her price. There are several reasons this typical seller's mind-set may not always apply with a lender.

First, the typical seller is usually trying to sell a property that is occupied. Occupied properties always look better. Vacant properties collect free newspapers on the porch and junk mail overflowing the mailbox. Vacant properties are an easy target for vandals.

Second, other business considerations may impact a lender's decision to sell. Lenders are subject to periodic audits by federal regulators. A lender may elect to dump some REOs prior to an audit. Lenders also have to maintain reserves based partially on nonperforming assets such as REOs. A lender may also elect to move some REOs quickly if, for whatever reason, their REO portfolio has grown to unacceptable levels. Finally, even a change in management can bring about a flurry of REO sales as a new executive takes a different approach to managing various aspects of the lending institution.

The point is that lenders can sometimes make sudden and dramatic changes in selling REOs that appear inexplicable to the outside investor. Therefore, it is important to stay in close touch with the lender if you have identified an REO property that you would like to buy.

REOs are the safest foreclosure opportunities for the new real estate investor. The lender will often sell below market value. There is less risk of unknown title defects. Many other debts against the property will have been canceled by the foreclosure process.

You should probably offer less than the asking price for most REOs. Always point out all the repairs and costs associated with bringing the property back to life. Start lower, and increase your offer only to what the property is worth to you.

A local real estate agent can help you locate REO properties. There are websites also available that list REO real estate. Some lenders offer listings of their REOs on their websites. The federal government also lists their REOs—properties that the Federal Housing Administration (FHA) or the Veterans Administration received because of their loan guarantees. Those and other homes offered for sale by the Federal Government are available online at: www.hud.gov/homes/homesforsale.cfm.

It may take a little work, but you can find REOs. Remember that other investors are also searching for them.

Real Deal

There are two perspectives that any investor may have toward foreclosures. One is the investor is riding in like the cavalry, helping the seller get out of a financial jamb. The other is the investor is preying on the weak. Only you can decide where to draw the line. Keep a clear conscience.

David purchased an apartment REO years ago. The former owner was dealing drugs with his tenants and was trading rent for sex. The property was seized by the local municipality for being a nuisance property. The bank began foreclosure. Somewhere in all of this the owner was shot six times in front of the building. Fortunately, he survived. The building fared less well. One of the two buildings sat through the winter with nearly every window broken. There were many frozen, broken plumbing pipes. Graffiti was everywhere. Drug dealers had removed drywall between apartments so they could disappear into the walls if they needed to. Garbage was everywhere. The property was almost entirely vacant.

David retained an attorney, reviewed the title, and bid at the auction, but was ultimately outbid by the bank. There were no other bidders. After the bank completed the sale confirmation process, David bought the property from the bank, made the repairs, and eventually returned the property to profitability. David continues to enjoy considerable cash flow to this day—the property increased in value by 50 percent once the repairs were made.

Dealing With Owners in Trouble

Property owners can get into financial difficulties for many reasons. Job loss, employer downsizing, pay cuts, periods of illness, job relocation, divorce, or death of a family member are just some reasons that could have changed a homeowner's financial situation.

If you are going to work as an investor with properties in the first three stages of foreclosure, you will be dealing with a property owner who is in financial distress. Their life has somehow suddenly changed and they are facing an unpleasant future that probably includes the loss of their home.

Buyer Beware

The owner of the property can always sell the property to someone else up to the time of the courthouse sale. Be aware that your work could be for nothing if the owner is able to complete a sale or refinance the property.

Many real estate investors wrongly believe that they are dealing with the bank or lender when a foreclosure has commenced. The property owner still is in control of the property up to the moment of the courthouse sale. Unless the bank owns the property—which only occurs in stage four after the auction—the owner (borrower) is still in control of the property, has the right to it, and is the only party that can sell it.

Property owners facing foreclosure are often confused, angry, upset, bewildered, bitter, or frightened. They do not know what to do or which way to turn. Many times, they just want out from under the legal pressure facing them. Often they need some money to move out and try to start their lives again.

Keep in mind that when you speak to someone facing foreclosure, there may be many emotions. To be a successful investor working with owners facing foreclosure, you need to help solve their problems for them.

You may contact owners in various stages of foreclosure, either deliberately or unexpectedly. Sometimes owners in foreclosure advertise their homes for sale, and you might learn about their foreclosure when inquiring about the property. Another way you may come in contact with a property owner facing foreclosure is through calls generated from your bandit signs, advertising, or brochures.

You might make deliberate contact by sending a simple postcard or letter to property owners who have just been served a foreclosure notice. You can develop this list easily by visiting the county courthouses and looking at the docket of recently filed foreclosure actions. You can also develop the list by reading the local legal newspaper (each court jurisdiction has some form of local legal newspaper that publishes the most recent court filings). Lists are also available on the Internet at various foreclosure websites.

Be aware that other investors are also trying to contact the property owner. Your letter may only be one of many the owner receives.

Your message can be simple: I am a local real estate investor and I buy houses—regardless of condition. I can offer a quick cash settlement. Call me at 555-555-5555.

Try to answer your telephone rather than use voice mail or an answering machine. Most people in desperate financial trouble would rather speak to a real person than leave a message. Of course, sometimes you have to use a recording device, but try to answer as many calls as you can.

It may take several contacts until you receive a response from the property owner. For that reason, it might be better for you send a follow-up letter or two before giving up.

You can also try to contact the property owner by telephone. If all else fails, you can also stop at the property and knock on the door. If the property owner is not at home, leave a written message asking the owner to call you.

Foreclosure Pitfalls

One problem any real estate investor faces when working with foreclosures is the likelihood of other investors trying to contact the owner and buy the property. Working from published lists will also put you in competition with other real estate investors. Additionally, count on competing bidders at the foreclosure auction.

If you are able to contact a property owner facing foreclosure, consider some of the other likely problems you might need to overcome:

- **Outstanding Mechanic's Liens.** There might have been repairs made to the property, and the owner did not make payment to the contractor(s) doing the work. In an attempt to collect, the contractor(s) placed a mechanic's lien on the property. Mechanic's liens are typically wiped out if the foreclosure is finalized.
- **Municipal Liens.** Foreclosed properties often have municipal liens placed on them for things such as unpaid water or sewer service. Sometimes, the landowner did not do required maintenance, so the local municipality did the work and billed the owner for it. When they did not pay, the municipality filed a lien against the property or added the charge to the property tax bill. Most municipal liens are not wiped out by foreclosure.
- **Unpaid Property Tax Liens.** The property taxes may not have been paid, creating an additional lien against the property. These tax liens are rarely wiped out by foreclosure.
- **IRS Liens.** The Internal Revenue Service, seeking payment of unpaid taxes, may have filed a lien against the property. The repercussions of these liens and how to avoid them are covered later in this section.
- **Severe Maintenance Needs.** The property may need major maintenance or repairs. If the property owners were unable to pay the monthly loan payment, they may also have been unable to afford to maintain or repair the property.

- **Unpaid Homeowner Association Dues.** Often, failure to pay homeowner association dues and fees can result in substantial fines.
- **Building Code Violations.** The plumbing, heating, and electrical systems may be damaged, outdated, etc.
- **Deliberate damage.** The occupants may have deliberately damaged the property in retaliation once they found out they were going to lose it.
- **Uncooperative owners.** If you are bidding at the auction and the owner is uncooperative, you may not have the opportunity to inspect the inside of the property before you bid. Bidding on a foreclosed property you have not been able to thoroughly inspect is not recommended for the beginning investor.

Always keep in mind that property owners in foreclosure probably had a sudden change in their lives which caused their financial circumstances to change. After all, they were able to qualify for the loan to buy the property. It is just now that something happened that prevented them from making their payments. And if they were unable to pay their mortgage payment, it is likely that many other things have gone unpaid, too.

Be in control when you inspect any property. There are several items you should always carry with you. They include …

- A flashlight.
- A legal pad or clipboard so you can make notes (don't forget pens).
- A tape measure.
- A digital camera.

Take plenty of notes. Write down everything. This is important when looking at properties in the stages of foreclosure before the auction. Remember, the seller is in a difficult position. As a result, the seller may attempt to hide problems with the property. Additionally, the seller is likely to be uncollectable, unable to satisfy any post-closing judgment you may win as a result of their unscrupulous behavior. Therefore, the financial constraints that keep other sellers honest may not apply here.

Solving the Foreclosed Property Owner's Problem

To be successful as a real estate investor working with foreclosed properties, you have to help solve the property owner's problems. Alternatively, if there are too many debts and some of those debts can be removed by the foreclosure process, you may be better off bidding at the auction or buying after the auction from the lender if the lender is the successful bidder. A property owner facing foreclosure is one of the most motivated sellers you can locate.

A motivated seller is a property owner who has a strong incentive to make a deal to sell their real estate. Realize that not all property owners in foreclosure may be ready to admit the problems they are facing. Some have not yet come to reality. They may believe that somehow they will be rescued, or are simply denying the inevitable.

A property owner in foreclosure who realizes the problem is likely to be eager to deal with an investor or any other buyer. At first, the owner may have an inflated opinion about the value of their property. Of course, they want to sell it for as much as possible. Yet this troubled owner may not understand all the obligations that he or she would need to satisfy to deliver clear title to a buyer.

At some point in the process, you are going to need to have a frank conversation with the seller about his or her situation. The conversation should include the owner's attempts to sell the property and the results of those efforts. Find out what the seller's full obligation to the lender is if you can. The nature of your conversation should not be just based on what the seller tells you, but also based on your research into building code violations, tax liens, and other unpaid liens against the property. You will read about how to research these liens later in this section.

Many times, the total obligations the seller needs to satisfy exceed even the lofty projections of the seller's idea of value. This situation defines why the owner is in foreclosure. There are seemingly no other remedies available. The situation appears hopeless.

However, there may be remedies available to you as an investor that may not be available to the property owner. Understand the emotions and frustrations that come with most foreclosures are not just limited to the property owner. Often, the lien holders are experiencing those emotions too. Contractors may have done their work and not been paid. Municipal officials may be upset about repairs that have not been made. The lender may be upset as well.

These lien holders have good reason to be angry. If the foreclosure proceeds to its conclusion, they may get paid nothing. But these lien holders are angry with the property owner, not with you. You may be able to negotiate remedies with these individuals the seller would not be able to. You may be able to persuade these lien holders to settle their claims for a fraction of their value. After all, something is better than nothing. If enough liens can be reduced by a sufficient amount, then the total indebtedness against the property may be reduced to an amount below the property's value, restoring an equity position to the property and creating a profit opportunity for you.

Taking the Next Steps

Keep in mind there could be more obligations that might have to be paid (sewerage service, water, trash, homeowners associations, etc.) before the property can be transferred. Check the courthouse for all liens recorded against the property. A title insurance agent can help you discover these obligations.

Determine what the loan payoff amount is at the moment. Ask the owner to give you written authorization to speak to the lender. Also, estimate what added costs the owner would need to pay to transfer the property to the buyer. Such additional cost might include tenant security deposits, transfer taxes, and title insurance.

From your inspection, determine what the costs of repairs and necessary maintenance might be. Also, find out the likely market value. After gathering this information, you can finally determine the equity position of the property owner. An example is in the table that follows:

Probable Market Value	$100,000
Repairs Needed	$4,500
Transfer Costs	$2,000
Current Payoff of Loan	$79,245
Unpaid Liens	$1,319
Total	$87,064
Equity Position	$12,936

In this example, the owner of this property has approximately $12,936 of equity available in the property. Once you know the equity available, you can determine if this is a piece of real estate you want to consider.

Negotiating With the Owner

The equity will usually determine what you can, or cannot do, with the property. Then you could make offers based on different scenarios:

- If the owner just wants out, you could offer to take over the property. You would offer to pay the owner the loan payoff and liens, and pay all closing costs. After paying for the repairs, you would sell the property or keep it for cash flow, and then start earning your profit.
- If the owner has an equity position that he or she wants to recover, you can just negotiate to buy the property as you would any other. Just be certain that your seller is able to clear all liens against the property so he or she can deliver clear title to you at closing.
- If there is no equity or a negative equity situation, you could take over the property if the lender and other lien holders will sell on a *short sale* basis.

def•i•ni•tion

A **short sale** is when you purchase the property and the lender or other lien holders agree to accept less than what the full payoff amount is.

A short sale will take more of your time. You need to negotiate with the lender (or their attorney) and other lien holders to persuade them to accept a discount on what they are owed. Your negotiating points would include the high cost of taking over the property, the sale, the costs of selling the property, time, the ability to collect the full amount owed, etc.

Before attempting to make offers on properties in foreclosure, you need to speak with a local attorney who specializes in real estate law and is experienced in foreclosures. You need to understand what can and cannot be done. You cannot expect to close every offer you make when proposing a short sale. At best, expect to close no more than 1 out of 2—if you do better, great!

As you learned earlier, you need to have an attorney on your side. You should have your attorney review any sales agreement before you sign it and present it to the property owner in foreclosure. Your attorney can also provide you with a release form that authorizes you to speak to the foreclosed owner's lender. Do not proceed with any foreclosure deal that you have not discussed first with your attorney.

You should also be aware of trends in law that give the property owner additional rights. The property owner in foreclosure is acting under duress, and can claim so later. Some states have begun to pass laws to prevent predatory investors from taking advantage of property owners in such financial distress. This is another reason you are advised to seek assistance from your attorney on the proper way to work with foreclosure properties in your area.

Bidding at a Real Estate Auction

The auction is the final step in the foreclosure process, but most foreclosures never make it this far. Once the lender has commenced legal action, the property owner resolves the outstanding debt. Mostly, the property is sold or refinanced, the debt is satisfied, and the foreclosure suit is ended. But not always. Sometimes the property is sold at a public auction at the courthouse.

At the last minute, the property owner could file for bankruptcy protection. This would delay the public sale—it is sometimes specifically done to stop the sale from proceeding.

At a public sale, there is always at least one bidder—a bidder to represent the interests of the lender. Depending on the locale and customs of the court, that bidder might be the auctioneer, or an attorney representing the lender. Often the only bid received is the one from the lender's representative in the outstanding amount of the loan.

The lender's representative will usually always begin the bidding at the amount of the outstanding loan.

There could be other bidders bidding on the property. The auctioneer would invite an opening bid, and any subsequent bids, until a final bid amount has been determined. At that point, the auction for the sale of the property is completed. If you are the highest bidder, you still may not yet own the property. The property may still have to go through a confirmation process, depending on the laws in your state. But assuming whatever post-auction procedures occur successfully, you become the new owner of the property.

The auction will be subject to several specific requirements. The exact requirements vary by jurisdiction, but typically any successful bidder must be prepared to make a 10 percent down payment of the bid price in the form of a cashier's check on the day of the auction. The balance is due in 30 days. Should you fail to perform, you could lose your 10 percent down payment.

Because of the timing constraints and the potential for losing the 10 percent down payment, a wise investor will arrange for financing before ever bidding at the auction.

Buyer Beware

The title you receive may not be free and clear of all liens. Again, this is why you need an attorney who specializes in foreclosures.

Let's assume that a property is worth $200,000 (fair market value). A foreclosure was commenced for a loan where $100,000 is still owed. The property went to a courthouse auction.

The first bid received was $100,000 for the outstanding loan. If no one else bids, the property will be transferred to the lender and become an REO. The lender will eventually sell the property.

If there were additional bidders in this example, suppose the final bid was $125,000. The successful bidder bought the property—worth $200,000—for $125,000. Their payment goes to pay off the loan ($100,000). The remaining $25,000 is distributed to the property owner.

The successful bidder can then sell the property for $200,000, earning a net profit of $75,000. In the real world, this does not happen often, but it can and does occur.

The more equity in the property, the more likely there will be competitive bids. Other real estate investors are also looking at the equity that is on the table, and will do their best to capture it.

What sounds like an easy way to make a fast profit in real estate investing has some pitfalls. For example, you must usually provide a minimum of 10 percent of your bid in certified funds to the auctioneer at the time your bid is accepted. You must conclude the sale within a specified time—usually 30 days.

This is not a beginner's game. If you do not conclude the sale, you could lose your 10 percent down payment.

Before trying to acquire a property this way, make sure you have a clear understanding of the terms of the auction. Discuss this with your attorney. Make sure you understand the terms of the sale. Make sure that you understand which liens will not be removed by the foreclosure action, and if there could be any problems with the title to the property.

Always be cautious of liens placed against the property. Tax liens, in particular, remain fully enforceable against the real estate, even when a foreclosure occurs.

Property tax liens are not the only liens that should concern you. The Internal Revenue Service also has special powers to collect income tax, including placing liens on properties. If the title report reveals the

Author's Advice

The unwary real estate investor can suffer significant losses after acquiring the property at auction if the property was subject to tax liens that he failed to discover. These liens are always part of the public record.

existence of a tax lien, determine if the IRS has been duly notified of the pending foreclosure. If the IRS has been notified at least 25 days before the sale, current law allows the agency to seize the property to cure the lien for up to 120 days following the sale. If this were to happen to you, you would be entitled to a refund of all of your money with interest. Should the IRS not proceed with a seizure, their right to do so expires after the 120th day following the sale.

But there is a big catch. If the Internal Revenue Service was not notified properly of the public auction, their lien remains in place as long as it is on file in the county recorder's office. If you have purchased the real estate and the IRS opted to enforce its lien against the property, you would not be compensated. In effect, you get to pay someone else's taxes for them.

Many times, scheduled auctions are cancelled. The property owner may have satisfied the debt or a legal procedure may have postponed the sale. It is best to check the day before to make sure the auction is still scheduled.

You can find information about any public-scheduled auction in the courthouse and often in the legal notice sections of circulated newspapers.

The Least You Need To Know

- There will be keen competition from other real estate investors looking for foreclosed properties.
- Buying foreclosed properties at or before public auctions is tricky and could be risky.
- You need to consult with your attorney to understand how foreclosure works in your area in general and for guidance through your purchase in particular.
- REO properties are the safest foreclosure stage for a new real estate investor.

Chapter 8

The Numbers Game

In This Chapter

- Determining when to buy a property
- Understanding wholesale pricing of real estate
- Making real estate deals work profitably
- Determining your costs

Buying real estate as an investment is a numbers game. Either the deal makes sense, or it does not.

Basic math skills and a financial calculator are what it takes to evaluate the numbers on each deal. Sometimes it takes a little more work than other times. Creative thinking will sometimes make a marginal deal look better.

Like it says in the song *The Gambler*, "you got to know when to hold 'em, know when to fold 'em." That applies so well in real estate investing. Sometimes, it makes sense to say no, and just throw the cards away. In this chapter, you'll learn that's how it works in real estate investing, too.

When It Makes Sense to Buy

As a real estate investor, you should be constantly looking at properties that you would consider buying. Obviously, you will not be purchasing everything you look at—in fact, you will only buy a tiny fraction of all the properties you consider. The more properties you look at, the smaller that fraction will be.

When it comes to acquiring properties—whether you will hold them and collect rent, or resell them for a profit—you will be buying them in one of the following categories:

- Retail Pricing
- Wholesale Pricing
- Distressed Pricing

Retail Pricing

This is the simplest and most common form of real estate investing. You buy a property at the current market value. The retail price would be best defined as the price as determined by other recent comparable sales. In other words, the retail buyer wound up paying about the same as what other buyers paid, or the fair market value for the property. Then the buyer sits back and waits for the market value of the property to increase.

This is what most people do when it comes to buying their own home. They purchase a property, live in it, and if all goes well, they eventually sell it for more than they paid for it. This is real estate investing in its most basic form.

With home prices soaring over the past several years, this strategy has been a real moneymaker. The formula is simple: buy it, hang on to it, and sell it again when the price is right.

There are some pitfalls to this strategy. First, relying on appreciation is always risky. Should there be a slowdown, or reversal, there goes the profit. The rate of appreciation affects the return. If appreciation at the rate of 20 percent occurs each year, it's a great strategy. If the appreciation rate is a modest 2 percent, costs of buying and selling can easily destroy any profit potential, if your holding period is short.

Buyer Beware

Negative cash flow is a formula for trouble in real estate investing.

The second pitfall is for the real estate investor who plans to rent the property. The problem here is that rents have not always kept up with the costs of acquiring the property. In the prereal estate boom in many parts of the country, landlords could count on the rents received to cover the costs of the mortgage payment, insurance, taxes, and other expenses.

In many parts of the country, it is tough to rent out a home for what it costs to operate it. This creates a negative cash flow situation.

Wholesale Pricing

Another strategy when buying properties for real estate investment is to buy at wholesale pricing. In other words, you hunt for bargains. You always want to buy for less than the retail price.

The problem with this strategy is finding the bargains. Who would be willing to sell their property for less than what it is worth?

One answer is a motivated seller. Some people, because of their situation, will be most willing to do nearly anything to sell their property just to get rid of it—and the responsibility of ownership. Most motivated sellers are facing some financial hardship or crisis.

In the previous chapter, you learned about investing in foreclosures. Of course, people facing foreclosure are often highly motivated sellers.

Another source of motivated sellers are other real estate investors who have become frustrated with the business. Some investors, in search of wholesale-priced properties, call landlords advertising a property for rent. They inquire as to the interest of the property owner in selling their property. They hope to find an investor frustrated with searching for another renter who is now willing to sell the property at a discounted price.

Author's Advice

There are many myths about motivated sellers. Other sources of motivated sellers often cited include those individuals suffering from job loss, illness, or divorce, among other calamities. Forgetting the ethical considerations to this approach, a question needs to be asked about exactly how you go about finding such individuals. While you may meet some by chance over the course of an investing career, you will ultimately be more successful by finding opportunities where you can add value than by scouting for chances to steal real estate from the supposedly desperate.

Yet another strategy is to buy properties in a blighted area, fix them up, and hope the area improves. This works well in areas undergoing redevelopment, or a real estate boom. For example, a beach town is a good location for buying in a blighted area.

Because the demand is great for waterfront properties, and the prices are too high for many, redeveloped properties a few blocks away may suddenly become appealing.

The problems with buying property at wholesale prices are fourfold. They are …

- **The competition.** Everyone wants to buy a property for less than the market value. The bigger the bargain, the more likely that competition will either bid up the price or snap up the deal before you have a chance to buy.
- **Finding the properties**. Most of the work is in locating the properties. Few people advertise or list a property below its market value. Most of the time the real estate investor has to be aggressive in searching for properties that can be purchased below fair market value.
- **The property condition.** Many times, properties that can be purchased below fair market value have significant repair or maintenance issues. Buying one could prove to be a significant economic burden because of the repairs that might need to be made.
- **The risk.** Is that neighborhood headed for brighter days or will it retain its blighted ways? The challenge is to have the vision to see the potential in an area before anyone else does. The further challenge is not to be wrong about your vision!

Distressed Pricing

Another type of pricing for a property is when the asking price is set extremely low. In simple terms, the property and the pricing are distressed. The reasons could vary. Often the property has fallen into total disrepair, and needs major work to make it habitable. It could be unsafe, in violation of the building codes, and need major updates. Sometimes the costs of repair are significant—from the need for a new roof to replacement of siding, plumbing, heating, electrical systems, etc.

Many times these properties are offered for sale as a "rehabber" or "handyman's special." The asking price often reflects the shape of the property. Often these properties can offer opportunity to people who buy them if they are willing to pour money into them to make them more marketable. Of course, you need the financial wherewithal or borrowing capacity to fund such a project. However, updating a kitchen or changing a poor floor plan can make a substantial difference. You already read about the investor who buys homes without a garage but with the room and potential to add a garage. This investor has found a niche that allows him to add significant value and reposition the property for greater cash flow and resale profitability.

The obvious pitfall is that it may cost far more in time and money than you think to fix up and repair the property. There will be far more repairs needed than what you first see. Finding capable and reputable contractors to get the work done quickly is often another challenge.

The other issue is finding the money to invest in these types of properties. You will find it difficult if not impossible to obtain conventional financing to take on a major rehab as your first investment unless you are already in the building trades or have similar related experience. There are several ways to overcome this dilemma. The best way is if you are intending to occupy the property as your own home. Alternatively, if you have a track record, you can leverage this experience to help persuade a lender to back you. For example, if you helped friends with an extensive remodeling project or you completed such a project yourself in your own home, that experience coupled with a few before and after pictures (if you have them) could make a powerful argument in favor of your loan proposal.

On the other hand, if you retain a professional such as a home inspector, architect, or building engineer to define the scope of the job and then back up your renovation plans with detailed estimates from qualified contractors, you may be able to obtain financing. Because of the unique circumstances, you may not be in a position to shop for the best financing rates and terms, but instead be restricted to the one lender willing to take a gamble on your dream.

Should You Invest Now?

If you want to learn to play tennis, practice drills and calisthenics are all well and good, but at some point you have to go out on the court, pick up a racquet, and serve the ball. In real estate, it's the same way. The question is, when should you go from beginner to buyer? When do you make the leap from looker to landlord? The question you must ask yourself is, "should I invest now?"

The answer is simple: Yes, if the deal makes sense.

You already read in Chapter 2 about knowledge, knowledge, knowledge. If you have done your homework and have become the expert you need to be in your investment circle, you will know when you have found a deal. Having a mentor or adviser as a sounding board is a great way to get feedback on your investing ideas. In the end, you

Author's Advice

Often, the deal opportunity may define the kind of investor you become. David has always had it in mind to buy and hold and invest for cash flow. However, he has come across deals that were more suited to buying, fixing, and selling.

should be able to develop a compelling case based on facts and research about why any particular investment should be successful. Real estate investing is no place for playing hunches.

You have to decide what kind of real estate investor you are going to be. If you are going to acquire properties and hold them for the rental income (and enjoy the financial benefit of any appreciation), the deal may need to look a bit different from buying a property to rehab and resell at a profit.

Making Deals Work

Let the financial calculations begin! We are going to examine several deals, and see how we might be able to make marginal deals work better.

Deal #1: A $100,000 Single-Family Home

To purchase, you need to put down $5,000 and get a mortgage for the remaining 95 percent. At 7% interest, the monthly payment is $632.04 for 30 years. Taxes are $150 per month, and insurance is $15.

One tool every investor needs is a financial calculator and the instruction in how to use one. Financial calculators are available in just about any electronics store, office supply center, or the electronics section of many department stores. Most computer electronic spreadsheets are also capable of performing these functions. The calculators and computer software will come with instructions on how to use them, but if you feel like you need additional instruction, show up at your local apartment association meeting and there will be plenty of fellow investors there willing to give you a hands-on primer. You should get such a calculator now and practice on it by confirming the computations in these examples as you go along.

Author's Advice

A financial calculator is great for evaluating deals on-the-fly, like when you first drive past them. For more in-depth analysis, an electronic spreadsheet is great for comparing deals side by side.

To summarize, this is how the deal looks:

Purchase Price:	$100,000
Down Payment:	$5,000
Amount Financed:	$95,000
Loan Payment:	$632.04 (7% at 30 years)
Taxes:	$150.00
Insurance:	$15.00
Total PITI:	$797.04

This property will rent for $850.00 per month. On the surface, this looks like a marginal deal—generating about $53 a month in positive cash flow. But there is a problem. You did not add in the cost of Private Mortgage Insurance (PMI). With FHA loans, the mortgage insurance is called Mortgage Insurance Premium, or MIP.

def•i•ni•tion

PITI is short for principal, interest, taxes, and insurance.

In this example, the lender requires PMI. A typical monthly PMI premium is 0.78% of the initial mortgage amount divided by 12. As the down payment increases, the PMI premium percentage decreases. However, this example assumes the .78% premium rate. To calculate the monthly premium, do the math: .0078 × $95,000= $741 / 12 = $61.75.

Now this marginal deal has become a negative cash flow situation. This now looks like a deal to pass. Or is it?

What if you eliminated the need for the PMI? Could this become a workable deal? Suppose you only borrowed $80,000 from the lender, and then borrowed the remaining $15,000 from another lender, possibly the seller, on a second mortgage. Let's look at the loan:

$80,000 borrowed at 7% for 30 years = $532.24 monthly payment

$15,000 borrowed at 7% for 30 years = $ 99.80 monthly payment

Total monthly payments: $632.04 but with no PMI required.

PMI is only required when the borrower is requesting a loan for more than 80 percent of the total value. Because there would be a first and second mortgage in this example, there first mortgage lender would not require the PMI.

Author's Advice

In the real world, an institutional lender would charge a higher interest rate for a second mortgage than for the first mortgage. However, most second mortgages are funded by the seller and the interest rate charged is a matter of negotiation. The point of the example is important: by applying a different financing strategy, a deal can become more workable.

Here's another example of how creative thinking—thinking outside the box—can change the way a deal might work:

Deal #2: Changing the Floor Plan

You can buy a property for $150,000—the fair market value is $160,000. It looks like a good property, needing only some minor repairs and cleanup. It should not cost more than $1,000 to get it ready for resale. The reason you can get it for $10,000 less than market value is that the owner has been transferred out of state for her job, and she does not want to keep the property and make double housing payments.

In some areas of the country, closing costs are quite low. But for this example, assume that closing costs will absorb about 5 percent of the value to buy the property. Closing costs make this look like a deal breaker. By paying $7,500 in closing costs, adding a $1,000 in cleanup and repairs, you have only $1,500 potential profit. If you sold the property, your costs associated with the sale would destroy any chance of even a marginal profit.

The solution: the property is a 2 bedroom, 1½ bath unit. The floor plan includes a den area, which the current owner uses as a home office. It is about 12'×12', has no door, and no closet. You call your favorite local contractor and find out that installation of a door and a closet would cost $1,000.

Now if you bought the property for $150,000, paid the $7,500 closing costs, paid $1,000 for clean up and minor repairs, and another $1,000 to convert this den into a third bedroom, you would have $159,500 into the property. But it is no longer worth $160,000. Three bedroom homes in this neighborhood have been selling for $180,000. Suddenly, by thinking out of the box, a property you were likely to pass on could turn a $20,000 profit.

Creative thinking, combined with your knowledge of the local area, can often turn a marginal deal into a profitable one. As an active real estate investor, it makes sense to look at properties and your investments creatively. You could see things that others overlook. This opens the door of possibilities for you.

What Is This Really Going to Cost?

Always ask yourself, "what is this really going to cost?" Don't take the word of others—check it out yourself. Just because a property owner suggests that removing a beehive "won't cost more than $25," does not mean you can find anyone to do it for that price.

Verify everything. Make telephone calls. Determine for yourself what the cost will be.

Many times, you can get a lower estimate just by asking for a better price. "Can you do any better?" is a simple question that often follows with a better figure. This works with contractors, service businesses, and even lenders.

Author's Advice

Remember, everything is negotiable.

You cannot expect anyone to work for you for free. Costs have to be paid, and it is fair for everyone involved to make a profit (just as you hope to do). But if you can get the same quality of work done by someone else for less, do it. Every dollar you save is money kept in your pocket.

As an investor, the challenge is to achieve Cadillac quality on a Chevy budget. The only thing better than buying on sale is to not have to buy at all. Take advantage of the sales, but don't maintain any unnecessary supply of inventories that you don't need. For routine parts and supplies, let the hardware store be your warehouse. Inventoried items tend to get lost, stolen, wasted, or spoiled.

The key is to watch your costs.

Watch for fees that show up unexpectedly from everyone you deal with—and always be prepared to question them.

How Much Is Too Much?

Sometime in your career as a real estate investor, you are going to question how much you should be spending on a property. Somehow, you have to establish your own threshold.

That threshold will depend on many different factors. Some of them include your personal goals, your financial situation, and what kind of real estate investor you are.

For example, if you decide to invest in properties for rehabbing and you want to do most of the work yourself, you are going to be limited as to how many properties you can rehab each year. If it takes an average of 90 days to rehab a property, the maximum you could do each year is four.

If you are acquiring properties to hold and collect rent, and have little cash to invest and use as a down payment, the number of deals you could make is limited. You might only be able to purchase one, and if your cash flow is nominal, it may be several years before you can acquire another income-producing property.

On the opposite side of the spectrum, how many properties are too many? Only you know what you can—and want—to do. Some real estate investors acquire more than 50 properties, and spend most of their working day managing their real estate, dealing with repairs, maintenance, and tenants.

Other investors have far fewer units, but still live a comfortable lifestyle from the income their real estate investments generate.

Only you can decide how much is enough. It will depend on the time you have to devote to real estate investing and how much money you want to earn as an investor.

The Least You Need To Know

- There is a big difference between retail, wholesale, and distressed pricing.
- Negative cash flow properties can lead to trouble.
- Different financing strategies can often make a marginal property profitable.
- Strategies are often different between buy and hold for rent properties and those properties to be flipped.
- Control your costs.

Chapter 9

Making the Offer to Buy

In This Chapter

- Understanding a purchase agreement
- Deciding on a price
- Making a deposit
- Determining contingencies and terms
- Negotiating the purchase

You have found the perfect real estate investment for your goals. You have inspected it. You did the math. It makes sense. There is no reason not to move forward. The time has come to buy a piece of real estate.

To do so, you must make an offer to buy it. This chapter explains the steps involved in creating an offer.

Creating Written Offers

The purchase agreement, also called a sales contract, is used to make offers to buy real estate. Before making your first offer, there are several things to consider. All offers to purchase real estate must be made in writing. The price and the parties to the transaction must be clearly identified.

Buyer Beware

Verbal deals are never binding or enforceable. As soon as you think you have a meeting of the minds with the seller, get it in writing, assuming your negotiations were not in writing from the start. Verbal agreements—when it comes to real estate—are not worth the piece of paper they are not written on.

The real estate must be clearly identified and the agreement must be dated. Most purchase agreements are multiple-page contracts. See an example of a purchase agreement in Appendix B.

You should become familiar with the ordinary purchase agreements used in your particular area. You can obtain a copy from …

- Your attorney.
- Your settlement/title company.
- Local stationary stores.
- A local real estate agent.
- Your state's Realtor's Association.

You need to read the entire agreement, and understand your rights and obligations as the buyer. Purchase agreements will vary from state to state because real estate laws differ. Certain provisions may be required in your area. The format will also differ in each locale.

Despite the differences of the actual form in each state, all will have some basic information:

- Buyer's and seller's name and address
- The address and legal description of the property
- The purchase price
- The down payment, financing information, and amount of the deposit
- A time limit for the offer to be accepted, for the buyer to arrange financing, the date of settlement or closing, and the date for possession of the property
- Contingencies of the sale

Approach a purchase agreement as a proposal. You are proposing to the owner of the property to buy it under the terms in the agreement. This proposal not only specifies the price you are willing to pay, but it also includes all the terms and conditions of the purchase.

Promises from the Seller

As the buyer of the real estate, you will want some promises and concessions from the seller. These are likely to include …

- A promise to provide clear title to the property (ownership).
- Proration of the real estate taxes, rents, fuel, water bills, and utilities.
- The type of deed to be given at closing.
- Any other requirements specific to your state, which might include an attorney review of the contract, disclosure of specific environmental hazards, or other state-specific clauses.
- The right to perform various inspections of both the property itself and the books and records associated with the operation of the property.

Promises from the Buyer

The offer that you make will ultimately obligate you to a number of promises as well, including the following:

- Promises to exercise good faith in performing inspections, obtaining financing, and removing other contract contingencies
- Promise to make earnest money deposit payments on time
- Promise to pay the balance of the purchase price by the date of closing

And remember, never sign any agreement or contract unless you understand it. Seek competent legal assistance whenever you need help to understand what you are agreeing to do.

Creating Contingencies

Most purchase agreements include some form of contingencies. If your purchase offer says something like, "this offer is contingent upon (or subject to) a certain event," you're actually saying that you will only go through with the purchase if that event occurs successfully.

Financing and satisfactory inspection reports are the most common contingencies contained in purchase agreements. The buyer must obtain specific financing from a lender by a specific date. If the loan cannot be secured, the buyer is no longer bound by the contract, and any deposit money is returned.

Another routine contingency is for various inspections of the property. The contingency might say something like, "The buyer must receive a satisfactory report by a home inspector within 15 days after acceptance of the offer" or "the buyer must obtain a favorable opinion of the condition of the furnace within ten days of acceptance of the offer." The seller must wait for the prescribed time for the inspector to submit the reports called for in the offer that satisfy you. If the report reveals significant flaws or problems, the sales contract may be void.

Author's Advice

You can ask for any contingency that you want from the seller in your purchase agreement.

Besides the price, dates, and contingencies, you can include other conditions of the sale. Some of the common terms include:

- What else do you want from the seller? For example, you might ask the seller to purchase a home warranty. You could ask the seller to assist your purchase by paying for some of the closing costs. You might ask for a repair to be made to the property.
- What else do you want included with the home? For example, you may want the refrigerator, window treatments, a pool table, and a dehumidifier to remain with the property.
- What is the final condition of the home at settlement? For example, you might want the carpets cleaned professionally and the furnace cleaned.
- What kind of seller financing do you want? For example, you may ask the seller to lend you $15,000 in the form of a second mortgage, to be paid back over 10 years at a rate of 7 percent.

Be careful about how you construct your contracts. If an advertisement for a property says the appliances and the basement pool table are included with the home, the seller is still not responsible for providing these items unless they were specifically named in the offer to purchase.

Property: Legal Terminology

The real estate profession uses three legal terms to describe property: personal property, real property, and fixtures.

- Personal property is just as it sounds. It is property that you can readily take with you like an automobile, a refrigerator, or a stove.
- Real property is what people are usually thinking about when they talk about real estate. Real property is land and the improvements on the land, such as paving, landscaping, and erected structures.
- Fixtures are personal property that is fixed to real property. For example, a garbage disposal is an item of personal property when you buy it in the store, but once you install it in your home it becomes a fixture, part of the real property.

Buyer Beware

Fixtures are an area for confusion. Many would argue that window treatments are fixtures, but you don't want to leave the disposition of such items to later debate. If anything looks like it might be remotely possible to be removed from the property, be safe and specifically list the item as included in your offer.

Fixtures and personal property can be a point of confusion and contention when buying a piece of property. Always clearly spell out in your offer to buy the items of personal property and any fixtures that you intend to be included in the deal.

Making Fair Offers

Let's assume, for a moment, that you want to make an offer to purchase a home that is offered for sale at $100,000, which is a fair price for the property. Sure you can offer a small amount—$500 even—but in reality, it will never be accepted. All you are doing is wasting time and alienating the seller. This does not make sense.

What does make sense is to make a reasonable offer for the property. As an investor, you do not need to be emotionally involved with the property, as you are likely to be if it is your home. As an investor, if your offer is not accepted, you just simply move on to the next property.

Consider that $100,000 price. Let's say you offer it, and ask for $3,000 in closing costs assistance. Is it the same as offering $97,000, and receiving no closing cost assistance from the seller? Psychologically for the seller, the answer might be no. You might be more likely to get the seller to agree to this concession by offering full price. Of course, if you need the $3,000 to make the deal work, there is a huge advantage for you in building in the $3,000 closing cost credit.

Buyer Beware

Remember that your written offer is a legally binding contract. Just as you want the seller to be bound to the agreement, you too will be bound by the agreement.

As you consider your offer, always think about everything that needs to be done to the property. Consider what you need to make the property marketable. And never forget: base your offer on what the property is worth to you, not to anyone else. Don't negotiate with yourself. Don't say no for the seller. In the end, even as we advise you to make reasonable offers, make sure the offer is reasonable in your own mind, regardless of what anyone else may think.

It is up to you to offer what you want for the property. The amount you are willing to pay for it could be totally different from the seller's asking price. It could also be worth more to you than what the owner is asking—and you would obviously not offer more than the asking price. As was just mentioned, one mistake beginners make is to negotiate with themselves. Never start saying to yourself, "the seller would never accept $XXX,XXX.XX." You may be right in your assumptions, but let the seller tell you so. Sometimes you will be pleasantly surprised by a seller's reaction.

Earnest Money

Earnest money is just what it sounds like. It's a deposit of money made to demonstrate a good faith intention to close the deal.

As you are working on the details of your offer, you will need to make a deposit on the property. The deposit must be at least $1 to bind both the buyer and seller legally to the terms and conditions of the purchase agreement.

The seller is going to want to see a larger deposit. Sellers assume the larger the deposit, the more sincere you are about purchasing the property.

You may want to make as small a deposit as possible, enabling you to hold onto your cash. One real estate investor uses a $20 bill. He staples it to the purchase agreement. That's the maximum earnest deposit he ever offers.

You can offer as little or as much as you want as earnest money when making an offer to purchase property, and you can use earnest money as part of your investment strategy. If you are pursuing multiple deals simultaneously, or if cash is tight, you will want to keep the earnest money low. However, if you have the cash available, a big earnest money payment may lend greater credibility to a low offer.

Your purchase agreement should state who holds the deposit until the closing. If a real estate agent is involved in the transaction, the agent will probably retain the earnest money in the broker's trust account. Assuming your agent is minimally ethical, placing an earnest money deposit in a broker's trust account is a safe bet. If no agent is involved, allowing the seller to hold earnest money may be problematic. A neutral third party should hold the deposit. The best party to hold the deposit is a title company or your attorney.

Make certain the purchase agreement states what happens to the deposit if the deal is not completed. If the seller does not accept your offer, or you or the seller cannot meet some contingency or condition, you will want your deposit money returned to you within a reasonable period.

Author's Advice

Consider asking the seller to pay as many of the purchase and sale expenses as possible. Do not let local traditions or customs get in your way. If you are told the "buyer always pays for the title insurance," that does not mean the seller cannot pay for it.

Withdrawals and Refusals to Present Your Offer

Can you ever take back an offer to purchase a property? In most cases, the answer is yes, right until the moment it is accepted. Sometimes you may also withdraw your offer if you have not yet been notified of acceptance.

If you do want to revoke your offer, be sure to consult with your attorney. You could lose your earnest money deposit, or worse, find yourself being sued for damages by the seller.

Occasionally, you may run into a real estate agent who flatly refuses to accept your purchase agreement and present it to the seller. This usually occurs with an inexperienced agent who has forgotten their training.

Should this happen to you, follow these steps:

1. Remind the agent that legally and ethically, the offer must be presented to the seller.

2. If the agent persists, advise the agent that you will report the matter to the broker for resolution, as well as the state licensing authority. Ask for the agent's and the broker's license numbers.
3. By now, the agent should have backed down. If not, ask to meet with the broker. Finally, go to the state licensing authority.
4. Another alternative is to retain another agent, unless of course it is the listing agent who is refusing to present your offer.

The agent is required to present the offer (no matter what they tell you). You may find this situation occurring when an inexperienced agent overpromised a potential seller a higher selling price. Now the agent must take a more realistic offer to the seller, knowing the seller wants more for the property.

The agent can recommend to the seller to accept, or not to accept, any offer. The agent, when forced to present an offer, is likely to recommend the offer be turned down. When you suspect that an agent will not present an offer fairly, add this verbiage to your sales agreement: buyer reserves the right to be present when this offer is presented to the seller.

You can then be there when the agent presents the offer, and explain why you made the offer for the property as you did.

The Seller's Response to Your Offer

After your offer is presented to the seller, you are likely to receive one of three responses:

- Acceptance of your offer
- Total rejection of your offer
- A counteroffer

If you receive an acceptance, congratulations! You are well on your way to buying a property! There is no legally binding contract until the seller, after receiving your written purchase agreement, signs an acceptance as it stands, unconditionally. Your purchase offer becomes a firm contract when you are notified of the seller's acceptance.

If your offer to purchase the property is rejected, that is the end of your commitment to move forward with the deal. The sellers cannot later change their minds and force you to purchase the property. If you receive just a rejection, you have two options:

- Submit another offer
- Move on to another property

If you receive a counteroffer, you need to review it and consider what the seller is asking of you. For example, you might have offered $90,000 on a property listed for $100,000. The seller counteroffers with a price of $95,000. You can accept it, reject it, or make another counteroffer. In essence, a counteroffer is a new offer to you from the seller.

Each time either the seller or buyer makes any change in the terms of the purchase agreement, the other side can accept or reject it, or submit a counteroffer again. The purchase agreement becomes a binding legal contract only when one of the two parties finally signs an unconditional acceptance of the other side's purchase proposal.

The give-and-take—the negotiation process—is just that. It is the process where both parties are trying to work out the sale and purchase of a piece of real estate.

For example, if the seller agrees with everything except the sale price, the proposed closing date, and the dehumidifier you want with the property, you may receive a written counteroffer, with the changes the seller prefers. For example, "Seller counteroffers with the price of $98,000. The closing shall occur on or before June 30th, and the seller will not leave the dehumidifier with the property." When you receive this counterproposal, you can accept it, reject it, or make your own counteroffer.

The process continues until each party agrees or rejects the offer and counteroffers.

Author's Advice

Keep in mind during the negotiation process the seller could be receiving other offers to purchase the property. Sellers are not legally obligated to disclose the terms of other offers to prospective buyers. In fact just the opposite tends to be true. If there are any real estate agents involved, those agents should not be disclosing the details of any offer with anyone.

Strengthening Your Negotiating Position

Negotiating a purchase goes back long before recorded history. Haggling over price and terms is a part of life. It is also a part of buying real estate.

There are several things you can do to put yourself in a stronger position to negotiate with a seller. They are:

- Be a cash buyer.
- Be preapproved for financing (more on this in Chapter 10).
- Be willing to put up a larger earnest money deposit.
- Be willing and able to conclude the sale in a short period of time.
- Do not include burdensome contingencies.

There are some additional things you can (and should) do to improve your position during negotiations. They are:

- Learn as much about the seller as possible. The more you know about a seller's motivation to sell the property, the stronger your negotiating position. For example, if you learn the seller has already purchased another property, the seller may be more likely to accept an offer that includes a fast settlement.
- Try not to reveal too much information about your thoughts to the seller or the agent. Do not confide your negotiating strategy. Keep your motivations to yourself. Watch what you say within earshot of either a real estate agent or a seller. Everything you say can, and will, be used in the bargaining process. For example, if you submit a purchase agreement with a figure lower than the asking price, don't tell the seller's real estate agent that you are willing to pay more for the property.
- Do not rush into any decision, no matter how tempting it may be.

Many experts discourage making a deliberate, lowball offer. While such an offer can always be presented, it can also sour the seller, and discourage any negotiation.

Closing the Deal

Once the purchase agreement has been accepted, both parties work toward closing the deal. While negotiations can be difficult or contentious, the buyer and seller should now come together, cooperating with each other to make the sale occur. The seller grants access to the property for inspectors and appraisers and provides information as required in the contract. The buyer applies for financing, providing financial documents to the lender so the loan can be approved.

On the date of the closing, legal documents are signed, money is transferred, and possession of the property passes from the seller to the buyer.

Congratulations landlord, and welcome to the ranks of real estate investor!

The Least You Need To Know

- Make sure you understand a purchase agreement before you sign it.
- You can make any offer you want.
- A purchase agreement is not legally binding until both parties agree without conditions.
- List any personal property you want included in the sale on the purchase agreement.
- Common contingencies include satisfactory inspection reports and a satisfactory loan commitment.
- Both parties can make counteroffers to the other's proposal.

Chapter 10

Fixing Up a Property to Sell

In This Chapter

- Buying properties to flip
- The problems with flipping properties
- Easy fixer-uppers
- Rehabbing properties
- Different ways to profit with flips

Many real estate investors like the idea of buying a property, and immediately selling it for a profit. The quick resale—the flip—is where they find their payday. Yes, flipping can be profitable.

But finding properties to make a quick flip is problematic. You must find properties and buy them at deep discounts. The so-called real estate gurus who appear on television may tell you to pay not more than 65 percent of the fair market value of a property. That way, when you flip it, you are assured of a profit.

For example, if you found a property that is worth $150,000, you should pay not more than $97,500 for it. Sounds easy enough. All you need to do is to find a distressed seller willing to throw away $52,500. Anything is possible, we suppose, but if your plan is to complete more than one such deal in a lifetime, you will need to develop some sophisticated strategies for finding, improving, and moving these flips.

This chapter will show you how to develop your value vision for spotting deals priced well below current or potential fair market value. You'll learn which improvements to make, and how to keep your rehab on budget.

Flipping a Property

Rather than buying and holding a property, collecting rent, and building equity, you can opt to buy properties to flip. There is nothing wrong with that decision. It is not illegal or improper.

You may have heard of illegal flipping. This is a misnomer, and something that has been wrongly reported recently by the press. What the media calls illegal flipping is more accurately characterized as loan fraud. This scheme involves getting inflated appraisals to qualify for inflated loans. There is nothing illegal about buying a property for one price and turning around and selling it for more than you paid for it. Any illegality stems from the fraud perpetrated on the lenders by unscrupulous appraisers and investors. The illegal transactions are not arms-length transactions to unrelated parties. Instead, a gang of investors conspires to sell a property repeatedly to one another, getting a higher appraisal and a bigger loan each time.

The concept of legally flipping a property is uncomplicated. Buy a property as cheaply as possible and sell it for as much as possible in minimal time. There are variations to this simple moneymaking model:

- Buy at a wholesale price, and sell at a wholesale price to another investor—making just a few thousand dollars on the transaction. Perhaps a better way to explain this is to charge a finder's fee—of $3,000 to $5,000. When you make an offer, you include the phrase "and assigns" after your name so you can assign the purchase agreement to another investor.
- Buy the property, freshen it by doing cosmetic repairs, and then sell it.
- Buy the property, and rehabilitate it by updating the mechanical systems, completing cosmetic repairs, and selling it.
- Buy the property, and make it better than it is by adding additional features and improvements.

The one common element of these various flip options is your desire to buy the property for as little as possible. Finding properties that are being sold below fair market value is always the challenge for the real estate investor who is engaged in flipping. To be successful, you are going to have to go beyond merely buying a property below its present fair market value. You need to have the vision to be able to see the potential fair market value in a property. Further, you have to have the ability to improve the property without spending more than the potential increase in value.

Finding these properties has been discussed in previous chapters. Buying properties at a discount is an obvious, effective strategy regardless of whether you intend to sell quickly or hold for the long-term. Expect major competition from other investors in finding these types of properties. The better the bargain price, the more likely there will be competition for the property.

Think about the problem. Everyone wants to buy low and sell high. Finding the properties where you can do just that is always the challenge.

Finding Your "Vision"

You can (and will) spend much time looking for properties that you can buy for 50 to 60 cents on the dollar. Can it be done? Sure, if you have the vision to see potential that everyone else may miss. Having the vision is key. There just are not many property owners ready to walk away from even marginal real estate at obvious, huge discounts. But there are plenty of owners who have lived in or owned a property for years without ever seeing the potential in them.

For you to understand "the vision thing," some historical background and then some specific examples will be helpful. Architectural styles change just the way clothing fashions change. Sometimes the changes are driven by changes in technology and other times the changes are purely a matter of taste. For example, the basement used to be where coal and a giant furnace were located. Today, smaller, more efficient furnaces fueled by natural gas are so unobtrusive that basements have been finished off to become another room in the house. This development reflects a change in technology. Appliances have evolved from copper brown to avocado green to harvest gold to almond to bisque with detours to include black and stainless steel along the way. These changes reflect merely changes in tastes.

Author's Advice

Buy white appliances. White is always in style.

The same way that clothing fashions from years ago can come back in style, housing trends also sometimes get recycled. Again, some examples will prove helpful. Years ago, standard flooring material was hardwood flooring. Carpeting was an expensive upgrade.

Today, no one waxes a hardwood floor anymore. Modern polyurethane finishes so completely protect wood floors that they are even used in kitchens. So what happened to the hardwood floors in all the old houses? When less expensive nylon carpeting became widely available, many of those wood floors were covered over in wall-to-wall carpet. After all, at the time hardwood floors were commonplace, but wall-to-wall carpet was the newest, latest, best thing. Besides, in those days, the materials and labor to install a wood floor were cheap. Fast-forward a few decades and the situation has reversed itself. Everyone has carpet and the elite upgrade is a hardwood floor.

What does this mean for the investor? Simply this: by understanding trends and fashions not only for today but also from yesterday, you may be able to discover hidden value. Again, some examples will paint the clearer picture. You have already been reading about one example, hardwood floors. You will not have to go through many older housing units before you come across some with hideous, stained, obsolete carpeting. Sometimes the carpet has been down so long that even the resident does not know what is under there. Obviously, new carpet always looks great, but if you can tear out an old piece of carpet and restore a wood floor, you can add value.

You have already been reading about one trend in value-added opportunities. Many older housing units may have recoverable wood floors hidden underneath the carpet. Other trends include changing floor plans, changing finishes, and changing styles.

Changing the Floor Plan

In the past, floor plans were sliced up into little pieces with each room in the house having its own four walls. The trend was to have many smaller, private rooms. The trend today is to have an open floor plan. Yesterday, perhaps the typical home had a narrow galley kitchen with a separate dining room, family room, living room, and even a den.

Today, these same rooms might be combined into an "L" shaped kitchen that opens to a dining area adjacent to a larger great room that may be equal in size to the old family room and living room combined. The den is just a nook tucked away in an open corner somewhere. The application here is that you may want to consider removing nonload-bearing walls to open a floor plan.

Dave just completed renovating an apartment building where he knew the kitchens were going to be replaced. Instead of duplicating the existing arrangement, a wall was removed to make a galley kitchen into an "L" shape. The apartment is no bigger than it was, but it looks huge in comparison to before.

Changing the Finishes

Finishes have changed the same way. In the sixties and seventies, wood wall paneling was all the rage. Today, that paneling looks old, dried out and faded, not to mention obsolete. The solution is not to get fresh paneling, the solution is to get rid of the paneling entirely. You would be surprised at the number of times paneling has been pulled off of a wall to reveal taped and finished drywall ready for paint. In one of Dave's buildings, a two-story lobby was paneled on one wall. The paneling looked drab and soaked up light like a sponge. Behind the paneling was finished drywall. Once the paneling was removed and the wall painted, the lobby looked bigger, brighter, and new.

Then there were the drop ceilings with acoustic tile that some building butcher installed 40 years ago to cover the cracks in the ceiling plaster. Never mind that he also covered the cove ceiling and the crown moldings, at least he did not have to look at those cracks anymore. The application here is that things that were once commonplace can be taken for granted. Years ago, even many modest middle-class homes had coved ceilings and crown molding. They were common enough that they were not always appreciated then. They are priceless now. Ditch the ceiling tiles and fix that plaster.

Changing the Style

Styles change, too. Today, faux painting is all the rage. It's simply incredible, the effects that can be achieved with a little talent and some paint. Many of these finishes require a high degree of skill and practice, but some techniques are easy. Most hardware stores and home improvement centers have inexpensive faux painting kits, some of which even come with instructional videos. Anyone who can use a paint roller can learn the techniques, and the process is nearly as quick as a conventional paint job. You will rarely see a faux finish in a rental dwelling. Typically, such finishes are reserved for luxury homes, but they can be reproduced even by the do-it-yourselfer at modest expense.

Real Deal

Anyone seeking opportunities to add value to real estate should be attending the local "parade of homes" type shows put on by local building associations. These "parades" are typically a new subdivision of homes selected by the local builder's association intended to display many model homes produced by many different builders. The opportunity for the investor is excellent. You can peruse these new homes at your own pace without being assaulted by an annoying salespeople. While you are there, take note of the latest trends. Often, the homes will be extensively decorated, even over-decorated.

There will be many trends that you will not be able to duplicate cost-effectively. But there will be other trends that you can practice on a budget, like faux painting. Some more recent trends that may be within an investor's budget include closet organizer systems. Today, these closet organizer systems are now moving into the garage. Finished basements are also hot. Finishing a basement only makes sense if there are sufficient ceiling heights and good natural lighting, which is to say that most rental properties will probably be disqualified. But you may want to paint the walls and floor. Again, some of the modern concrete stains and paints render amazing finishes.

Seeing the Potential

There cannot be enough emphasis placed on developing your vision for seeing potential. You are simply not going to find consistently deeply discounted properties selling well below their market value. But with a sharp eye for opportunity, you may be able to spot consistently plenty of properties selling well below their *potential* market value. Once you have sharpened your value-adding vision, consider some of the strategies for buying and flipping:

1. Maybe you do not have the time or the cash to exercise your vision. If so, determine if you are going to do any improvements to the property. If circumstances constrain you from improving, adopt a simple strategy of making an offer to buy the property, with the intention of assigning your contract. On acceptance, you later assign your contract to another buyer. This strategy does not excuse you from having a vision for what the property could be. Instead, what you are going to do is sell another buyer on the merits of your dream. For example, you agreed to buy a property for $60,000. After acceptance, you assign your contract to another investor at a value of $64,000. When the other real estate investor

closes, you receive $4,000 at closing. To pull this off, you need to have a list of active real estate investors in your area. You also need to include the words "or assigns" after your name on the purchase agreement. By doing so, you can assign the purchase agreement to whomever you want. It might not seem like much money, but if you did one of these every few months, you might consider yourself a successful real estate investor by the end of the year. One way to look at this is that you are collecting a "finder's fee" for your work.

2. Not every viable investment property lends itself to a visionary metamorphosis. Sometimes just a cosmetic makeover is all that is required. This strategy works best when the investor is going to do most (if not all) of the work. If you do not mind doing painting, wallpapering, cleaning, and scrubbing, this can be a good flipping strategy.
3. Buying a property that needs major rehab work is always a challenge, unless you have the time, money, and expertise. One way to do this—without the cash you need—is to use what's called hard money financing. This is described in more detail in Chapter 11. One of the problems you need to solve is to have reliable contractors available to do the work quickly and economically.
4. Flipping a property that has been fundamentally changed—by remedying underuse—can be profitable. Under use includes the small house on the big lot or the changes in use (office to residential and vice versa) discussed previously. With some imagination, the possibilities could be endless. However, you usually are paying more for the property and not relying as much on getting the property at a steep discount. And you have to have the vision for what could be.

The problem for the real estate investor interested in flipping remains finding the properties and getting them for pennies on the dollar. Properties that need total rehabs are often easier to locate. These are often in the questionable neighborhoods and have been nearly abandoned by their owners.

They usually take far more than some paint and cleaning of the windows. They usually need an overhaul. The real estate investor may need a general contractor to handle the scope of the work to be done. Kitchens and bathrooms often need total renovations. New roofs are often needed, too. Some of the properties are burnouts, and remain only as vacant shells. Usually windows and doors need to be replaced. Most of the work is well beyond the scope of a weekend of work to freshen the property.

Real Deal

If you find a property that just need a freshening, and can be flipped profitably, buy it.

When it comes to flipping, everything rests on your ability to buy a property at a huge discount to potential market value. This means that either you look for run-down housing that can be purchased at a deep discount, or you develop your vision to see diamonds in lumps of coal.

You'll find plenty of competition over the properties only in need of a quick cosmetic fix, but once you graduate to the heavy-duty rehab properties, the competition thins quickly.

You need to think out of the box. Underutilized properties are properties that are more than those with out-of-date colors, need landscaping, or just look bad—inside and out. These are the properties that are obsolete, underutilized, and ugly, but with some imagination and money, could be increased in value.

For example, you might find a property that has only two bedrooms and one bath. It has the possibility of adding another bath and a third bedroom in the attic. If it had it, the value of the property may instantly rise well beyond what the acquisition and improvements costs would be.

The possibilities are endless. This strategy gives you a new approach to flipping properties. And most likely you'll have far less competition from other real estate investors.

Most real estate investors who flip properties relate that it requires making many offers before getting acceptances. Remember that you are offering far less than what the property should be worth. Be patient and stick to these strategies.

As soon as you have the property ready, you should be able to sell it—at a profit. On closing day, you receive your paycheck for your work. The size of the paycheck will be determined by what your sale price is, less the cost of selling, less your acquisitions costs, and repairs.

You could also change your mind about selling the property you bought to flip. If you decide to keep the property, you should be able to rent the property and realize positive cash flow. This happens often to real estate investors. They buy the property to flip, but then decide to keep it for the ongoing rental income.

Anybody can buy a property for fair market value. There is no magic—it's just common sense. For example, if a property is offered for sale at $100,000 (which is its fair market value), and you buy it at $100,000, good for you. But if you are going to flip properties successfully for a profit, you need to purchase the property for less than the potential fair market value. How much less you buy it for is what will determine your profit.

Fair market value is defined as the price that would be achieved in the marketplace between an unrelated buyer and seller after allowing sufficient time for marketing the property. The difference between your purchase price and the actual fair market value is called the spread. As an investor, you want as large a spread as possible on each deal.

There is nothing wrong with buying a property at its fair market value—but it does not make sense to do so when the property has been neglected and allowed to fall into disrepair.

Author's Advice

Investing in neglected properties is particularly good for those investors who are handy and can do simple home repairs, including painting.

A number of years ago, David bought seven townhouse-style duplexes from an estate. The buildings were 40 years old and in poor condition. All the properties had gravel driveways and a yard full of weeds. The interiors had been equally neglected. Carpets were in poor condition. Bathrooms were obsolete and badly deteriorated. The kitchens were a disaster. New kitchen cabinets would be required. There was no air conditioning. David thought the buildings would be worth $240,000 each once restored to move-in condition. His plan was to buy them, fix them up, and resell them to individual buyers who would probably live in one side of the duplex and rent out the other side. However, as a fallback position, David also felt that if the units would not sell, he could keep the buildings and rent them out with positive cash flow. David bought the buildings for $180,000 each in anticipation of spending $20,000 each in repairs. If the buildings could be sold for $240,000, then there was a profit potential of $40,000 per building.

David purchased the properties and immediately set to work. He started on the exteriors the day after closing by having an asphalt contractor put in new driveways. The landscaping was quickly brought under control. Work began on the interiors in the vacant units. New paint, carpet, central air conditioning, and new kitchens with all new appliances went into every single unit. Each bathroom was similarly remodeled.

The properties were restored to better than new condition. Unfortunately, the job had cost twice what David had budgeted. Could the properties be sold for a little more to recover the extra costs? It was time to put the properties on the market and find out.

Indeed, David was able to sell each of the buildings for $260,000 or more, enabling him to recover the extra costs and still maintain the desired profit margin. The final deal looked like this:

Acquisition Cost:	$180,000 per building
Repairs and Upgrades:	$40,000 per building
Total Final Cost:	$220,000 per building
Sale Price:	$260,000 per building
Less Total Final Cost:	$220,000 per building
Profit:	$40,000 per building

Note that in this example, the final repair cost was twice what was anticipated, even for an experienced investor. The project also took twice as long as David thought it would. Everything worked out well in the end, but David still jokes that he will never drive down the street where these properties are located ever again.

If you are buying properties to resell quickly at a profit, be prepared to spend a lot of time doing so. And remember the only way you make money with this real estate investing strategy is to be buying and selling constantly. You only have a payday when you sell your property at a profit.

What Improvements to Make

If you are flipping properties, and your strategy is to fix them up, you must decide which improvements to make. Obviously, you need to make enough to sell the property at a profit. You do not want to overimprove the property, but you also do not want to skimp and neglect obvious defects. This is important if you are thinking the property is likely to be sold to a first-time homebuyer. Most new homebuyers scrimp and save to get enough money to make a down payment. They cannot afford a major postclosing repair. If there is an obvious defect, fix it.

Easy Ways to Improve a Property

There are some easy ways to improve a property and make it more appealing to potential buyers. Some of the quick and easy things you can do include:

- Replacing outdated appliances
- Updating lighting fixtures
- Painting

- Replacing torn screens
- Installing new screen doors
- Fixing all doors and windows
- Completely freshening the entry door area
- Replacing carpet or linoleum floors
- Eliminating any unpleasant odors
- Cleaning and polishing
- Updating window treatments
- Adding appliances such a dishwasher or space-saver microwave

You need to work the clean-up process. As soon as you get your hands on a neglected property, there are many things you can do to get it cleaned up quickly, easily, and inexpensively:

- Rent a dumpster to haul away trash, debris, and landscape debris.
- Cut the lawn, get rid of the weeds, and improve the shrubbery (many landscape supply stores will help you design a landscape plan for free).
- Have a "fill the dumpster day" with the children in your family. Recruit your own children, nephews, nieces, or grandchildren to help fill it. Pay them for their labor. Buy them some pizza for lunch. Turn it into a party. You will be surprised how much you can get done just by having extra help around to carry stuff and throw it in the dumpster. And you are helping all the kids learn how to make honest money.
- Dig out old shrubbery that cannot be saved. Often it is better to replace with a smaller, in shape plant than to try to trim up an unruly bush that has grown out of shape.
- Pay attention to the entrance and main door. Invest in some brass street numbers. Clean up or replace the doorknob, lock, and any outdoor entrance light.
- Add mulch to the new landscaping. Give the plants a boost with some fertilizer.
- Feed and water the lawn.
- Replant any bare spots in the lawn with grass seed or sod.

- Throw away any badly stained, torn, or soiled carpet. (If there are hardwood floors, clean, polish, and refinish them as necessary.)
- Replace the stove if it is old, out-of-date, or unable to be cleaned. (You may be able to find a deal on a scratch-and-dent appliance—and if the dent is on the side that cannot be seen because of a cabinet, save the dollars and buy it.)
- Remember that paint is cheap. Paint whatever needs it. Buy good quality paint to freshen the outside. When doing interior walls, always use a neutral color such as white or off-white.
- If the property has wall-to-wall carpet, schedule a professional cleaning.
- Schedule any contractors you need to get the cleanup and maintenance done as soon as possible after taking possession.
- As soon as the outside is cleaned up, erect the "for sale" sign (either your own, or if you are going to have real estate agent sell it, list the property) or a "for rent" sign, depending on your goals.
- Tubs can be resurfaced to bring new life to the bathroom.
- Consider kitchen cabinet refinishing to brighten a kitchen and make it more appealing.
- Do not overlook what cleaning can do—and cleaning is always the least expensive option.

Always complete the outside work first. The better the home looks outside, the sooner you will attract interest from others in the property.

Renovations

When considering renovations, make those that are necessary. They usually involve the kitchen and bath. Opening walls is also possible, and can drastically change the appearance of the interior. Gutting a kitchen is more than a weekend project, but can be done by people with some advanced handyman skills. Many small contractors can remove old cabinets. A new floor, fresh paint, new cabinets, countertops, and appliances can add real value to the property. Such improvements can change the entire appearance and breathe new life into the home.

What Improvements to Avoid

When considering flipping, you do not want to make improvements that do not add value to the property. Forget personal taste, and choose functional rather than extravagant items. For example, if you are replacing the dining room light fixture, don't purchase one for $15, but you don't need to spend $500 for one, either. Use common sense in everything you do insofar as making improvements. This basic philosophy can be applied in every room of the property, as well as the exterior. Don't buy cheap, but don't overimprove the property, either. Every dollar you spend is money that will come out of your bottom line.

The Least You Need to Know

- There is nothing illegal or improper about flipping a property.
- Finding properties at a significant discount is a challenge.
- Develop your vision for seeing potential in underutilized properties that can be bought far below their potential market value.
- The only way you can make money flipping properties is when you actually sell the property you bought, unless you keep it for rental income.
- You can buy a property and sell it to another investor without ever doing any repairs (use the phrase "and assigns" in the contract).
- Many properties bought to flip will require significant repairs.

Part 3 Locating the Money

To buy real estate, you need money. Luckily, and unlike any other investment opportunity, you can use someone else's money to buy the property. It is just a matter of arranging the loan and borrowing the money.

In this part of the book, you will learn all about real estate financing, and the various ways to finance your real estate investments.

Chapter 11

Traditional Financing

In This Chapter

- Preparing to apply for a mortgage
- Options available when borrowing
- Knowing what documents you will need
- Understanding your credit report
- Locating better financing deals

Investing in real estate requires money. Depending on how many investments you want to make, or how much each piece of real estate costs, you may need a lot of money.

Of course, you can use your own money to invest in real estate. However, few real estate investors do that. Most borrow the money they need to buy the properties they want. Even Donald Trump borrows heavily to fund his real estate investments.

Getting the money you need to buy real estate is not as difficult as you might think. You just need to know how to ask for it.

In this chapter, you'll learn all about traditional financing options and how to prepare to apply for a loan to maximize the odds of approval. You'll also explore the mysteries of credit scoring and reporting and how you can improve your credit score.

Getting Ready to Apply

Before applying for any loan, you can find out the lender's underwriting criteria. That way, you can know what the lender is going to say about your application before you present it. If you have followed the lender's underwriting criteria, you can have confidence about being approved for the loan. By following the underwriting criteria, you can be quickly and easily approved each time you ask for a loan. Start looking at a loan package just as a lender does. When you do, you will find the path to obtaining financing simple and easy.

The lending industry is regulated, creating much bureaucracy. Also, there is an underlying concern with making sure the borrower can repay the obligation. So lenders have rules in place and procedures that must be followed to comply with these regulations and ensure repayment of the loan.

The Perfect Loan

At first, if you think about it, lending money is a foolish thing to do. Would you lend $100 to a total stranger?

Often, that is what you are asking a mortgage lender to do. The only difference is that you are asking for a lot more than just $100. You are asking for tens of thousands or even hundreds of thousands of dollars. Why should they even consider lending it to you?

To understand the lender's thinking, first consider what a lender would think is a perfect loan:

A Perfect Home Loan	
Property to be purchased:	1234 West Main Street, Anytown, USA
Type of Loan:	Primary Residence
Fair Market Value:	$200,000
Amount of Loan:	$160,000
Source of Down Payment:	Proceeds of sale of current home
Borrower's Employment:	Worked for past 14 years as engineer at XYZ Corporation

Borrower's Income:	$85,000 per year
Borrower's Credit Score:	711 (High score, no blemishes)
Total Monthly Obligations:	$205
Other Assets:	$120,000 Savings Accounts, IRA

Analyze the loan in the preceding table. As you look at it, notice the key points:

- The property (the collateral for the loan) is a middle-America home, in a desirable location.
- The borrower is asking for a loan of 80 percent of the value of the collateral.
- The property will be the borrower's primary residence.
- The borrower is using $40,000 of his own money to purchase the property.
- The borrower has excellent earning potential, having been employed at the same place for the past 14 years. There is no reason to think the borrower's income is not likely to continue.
- The borrower earns more than enough money to afford the property and make the monthly payment.
- The borrower has an excellent credit rating—another reason to believe the borrower will faithfully make the monthly payment on time.
- The borrower has only a few other monthly obligations ($205).
- The borrower has other financial assets.

As you analyze this borrower, the property, and the loan, there is no reason not to approve it. To any lender, this is a perfect loan.

When a lender makes a loan, they want you to pay it back, on time, each month as you agreed. If you make your monthly payment, the lender is happy.

What if something happened to the borrower that rendered him or her unable to repay the loan? The lender would be in a good position. If worse comes to worse, and the lender gets the collateral back, they now have title to a $200,000 property that cost them only $160,000. Even if it cost $20,000 to dispose of the property, the bank should be able to recover their $160,000. They could sell a $200,000 property for $180,000, and still break even.

Author's Advice

Lenders believe most borrowers will do everything they can to save their primary residence.

But before the loan ever goes into default, the borrower has plenty of reason to keep the loan current. The borrower not only has the money in savings to make payments, the borrower has $40,000 of his own money to protect. Plus, it is his primary residence—the place where he lives.

This loan scenario is a perfect loan for a lender. This borrower would receive the best rate available from most lenders. Borrowers with a strong credit application such as in the preceding example can expect the best rates from a lender.

Lending to Real Estate Investors

Imagine for a moment that you had $50 million to lend to people buying real estate. Who would you lend it to?

Most likely you would not want to lose any of your $50 million dollars. You would only want to lend it to those people you think would pay it back. Right?

So you try to lend it to those applicants with a perfect loan scenario. To get their business, you have to give them your best possible rate. You may find that owing to the competitive nature of the lending business, not all of the $50 million can be loaned out to borrowers with the strongest credit applications. Alternatively, the lending institution may make a business decision to pursue other lending opportunities that offer a higher return—at a commensurate higher risk. After several months, you are still lending money, but you can't find enough perfect loans to make. You do not want any part of the $50 million to be idle—you need to lend it and make the money work.

So you start offering different loan programs. You agree to start making loans that are less than perfect, perhaps to someone with good, but not perfect credit. You might lend to someone who only puts 10 percent down, or to someone who is not planning to live in the property. Each concession you agree to creates more risk for you.

For example, when someone borrows money for an investment property, it is easier to walk away from that property than it is to walk away from your own home. Everyone needs to live somewhere, but not everyone needs an investment property. In other words, there is additional risk involved when lending on less than a perfect loan. To make up for this extra risk, you charge a higher loan rate. You may develop many different special types of loan programs. The following is a typical loan program offered by a lender:

Investor Loan Program

Multiunit (1-4 units)
Nonowner Occupied
FICO 660
Maximum Loan Amount: $350,000
95% LTV

The loan program described here is one designed for real estate investors. To qualify, you need a credit score of 660. You need 5 percent down payment, and the loan amount cannot exceed $350,000.

As you can see, lending to a real estate investor does not equate to a perfect loan, but that does not mean there are not programs available from lenders. In fact, you will be amazed at how many different loan programs are made available to you.

Key Personnel at the Lender

Depending on the type of lender where you apply for a loan, you may be in contact with any number of people. Some of the key people at the lender are:

- **Loan officer.** Sometimes also called the loan originator, this is the person responsible for collecting all the necessary information. This is your primary contact at the lender's office. This is the person who will take your application, answer your questions, and offer different loan programs to you based on your situation. This individual may be paid by commission.
- **Loan processor.** This person handles all the paperwork for your loan. Working behind the scenes, the loan processor makes sure all the lender's rules are followed, and orders the appraisal, credit reports, title insurance, etc.
- **Underwriter.** This is the person who decides whether you get the loan or not. The underwriter reviews all the information collected by the loan officer and the loan processor, and determines whether or not you meet the criteria to get the loan. You, as a borrower, typically will not have contact with the underwriter.

Your Mortgage Options

During the application process, you are going to be asked what mortgage you want. The loan officer will offer advice on the variety of loan products available.

You are going to find a lender by recommendation or by their advertisements. Often, the lender will advertise their programs in listing such as:

A Typical Lender Advertisement

ABC Funding (555-555-5555)				
30 Year Fix	5.75	0/0	5%	$0/$275
30 Year Fix	5.5	1/1	5%	$0/$275
15 Year Fix	5.0	1/1	10%	$0/$275
3/1 ARM	3.75	1/0	5%	$35/$300
5/1 ARM	4.375	0/1	5%	$35/$300
30 Year FHA	5.75	1/0	3%	$35/$275

The typical lender advertisement usually lists the term of the mortgage (30 or 15 years), the interest rate, the number of points (discount and origination points), the required down payment, the credit report, and the application or appraisal fee. Notice some of the terms used, such as ARM, which stands for adjustable rate mortgage.

Points are a financial term that means percentage. One point is 1 percent. A one point origination fee equates to 1 percent of the loan amount paid to the lender to issue the loan. A discount point allows the borrower to get a lower interest rate by paying a percentage (points) for the lower rate.

In this example, ABC Funding is offering a 30-year Fixed Rate Mortgage at 5.75% interest. To get this loan, there are no points to pay. You need 5% down payment, and the application fee is $275.

Real estate investors often seek loan terms that offer 30-year financing and a minimum down payment. Minimal closing costs are also quite desirable.

When you complete your loan application, you should know what loan you are seeking.

Before starting the loan application process, it is best to ask the loan officer several important questions. Just as you are going to be interviewed, you, too, should interview the lender. Do not be timid. This is just business. You need to learn what types of loans the lender offers, what interest rate they charge, and at what terms. You do not want to waste your time (or money) seeking financing for a non-owner occupied property, if the lender does not offer that financing.

Here are some questions you should ask of any potential lender:

- What kinds of loans do you offer?
- What types of payment schedules are offered?
- Do you offer fixed-rate or adjustable-rate loans?
- What is the current interest rate for a 30-year fixed-rate loan? For a one-year adjustable?
- What points are charged to originate the loan?
- Do the rates offered include any discount points?
- How much is the application fee?
- What lender fees will be charged when the loan closes?
- Will the loan require mortgage insurance? If so, how much is that monthly fee?
- Can rates be locked in? If so, when can the interest rate be locked in? How long will the lender lock in the rate?
- If rates decline after your rate is locked in, can you get the lower rate?
- Are there any prepayment penalties if the loan is paid off early?
- Are there any escrow requirements?
- How long does it take to process the loan?

Author's Advice

Rates will not vary that much between lenders—although it always pays to shop. What will greatly vary are their loan programs and the fees they charge. Always understand all the options, and exactly how much they will be charging you to close your loan.

Does it ever make sense for investors to pay points? These pesky fees are paid at the time the loan is originated. You will find them listed as origination points or discount points.

All points are paid to the lender. The origination fee is for issuing the loan (and the money collected often pays for the loan officer's commission). The discount fee is paid to get a lower interest rate.

If you are planning to purchase a property and hold on to it, it may pay you to agree to pay discount points. Compare the monthly payment to determine if it makes sense. Consider this example:

Loan 1: $100,000 loan, no points, 7% interest = $665.30 monthly payment for 30 years.

Loan 2: $100,000 loan, 1 point, 6.5% interest = $632.07 monthly payment for 30 years.

There is a difference of $33.23 per month. The one point would cost $1,000 (1 point = 1%. 1% of $100,000 is $1000). Divide $1000 by $33.23. The math is 30.09. So in the 31st month, you would be saving money by paying the point.

In this example, if you agreed to pay one point, you would save money in about two-and-one-half years. It would make sense to pay the point if you were going to keep the financing on the property for a period longer than that.

If you are going to buy a property and resell it, it never makes sense to pay discount points.

Many times, you can ask for, and receive, closing cost assistance from the seller. You can use that assistance to pay for points.

You will be amazed at how lenders vary in what they charge for fees and costs. Some can become creative in names for their fees. The bottom line is that it all costs you money.

There are some fees that cannot be avoided. For example, if your local courthouse charges $100 to record a deed, that $100 has to be paid by someone.

The appraiser has to be paid for the appraisal. If you do not pay the fee, someone has to pay. It could be the seller, or the lender. If the lender agrees to pay it, you can be sure they are making up for that cost somewhere else.

Always get a written estimate of the lender's fees. For residential dwellings four units and under, the lender has an obligation to give you a good faith estimate of all of your closing costs. Be sure to compare these estimates to the final costs at the time the loan closes. Be prepared to challenge any additional charges, or sudden increases in fees.

What Banks Want

At the beginning of the process of applying for a mortgage, the loan officer will help you complete the application. Most lenders use a four-page application printed on legal size paper. The loan application is often called the 1003 (pronounced the ten-oh-three).

The loan officer is likely to type your information on a computer screen and produce the 1003 from a software package. Of course, some complete the application by hand. You might be asked to fill out the application yourself. It all depends on the lender's procedure.

During the interview, the loan officer will be asking you many questions. Whatever you put down on the application, they will want to verify.

In addition to the loan application, the loan office will ask you to provide specific documentation. The exact requirements will vary, based on the lender's procedures. For example, one lender might ask for just a copy of your last pay stub, while another may ask for a month's worth of pay stubs.

Some of the things you are likely to be asked to provide include …

- Your most recent pay stubs, as well as the names and addresses of your previous employers (for the last five years).
- Your W-2 forms for the past two years.
- A copy of the purchase agreement executed by you and the seller.
- Copies of stock accounts, 401(k)s, IRAs, and other financial assets.
- Copies of your bank statements for the past three months. If there is a large deposit, be prepared to document the source of that deposit.
- If you are self-employed, be prepared to provide copies of your past two year's tax returns.

Depending on your situation, you may need to produce other documents. For example, if you must pay court-ordered child support, you may need a copy of your court order. You might need signed copies of lease agreements if you are collecting rent from tenants.

You are also likely to need to give the loan officer a check, usually for the appraisal of the property, and perhaps for a credit report or an application fee.

What Banks Do Not Want

The borrower cannot give the appraisal to the lender. If you already paid for one, that's too bad. The lender always orders the appraisal, in order to avoid any conflicts of interest or improper manipulation by the borrower. The reason is simple: this is the collateral for the loan. The lender must receive the appraisal directly from the appraiser.

> **Real Deal**
>
> You do not need to reveal all of your assets—you only need to reveal enough for approval of your loan. However, you are not allowed to hide your indebtedness.

Be prepared to provide any additional documentation requested by the loan officer. When you have completed the application, you will know what else you'll need to provide to the lender for your loan to be approved. It's always best to get the documents to the lender as soon as possible.

You should develop your own financial statement. You may find it convenient to keep your statement in a computerized electronic spreadsheet to make updating and reporting your financial condition easier. Keep the statement current.

If you put together your own statement, be prepared to back it up with proof of your assets and liabilities. Place conservative value estimates on your assets and do not list unusual assets. For example, David has actually seen an investor who included his beer can collection on his financial statement. That is not the type of asset the lender is looking for on the 1003.

Why Bankers Love You

Look at a standard, 6.5% mortgage for $200,000 financed for 30 years. Assume you never pay the loan off early. Not only do you pay back the $200,000, but you will also pay $255,085.82 in interest.

The loan is structured in such a way that you pay mostly interest in the early years of the loan. So if you pay it off, the lender wins by collecting mostly interest.

Many banks sell their mortgages on the secondary market. They keep any loan origination fees and pass along the interest rate benefit when the mortgage is sold. Under these circumstances, the lender has no default risk because they do not own the mortgage. No wonder the bank will love you. That's why they give you a free pen when you apply for the loan.

There is nothing wrong with all of this—again, it's just business. But keep in mind that you are a customer and you will be helping the lender to profit handsomely from your loan.

Mortgage Companies Versus Banks

There are more than just banks in the business of lending money to borrowers to purchase real estate. Some credit unions and private (or publicly traded) mortgage companies also make loans.

It doesn't make a difference where the money comes from, but only how much it costs you to borrow the money.

Although your friendly hometown banker may want your business, if a mortgage company offers a lower cost loan, there is no reason not to accept it.

The key for a real estate investor is to locate lenders who want to give the loans you need. You should always seek competitive bids, even if you have other loans from a lender. Keep the lenders bidding on your business. Make them earn your loyalty.

Finding the Best Financing Deals

You can find financing deals from various places. You might ask for a referral from a real estate agent. Most agents know two or three loan officers and can make a quick referral. You may also use the Internet to find competing rates. Sites like Lending Tree (www.lendingtree.com) are well known for matching borrowers with lenders. Understand that many of the Internet sites are simply lead generators for lenders and their loan officers. The websites charge for the leads, and again, that cost must be passed on to you.

Advertisements in the local real estate section of your newspaper are another good source of potential lenders. Keep your eyes open for new sources of potential loans.

Know Your Credit Scores Before You Apply

There are three major credit bureaus—Experian, TransUnion, and Equifax. Credit bureaus report what is in their files about your past credit history and provide a score based on that information. These credit scores are often called *FICO scores* because the credit bureau scores used in the United States are produced from software developed by Fair, Isaacs Co.

Those FICO scores are the credit scores most lenders use to determine your credit risk. Each FICO score is based on the information the credit bureau receives from lenders and keeps on file about you. As this information changes, your credit FICO scores change as well.

def•i•ni•tion

FICO scores have other names. Each of the three major credit bureaus producing the score uses a different name for the score.
Credit Reporting Agency FICO Score:
Equifax - BEACON
Experian - Experian/Fair Isaac Risk Model
TransUnion - EMPIRICA

Most lenders use a combination of the three scores to determine your FICO. (Some use the middle score, others use the top two—each lender has their own policy.)

It is to your advantage to maintain as high of a credit score as possible. The better your score, the better interest rate and loan programs you will be offered.

As you improve your FICO scores, you pay less interest. See the table that follows for an example.

This table illustrates how your FICO score can vary your loan payment. On a $150,000 30-year, fixed-rate mortgage:

Your FICO Score	Your Interest Rate	Your Monthly Payment
760–850	5.59%	$860
700–759	5.81%	$881
680–699	5.99%	$898
660–679	6.2%	$919
640–659	6.63%	$961
620–639	7.18%	$1,016

Improving Your FICO Scores

According to the Fair, Isaacs Co., there are many things you can do to improve your FICO scores. They include:

- Pay your bills on time and as you agreed to do. Delinquent payments and collections will have a major negative impact on your score.
- If you have missed any payments, get current, and stay current. The good news is the longer you pay your bills on time, the better your score will be.

- Be aware that paying off a collection account will not remove it from your credit report. It will stay on your report for seven years.
- Keep balances low on credit cards and other revolving credit. High outstanding debt can adversely affect a score.
- Pay off your debt rather than moving it around. The most effective way to improve your credit score is by paying down your revolving credit. Owing the same amount but having fewer open accounts may lower your score.
- Do not close unused credit cards as a short-term strategy to raise your score.
- Do not open new credit cards that you do not need just to increase your available credit. This approach could backfire on you by lowering your score.
- If you have been managing credit for a short time, do not open many new accounts too rapidly. New accounts will lower your average account age, which will have a larger effect on your score than if you do not have much other credit information. In addition, rapid account buildup can look risky if you are a new credit user.
- Do your rate shopping for a given loan within a focused period. FICO scores distinguish between a search for a single loan and a search for many new credit lines, in part by the time over which inquiries occur.
- Re-establish your credit history if you have had problems in the past. Opening new accounts responsibly and paying them off on time will eventually raise your score.
- Apply for and open new credit accounts only as you need them. Do not open accounts just to have a better credit mix—it probably will not raise your credit score.
- Have credit cards—but manage them responsibly. In general, having credit cards and installment loans (and paying timely payments) will raise your credit score. According to the experts, someone with no credit cards tends to be higher risk than someone who has managed credit cards responsibly over the past years.
- Closing an account does not make it go away. A closed account may still show up on your credit report, and may be considered by the score.

Calculating FICO Scores

The actual methodology of how a FICO credit score is determined is a trade secret. Manipulating statistical data with the software the company developed determines the score. The general formula used to calculate your FICO score includes information based on these factors:

- 35% on your payment history
- 30% on the amount you currently owe lenders
- 15% on the length of your credit history
- 10% on the number of new credit accounts you've opened or applied for (fewer is better)
- 10% on the mix of credit accounts you have (mortgages, credit cards, installment loans, etc.)

Understanding Actual FICO Scores

FICO scores range between 300 and 850. Ratings are as follows:

- Excellent: Over 750
- Very Good: 720 to 750
- Acceptable: 660 to 720
- Uncertain: 620 to 660
- Risky: less than 620

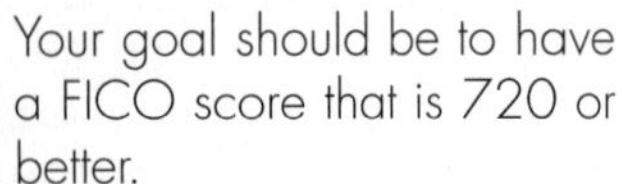

Author's Advice

Your goal should be to have a FICO score that is 720 or better.

It is important that you know what is being reported by each of the three major credit bureaus. For that reason, you should review your credit file each year. With credit fraud and identity theft at an all-time high, you need to carefully watch your credit reports and make sure the information reported is accurate.

Each person is now allowed to get one free credit report each year from each of the three bureaus. A recent amendment to the federal Fair Credit Reporting Act (FCRA) requires each of the nationwide consumer reporting companies to provide you with a free copy of your credit report, at your request. Reports will not automatically be sent out. Each consumer must request their reports one of these three ways:

- Visit www.annualcreditreport.com, which is the only authorized source for consumers to access their annual credit report online for free.
- Call 1-877-322-8228.

- Complete the form on the back of the Annual Credit Report Request brochure, available from the Federal Trade Commission (online or by writing), and mail it to: Annual Credit Report Request Service, PO Box 105281, Atlanta, GA, 30348-5281.

This new law does not interfere with previous regulations that entitle you to a copy of your credit if you have been denied credit. Some states also have laws that entitle their residents to free copies of their credit reports. Each of the three bureaus has policies for how you can receive your credit report.

Here is the contact information for the three credit bureaus:

Equifax
Equifax Credit Information Services, Inc
PO Box 740241
Atlanta, GA 30374
1-888-766-0008
www.equifax.com

Experian (formerly TRW)
National Consumer Assistance Center
PO Box 2002
Allen, TX 75013
1-888-397-3742
www.experian.com

TransUnion LLC
Consumer Disclosure Center
PO Box 1000
Chester, PA 19022
1-800-888-4213
www.tuc.com

You have the right to contest any faulty information contained on your credit report. According to federal law, each of the bureaus must investigate and verify the information, or remove it. If you find a mistake on your credit report, send a separate letter to each credit bureau where a mistake is found.

Real Deal

Correct errors on your credit report quickly. Even the smallest error could seriously hurt your credit chances and likely cost you more money.

Any error that you report to the credit bureau must be fully investigated by the credit bureau with the creditor who supplied the data. The bureau will remove from your credit report any errors a creditor admits are there.

If you disagree with the findings of the credit bureau's investigation, you have the right to file a short statement in your credit record giving your side of the story. Future reports to creditors must include your statement.

The primary reason a request for a loan is denied is the credit report. Sometimes, the smallest changes or corrections can make the difference between the loan being approved or denied. The denial will stop your purchase. Do not let your deal turn sour and be denied the purchase of your real estate investment property because of bad information on your credit report.

Author's Advice

Begin work on your credit report immediately. Whether you plan to acquire your first investment property immediately or six months from now, it is never too early to begin monitoring and improving your credit report.

You can contact the Fair, Isaacs Co. via their website and purchase your FICO score in various formats. The company offers different products that allow you to see and monitor your FICO score. Their website is www.myfico.com. You can also write to the company at Fair Isaac, Corporate Headquarters, 901 Marquette Avenue, Suite 3200, Minneapolis, MN 55402. Their telephone number is 612-758-5200.

The Least You Need to Know

- Learn to think like a lender to improve your odds of getting approved.
- Be prepared to provide documentation to the loan officer when completing your loan application.
- Shop for the best rates and terms from the lenders.
- Check your credit report, and fix any errors quickly.
- Know your FICO score, and improve it so you can get the best loans.

Chapter 12

Other Investor Financing Options

In This Chapter

- Finding money other than from a bank
- Working with a mortgage broker
- Using seller financing
- Creative financing options
- Special government programs

Up to this point, you have learned the traditional methods of investing in real estate, and how to finance the properties with traditional loans. There is nothing wrong with being a traditionalist. If it works for you, great.

But sometimes you need to be a nontraditionalist, especially when it comes to real estate investing. Sometimes, you cannot find a conventional bank or mortgage company to say yes to a loan, either because of your credit circumstances or because the collateral is not what they want or will accept.

For example, you might have an opportunity to invest in 25 acres of prime real estate at one-half of the potential fair market value. Nevertheless, the bank says no. Perhaps the bank does not see the same potential for the land, or maybe your lender is concerned about your experience level. For whatever reason, you cannot get the loan.

Despite these difficulties, there is no reason to let this deal slip between your fingers. You just need to find another source of funding. In this chapter, it's time to learn about nontraditional ways to finance real estate.

Mortgage Brokers

One of your biggest allies as a real estate investor is the *mortgage broker*. A good one can help you advance your real estate investing quickly and easily.

Today, mortgage brokers account for about 65 percent of the loans originated each year. According the National Association of Mortgage Brokers, the mortgage broker concept took hold in the early 1990s with *subprime* lending.

def•i•ni•tion

A **mortgage broker** is a person or company that specializes in mortgage loan originations and receives a commission for matching the borrower with a lender. The mortgage broker usually performs some or most of the loan processing functions such as taking the loan application, ordering a credit report, appraisal, and title report. The mortgage broker does not underwrite the loan, and does not use his or her own money to fund the loan.

A **subprime** loan is a loan made to someone with less than perfect credit, or someone who cannot easily verify his or her income.

Borrowers with damaged or imperfect credit turn to a mortgage broker to help them find a loan. Because a broker has multiple contacts with many different lenders, the broker can usually find a loan program for the borrower.

The broker business has expanded and now the brokers regularly compete with your local bank. Mortgage brokers offer A loans (perfect credit), Alt-A loans (loans to those with almost perfect credit, but perhaps with a few small blemishes), and B and C loans as well. Most banks will take only A or Alt-A loans.

Brokers have also found a niche in matching certain property types with lenders. This is of particular interest to real estate investors. For example, fewer banks are willing to consider lending on a property with five or more residential units, or mixed-use properties, such as a building with retail space on the first floor and residential units on the second floor. Mortgage brokers can often secure the financing for these types of properties. The more unique the property, the more likely that you may need one of these niche lenders. Just be sure the mortgage broker you are dealing with has placed plenty of loans on properties similar to the kind that you are trying to finance. Most mortgage brokers are arranging financing for single-family homes.

A mortgage broker receives his or her compensation when the loan closes. The broker receives origination fees (points), or a yield spread premium (YSP). This is a fee paid by the lender for originating the loan, based on the interest rate. For example, a loan with an 8 percent rate might pay the broker 2 points of the loan amount in a yield spread premium. The same loan with a 7.5 percent rate might pay just 1 point, while a 7 percent rate might pay nothing.

You should never have to pay a retainer or any other fee up front to a mortgage broker. The only money a loan applicant should give to a broker on making application for financing is an amount sufficient to pay for a credit report and an appraisal. The mortgage broker receives his or her fee at the closing of your loan.

Sometimes a mortgage broker can get the best rate and sometimes a borrower can find a better loan by dealing directly with a lender, avoiding a mortgage broker (and the broker's commission). It always pays to shop around. As you learned earlier, one of the key differences between working with a mortgage broker versus working directly with a lender is that the mortgage broker is not the final decision maker. So long as the mortgage broker is experienced in placing loans of the type that you need, this disconnection from the final decision maker is not important. But this situation underscores the need for you to be certain that your mortgage broker is experienced in placing your type of loan.

At least some mortgage brokers should be interested in your business because you offer the opportunity for repeat business. You should be interested in a broker because most have special programs designed just for investors.

Each of the fifty states license mortgage brokers where they operate. They must comply with their state, as well as Federal regulations.

Author's Advice

A mortgage broker will usually always steer you to the lender with the best deal available. From their experience, they also know which lender will offer you the best terms and is most likely to approve your loan.

Another benefit to using a mortgage broker is that they are more likely used to dealing with problem applications. They have the experience to assist a borrower with credit problems or other issues.

Do not overlook the value a mortgage broker can offer to you in finding financing.

Government Programs

Some government programs may be of interest to real estate investors. While most programs are designed to help first-time homebuyers, there are ways you can work with these special programs. Sometimes they are a source of potential investment properties. Real estate investors should understand the financing and foreclosure availability of the government programs.

FHA and the Investor

The Federal Housing Administration (FHA) does not have a specific program designed for investors. But the FHA will insure up to a four-unit property. The FHA requires that you live in one of the units. However, this allows you to purchase your first investment property with as little as a 3 percent down payment. In addition, you do not need to have perfect credit to qualify for an FHA loan. And the further good news is that you can use the income from the other units to qualify for the loan.

Another program just recently announced by the FHA is its 203K Streamline program. Buyers can include at least $5,000 (but not more than $15,000) of repairs into the purchase of the property. Based on the appraisal, you can also finance a new roof, a kitchen upgrade, or perhaps a new bath. Again, you would still need to live in the property, but it might be a way to start with your first investment property.

Sometimes confused with FHA programs, Housing and Urban Development (HUD) offers homes for sale for $1. The program, known as HUD's Dollar Homes, sells properties acquired by the Federal Housing Administration (which is part of HUD) because of foreclosure actions.

Single-family properties are made available through HUD's program whenever FHA is unable to sell the homes for six months. After 181 days on the market, HUD places the properties on the Dollar Homes program list. By selling the vacant homes for just $1, HUD makes it possible for families to fix up the homes and put them to good use at a considerable savings.

Only a nonprofit organization or local government can purchase these properties. However, investors may be able to partner with either the nonprofit or local government to rehab and sell the property to a first-time homebuyer. The lists of HUD Dollar Homes are located at www.hud.gov/offices/hsg/sfh/reo/homes.cfm.

VA Foreclosures

The Veterans Administration offers properties it has acquired from foreclosure to the public. Many times these properties are sold with VA financing—available to anyone, veteran or not. The properties can be bought with no down payment. However, there is a 2.25 percent funding fee charged by the VA.

For more information about the program, and to see a listing of current available properties, go to www.ocwen.com. Ocwen Financial Corporation currently handles the VA foreclosure properties.

Other Government Programs

There are often other government programs available from time to time. Some of these include:

- **Local Government Programs.** By getting involved in your investment circle, you will likely get to know the local government officials. Many times, they are concerned about rehabbing properties in the community. Often, local government programs make development grants available and look for real estate investors who will rehab properties, develop housing units for moderate income people, offer housing for people with disabilities, or create opportunities for people who are first-time homebuyers. Get involved with the local government within your investment circle.
- **USDA Foreclosures.** The United States Department of Agriculture offers properties for sale it has acquired through foreclosure. A current listing of properties available is located at www.resales.usda.gov.
- **State Programs.** Different states also have different programs available. These come and go, but in the past there have been land grants (requiring you to build a house on a vacant lot), programs that allow you to buy confiscated property, etc.

Seller Financing

Sometimes properties are offered for sale with the option of seller financing. For whatever reasons, the seller is willing to act as a bank and participate in carrying some or all of the financing on a property instead of insisting on receiving all cash. When seller financing is used, the seller does not lend money to the buyer as a traditional lender does, but rather extends credit against the purchase price of the property. The buyer executes a promissory note to the seller. The seller can offer a second mortgage to the buyer, or finance the full amount of the sale. The interest and other terms of the financing are negotiated between the buyer and seller.

If the seller is in a financial position to finance the entire purchase price, a quick closing is often possible.

Author's Advice

Always have your attorney review the promissory note and all other documents when seller financing is involved.

Over the past decade, seller financing has become less prevalent. With banks and lenders scrambling to find more customers, and loosening their credit requirements, there has been less of a need for seller financing. If interest rates climb, and lenders tighten credit requirements, it is likely that seller financing will regain popularity.

One advantage to seller financing is that such a deal will defer capital gains taxes for the seller. The advantage for the real estate investor is that often there will be fewer fees, a quick settlement, and less qualification headaches. Perhaps most importantly, many times the down payment can be less than a bank might require.

Seller financing is often a benefit coveted by many buyers. However, be wary. There are some pitfalls to seller financing. One of them is balloon payments.

Traditional lenders are often willing to make long-term, fully amortized loans. A fully amortized loan is a loan that is paid off over the term of the loan. For example, it would not be unusual for a bank to make a loan amortized over 30 years with a term of 30 years. In this example, the indebtedness is entirely paid off over the life or term of the loan.

Most seller-financing deals have a shorter term with a balloon payment. In other words, the seller may be willing to allow you to make payments over a 30-year amortization schedule, but the contract may require that you pay back the entire remaining balance of the loan after five years or some other period of time that is less than the fully amortized life of the loan. The large payment due at the end of the contract is the balloon payment.

Before approving any debt instrument that requires a balloon payment, you should have a plan for how you are going to pay back the balloon. One option is to refinance the property to obtain a new loan large enough to pay off the balloon payment. If the seller financing is a second mortgage, this strategy assumes that somehow the property is going to increase in value sufficiently to support a larger loan in the future. It also assumes the interest rates will be reasonable at the time the new loan is needed. If this is your remedy, make sure your assumptions about future appreciation are sound.

Another strategy is to sell the property before the balloon payment becomes due. Just make sure that you sell far enough before the balloon deadline that you don't become a motivated seller. A third alternative is to pay down the debt aggressively out of cash flow or out of your pocket, so the entire debt amount can be paid off before the balloon payment becomes due. Finally, if you have established a reliable payment history with the seller, you may be able to convince the seller to extend the contract further. However, you obviously cannot be guaranteed of the seller's generosity in this area.

When interest rates are low, as they have been for the last several years, the best thing to do is to lock in as low a rate as possible for as long a term as possible, unless you are not planning to hold the property for many years. Often, seller-financing packages are shorter-term deals. You may lose the opportunity to lock in a historically low interest rate.

Real Deal

Balloon payments got their name partly because naïve real estate investors who do not plan properly for paying off these balloon payments can go bust!

Underlying Financing

Underlying financing is a relevant concern only if the property the seller is selling has an existing mortgage. If there is an existing mortgage, you should be asking some questions about what will happen to the old debt once you buy the property. If seller financing is small compared with the entire purchase price, then the seller should be paying off the old debt with the balance of the sale proceeds and you should not have a problem. However, the larger the seller financing, the more likely it is the seller will not have the funds available to retire the old debt. This presents two problems. First, the old debt contract may have a due on sale clause. This contractual language prohibits the thing that you are trying to do—buy the property but leave the old loan in place. However, all is not lost if the old debt has a due on sale clause. You can approach the old lender and see if they will waive the due on sale provision. If the interest rate on the old loan is higher than current competitive rates, you might find the old lender happy to cooperate. If this lender is going to cooperate, they are likely to require the same scrutiny of your financial condition as you would encounter to qualify for a new loan.

The second problem to leaving the existing debt in place is the assurance you will need that this debt is still being paid. Remember, you are paying the seller each month and the seller is supposed to continue to pay the underlying original debt. But what if this seller is one of those motivated sellers that you were so proud of yourself for finding?

What if the financial duress he or she was experiencing does not end after the sale of the property to you? Will he or she be able or willing to keep making the payments on the old debt? Minimally, you will need two provisions in your contract to protect your interests. First, you need a provision that says the lender of the underlying debt will notify you of any default. Second, if there is a default, you must have the right to make payments directly to the bank, with any remaining portion of your payment paid to the seller.

One additional alternative is to just take over the old loan and make the payments directly to the bank. However, this alternative may fail if the old borrower is not released from liability. If the old borrower is still responsible for the old loan, then he or she is going to want the same kind of assurances that the old loan is still being paid, and will want the ability to make payments directly in the event of default.

Closing Costs

One of the advantages often cited about seller financing is the savings on ordinary closing costs. While this is usually true, recognize that what most often happens is that closing costs are deferred. Often, the buyer of a seller-financed property finds him or herself refinancing the property to pay off a balloon payment sooner than the buyer of a conventionally financed property would have.

Creating Notes

When you create a note, realize the seller could sell the note. Although the rate and terms cannot change, the owner can. However, note holders do not commonly sell their notes to someone else because they can typically only be sold at a considerable discount.

Hard Money Lenders

Imagine that you found a great investment property. All the properties in the neighborhood have a fair market value of $100,000. This property you are interested in buying is available for only $45,000. The reason is simple: it needs a new roof, and there was a fire in the kitchen. It will take about $15,000 to rehab the property.

This might be a great deal, but it might be hard to finance. Why? The collateral is in bad condition. Should the lender get the property back, it is going to take too much work to get it into shape for a resale.

What you may need to find is what's known in the industry as a hard money lender. A hard money lender is likely to be a private individual who has decided to invest his or her money in higher risk loans. These lenders are harder to find—they typically do not advertise in the yellow pages. However, a loan by a hard money lender may allow you to complete this transaction.

If you find a hard money lender, be prepared to pay hefty fees and interest to finance the deal. There is no standard among hard money lenders, but here are some of the parameters you may find:

- Interest rates: 12 to 18 percent, or at least higher than prevailing market rates.
- Balloon payment: typical, usually due after 1 or 2 years.
- Loan position: typically must be a first mortgage, not second.
- Maximum loan-to-value ratio: anywhere from 50 percent to 70 percent, but typically less than a traditional lender would allow.
- Points: 4 to 8, or higher than prevailing market rates.

Consider what a hard money lender could enable you to do with the deal presented here. If it took 180 days to rehab and sell the property, there is still plenty of profit to be made. A $60,000 loan—$45,000 for the purchase and $15,000 for the contracting work—with a 15 percent interest rate and 5 points would cost you $4,500 in interest, and $3,000 in points. But you have a property worth $100,000, and after paying off the loan of $60,000 and $7,500 in finance fees, there is a profit of $32,500. Not a bad profit and a great pay day in six months—even if you did pay 15 percent interest and 5 points.

Hard money lenders will usually only agree to deals where there is a larger equity position such as 35 percent or more. They also want to see fast turnarounds—they do not want to wait for long periods of time to get their money back.

Finding Hard Money Lenders

Finding a hard money lender takes some work, but it's not an impossible mission. There are some websites that list hard money lenders.

Another way to locate hard money lenders is to look for them locally. You can do this by …

- Searching for private lenders, rather than hard money lenders. Only people in the real estate industry know the term hard money lender.
- Seeking referrals to private lenders from other professionals. One of the best sources is other property owners. Maybe you can dig up a lead at a local apartment association meeting. Do some networking. Ask around.
- Contacting attorneys specializing in real estate law, who are another source of private lenders.
- Meeting with insurance agents specializing in property insurance. Because private lenders would be named as an additional insured on the insurance policy, your insurance agent may be able to assist you in locating private lenders.
- Checking with accountants. Accountants may also know of private lenders. Many times, their wealthier clients have cash available for short-term loans backed by real estate.
- Watching for advertisements for private lenders in the newspapers. Alternatively, you might place your own ad. A simple advertisement like, "Private Lender Sought for Short Term Loans, 15% interest paid, 100% secured by first mortgage on real estate" may be all you need to fund your deal.
- Taking note of any properties you see being rehabilitated in your investment circle. On your next visit to the courthouse, check for a recently recorded mortgage. A friendly title agent could help here, too. Sometimes rehabbed properties will be financed by a local private lender. You can then contact that person about the possibility of making loans to you in the future.
- Keeping an eye on the foreclosure lists. Any private lender who is foreclosing can be identified on such a list.

Finding private lenders will take some work, but again, it's not impossible to find them. Hard money lenders can help you make your deals.

Terms of Hard Money Loans

The terms of hard money loans can be whatever the borrower and lender agree. However, do not be naïve. A private lender is not going to take much risk without a large payday. Expect to pay above market interest rates. You may need to pay some points and accept a shorter term—usually less than a year—to pay back the loan.

Other Ways to Buy

There are still other ways to buy and control property without traditional financing. Sometimes, thinking out of the box can work wonders for investors.

Rent-to-Own

One form of acquiring a property is by renting it with an option to buy it. You are simply renting the property, and a portion of your rent can be applied to the agreed purchase price.

For example, you might agree to rent a property for $750 a month, and $100 of your rent applies toward the purchase price, which you and the owner agreed is $80,000. If you rented the property for 10 months, you would then need $79,000 to purchase the property (10 payments with $100 credit = $1,000. Purchase price of $80,000 – $1,000 credit = $79,000 balance.)

Make sure the property owner cannot sell the property to anyone other than you for the agreed price during the option period.

You can sell the property to someone else—at a profit. Suppose it took you the same 10 months to sell the property, and you sold it for $90,000 after some cleaning and fixing. The numbers would look like this:

$90,000 sales price from your buyer
$79,000 paid by you to property owner
$11,000 gross profit
$6,500 rent paid
(10 payments of $750 – $100 credit = $6,500)
$ 4,500 net profit

Of course, the sooner you sell (flip) the property, the higher your profit potential.

A property owner is likely to accept a rent-to-own deal when they need the monthly income from the rent to make their payments. Your rent check will cover their mortgage, insurance, taxes, etc. You can offer to take responsibility for the maintenance of the property, alleviating another headache they will no longer need to worry about.

Your strategy is to get the property in good shape quickly, so you can sell it and turn a profit on the transaction. Alternatively, if you wish to buy the property and get a mortgage to cash out the seller, begin by sitting down with a lender to make sure the lender is going to honor the various credits that you are building up toward your down payment. In essence, you are having your rent-to-own purchase preapproved by the bank. If you fail to arrange this financing and you cannot exercise your purchase opportunity, you may forfeit any credits you have earned during your tenancy.

Buyer Beware

Have your attorney prepare a rent-to-own lease for you to ensure your purchase option rights.

Using Options

An option is a contract that, in exchange for an option fee, gives the purchaser the opportunity to buy a property at a predetermined price for a fixed period of time. While the option is in effect, the seller continues to own, manage, and maintain the property. If the buyer elects to exercise his or her option, then and only then will the property change hands.

With an option, it is possible to obtain control of a property without owning it. This control is gained without having to qualify for a mortgage or pay anything more than an option fee.

The amount of the option fee is completely negotiable between yourself and the owner. You should be sure to have your option recorded at the register of deeds office or similar government agency in your jurisdiction. By recording the option, no one else can buy the property without first clearing your option.

While your option is in effect, there are three opportunities for earning a profit. You can exercise the option and buy the property. You can sell your option to another real estate investor. Finally, believe it or not, you could sell the option back to the seller.

You may want to exercise your option if you believe the property has increased in value to an amount equal to or greater than the agreed-upon price in the option. However, you do not have to exercise the option to profit. If the property has truly increased in value, you would also be able to sell your option to another investor at a profit.

Finally, if the seller is approached by another buyer with an offer that the seller would like to accept, the seller would not be able to accept this new offer without first clearing your option rights. Therefore, you might actually be able to profit by selling your option rights back to the seller.

There are three basic opportunities for using options. They are when you anticipate a rapid price increase, if you have inside information, and if you control a tenant.

- **Rapid price increases.** When employing this strategy, it will be important to have an option period for as long as possible. This strategy will not work if the public already anticipates rapid price appreciation. The fundamental premise of this strategy is that you believe prices are going to increase faster than what the seller thinks they will.
- **Inside information.** If you have advanced notice of sewer and water laterals being extended to previously unimproved vacant land, or if you know that new roads or freeway exits will be constructed, you may be able to act on this kind of information to gain control of the properties that are likely to benefit from these improvements if you can do so before the improvements become common public knowledge. Another example is assemblage. Assemblage is the technique of combining smaller parcels of real estate into a larger parcel that is worth more then the separate pieces. The problem is that one holdout could ruin the entire effort. The solution is to employ options to reduce your risk exposure.
- **Tenant control.** If a commercial property is vacant and you have control of a commercial tenant that would be willing to rent this space, you may be able to gain control of the property with an option, lease the space to your tenant, and be able to buy the property at a fraction of its new value. In some cases, the tenant that you control might be you if you already own a business or are thinking of starting one.

The Least You Need to Know

- A mortgage broker can help locate loans for the real estate investor.
- Seller financing, when available, offers flexible terms and a fast settlement.
- Watch out for balloon payments in seller-financing deals.
- Private lenders—often called hard money lenders—can help an investor purchase properties quickly and easily—but will charge high interest rates.
- Rent-to-own agreements and options can help an investor acquire properties without traditional financing.

Chapter 13

No Money Down—The Truth for Investors

In This Chapter

- Learning the truth about no money down investing
- Building your cash flow
- Buying from motivated sellers
- Ethically dealing with everyone

Yes, it is possible to buy a property with no money down. And now you will learn the truth about the claims of no money down real estate deals.

In this chapter, you will be introduced to different methods of buying property without any down payment. You have already learned some of these methods in earlier chapters, but now the techniques of buying with no money down will be discussed in detail. Moreover, the myths of no money down deals are identified and debunked.

What Is a No Money Down Deal?

In 1979, author Robert Allen published a book called, *Nothing Down*. That marked the beginning of the frenzy of people learning about *nothing down* buying techniques, and seeking no money down purchases of real estate.

def•i•ni•tion

Nothing down means buying real estate without any down payment. It does not necessarily mean that you will need no money at all to close a real estate transaction. For example, closing costs need to be paid.

Following the publication of *Nothing Down*, which was a highly popular book, many others began to hawk the idea of buying real estate with no money down. It really spawned a generation of so-called real estate gurus who were gladly selling books, cassettes, and seminars. To keep selling their materials and seminar seats, these gurus came up with many creative ideas to buy real estate with no money down.

Understanding Loan-to-Value

In real estate financing, there is a term known as the loan-to-value ratio. Real estate professionals call this LTV. This ratio compares the total of the loans to the value of the property. For example, a $75,000 loan on a $100,000 property is a 75 percent loan-to-value (LTV).

Sometimes, you may hear the term TLTV, or total-loan-to-value ratio. This is usually used when additional debts, such as a second or even a third mortgage, are secured by the property. For example, if there is a first mortgage on a $100,000 property of $75,000, and a second mortgage of $10,000, the TLTV is 85 percent ($75,000 first mortgage plus $10,000 second mortgage equals $85,000, divided by $100,000 = 85%).

In no money down deals, the actual amount of financing is 100 percent LTV. In other words, since you are putting nothing down, you need 100 percent financing to purchase the real estate.

What Is Wrong with 100 Percent Financing?

There is nothing wrong with buying real estate with no down payment—it is legal, and it isn't unethical.

The Federal Government has two programs that offer 100 percent financing on real estate purchases. The Veterans Administration guarantees 100 percent financing to veterans buying a home. The United States Department of Agriculture also offers 100 percent financing through its rural housing program.

Some private lenders also offer 100 percent financing programs. In the summer of 2005, Bank of America was offering Zero Down loans. Their 100 percent financing was available for applicants with good credit. Competing lenders were also offering 100 percent financing programs. Some offered an 80 percent first mortgage and a 20 percent second mortgage, which combined to provide 100 percent financing. Several other lenders were even offering 103 percent financing to borrowers with good credit.

Financing 100 percent of the real estate purchase price isn't impossible. Many lenders are ready to assist you to do so if the property is your primary residence. Properties not used as your primary residence are called non-owner occupied.

When the property is an investment property, 100 percent financing options from traditional lenders are limited. But they are available. The following is an example of a recent mortgage advertisement for non-owner occupied properties:

> 100% Non-Owner Occupied Guidelines
> 100%, one loan, no mortgage insurance for your rental purchases
> Purchase only
> Full documentation only
> Minimum score 680
> 100% one loan with no Mortgage Insurance
> 1-2 units, townhomes and 1-8 story condos
> Townhomes must be in a PUD
> No rural properties
> No deferred maintenance
> Interior photos required if property is vacant
> Appraisal to include rental analysis and rental comps
> 45% Debt to Income with 2 months reserves
> 50% Debt to Income with 6 months reserves
> Funds to close and reserves
> sourced and seasoned 2 months
> Max of 2 non-owner properties currently owned
> 3% seller contributions allowed
> Fixed rates only—ARM not available
> $70,000 minimum loan amount
> $300,000 maximum loan amount
> Interest only NOT available
> 1 year seller seasoning required

Sellers Offering 100 Percent Financing

It is also legal and permissible for sellers to offer 100 percent financing of their properties to someone purchasing it. If the seller agrees to 100 percent financing and does not want any down payment, so be it. The seller may or may not care if the property is being owner occupied or not. The kind of financing an individual seller may offer is up to his or her discretion and is completely negotiable.

Notice that just because a seller is willing to participate in a transaction involving 100 percent financing where there is no down payment does not necessarily mean the seller will not be getting any cash at the closing. For example, a seller might agree to sell his property for $100,000 and accept a second mortgage of $30,000. If the buyer is getting a $70,000 first mortgage, then there is 100 percent financing and no down payment. However, the seller still receives $70,000 in cash. This example assumes the seller had no debt on the property. But even if there was some debt, the seller would still receive at least some cash at closing, assuming the balance of the outstanding debt was less than $70,000.

One technique that was once fundamental to many no money down strategies was to assume the underlying debt. Again, in the example above, if the seller already had a $70,000 first mortgage and would be willing to accept a second mortgage for $30,000, then the buyer could purchase the property with no money down. One variation of this technique was to have the seller refinance the property prior to the sale and then have the buyer assume the new first mortgage. There might be any number of reasons for employing this technique. One of those reasons might be because many lenders might be reluctant to give an inexperienced investor a loan of $70,000 knowing the remaining portion of the purchase is being funded by a second mortgage, and the buyer is making no down payment. By having the seller refinance prior to closing and then having the buyer assume this new loan at closing, the problem is solved.

However, one of the trends in the mortgage industry is to include a due-on-sale clause in loan notes. This clause eliminates the ability to assume mortgages. Prior to the inclusion of this clause, it was easy for someone else to assume the mortgage, oftentimes with smaller closing costs. Sometimes, the interest rate was more favorable than the current market rate.

Common language used in a real estate loan states that, "the Lender may, at its option, declare immediately due and payable all sums secured by the Mortgage upon the sale or transfer, without the Lender's prior written consent, of all or any part of the Real Property, or any interest in the Real Property." The term, due-on-sale is perhaps misleading. In fact, as you can see from the actual language, the mortgage may be declared due if there is any transfer of any interest in the property, and not just the sale of the real estate.

Assumable mortgages are now nearly gone from the marketplace. However, it may still be possible to assume the loan. There are two opportunities for doing so. The first possibility is to go to the lender and see if they will waive the due-on-sale clause. The second alternative is to employ an unrecorded land contract or wrap around mortgage.

If you approach a lender about waiving the due-on-sale clause, the lender is likely to apply the same scrutiny to the deal as if you were applying for a new loan. However there may be two circumstances unique to an assumption that might induce the lender to waive the due-on-sale requirement. The first incentive is whether the loan being assumed has an interest rate higher than prevailing market rates. The second incentive is that the lender could still have the seller backing the loan if the lender did not release the seller from liability.

The second way to beat a due-on-sale clause is to employ an unrecorded land contract or an unrecorded wraparound mortgage, although these strategies are full of problems. A wraparound mortgage is a new mortgage that "wraps around" the existing mortgage, leaving the existing mortgage in place. The land contract does virtually the same thing. The underlying premise is that there would be no way for the lender to know about the sale, so there would be no opportunity for the lender to exercise the due-on-sale clause.

There are some people in the real estate industry who advocate making this move. In fact, a recent book about property flipping published by a major publishing house cheerfully points out that it isn't a criminal act to transfer a property while ignoring the due-on-sale clause.

Technically, ignoring the due-on-sale clause isn't a crime, but it is a contract violation for the seller. While you aren't violating the contract between the lender and seller, the seller is. Instead of being sent to jail, you would just become the victim of the lender's foreclosure on the seller! Unrecorded land contracts make little sense. There is no logical reason not to record the contract, except to avoid detection. That in itself should signal problems.

Anyone advising you to enter into an unrecorded land contract or wraparound mortgage to defeat a due-on-sale clause or for any other reason is dispensing terrible real estate investing advice. In life, none of our misdeeds seem so great as when we are caught doing them. If your scheme is discovered, not only will you have a legal problem, but even more importantly, your reputation with that lender will be ruined.

Buyer Beware

Never enter into an unrecorded land contract or an unrecorded wraparound mortgage or you may find yourself a party to a foreclosure action.

Lenders want the right to pick their borrowers, and to set the terms and conditions of their loans.

Loans insured by FHA or guaranteed by the VA have been and remain assumable. FHA loans closed before December 14, 1989, and VA loans closed before March 1, 1988 are assumable by anyone. Buyers who assume these mortgages do not have to meet any requirements at all, but the seller remains responsible for the mortgage if the buyer defaults.

Assumption of FHA and VA loans closed after these dates requires approval by the lender. The approval process is much the same as it is for a new borrower. Upon approval of the buyer and the sale of the property, the seller is relieved of liability. FHA permits lenders to charge a $500 assumption fee and a small fee for the credit report. The Veterans Administration permits the lender to charge a $255 processing fee and a $45 closing fee. The VA also receives a funding fee of ½ of 1 percent of the current loan balance.

Any property owner who sells and allows a mortgage assumption by the buyer without a release of liability is inviting problems. Even if the buyer does make the payments—and that is always the question—the seller's ability to obtain another mortgage will be limited by the continued liability on the assumed loan.

Lending Only 80 Percent LTV

Over the past century, the mortgage-lending industry has learned what has—and has not—worked when it comes to lending money. Over those decades, the industry has learned the most secure loans on single family, owner occupied properties are those with a 20 percent down payment. Lending only 80 percent of the value (80% LTV) makes the loans sufficiently safe. Loans are still available at a higher loan-to-value ratio, but by using private mortgage insurance (PMI), the lenders still make sure that they remain exposed to just 80 percent of the value of the property in the event of default.

Those that are lending more than 80 percent LTV are effectively offering a personal loan for the down payment amount. However, if the borrower is affluent, has the income, and possesses a good credit history, the lenders have been willing to lend more than the 80 percent—despite what they have learned over the years.

Abusing Motivated Sellers for Profit

Late night television offers the nation's insomniacs a series of products to buy—from jewelry to vacuums to coin collections. And then there are the infomercials offering educational products about finding riches in real estate investing.

Many of the infomercials feature settings in plush surroundings with palm trees and swimming pools. The lush backdrops tease the viewers while ordinary folks talk about how they are making lots of money in real estate investing because of the simple techniques they learned by using the featured guru's information. Even more enticing are the huge checks they show they received at a closing from one of their deals.

Author's Advice

Ever notice that it is always the student's closing and not the guru's? It is the student telling you how much money you can make … and not the expert—a fine line, but one that keeps the regulators away, and the shows on the air.

Buy real estate with no money down. Buy property with weak, poor, or no credit.

Is any of this possible?

Yes.

Is it likely?

No.

Some of the techniques the television gurus teach are, at best, questionable.

For example, one offers the advice, "find a partner." The idea here is that you would use a partner's money or credit, or both, to make deals. Other advice is to borrow some money from a family member. If you use either of these techniques and purchase real estate, you aren't doing a no money down deal, but rather doing a deal using someone else's money. It's just that you aren't putting any of your own money down. Acquiring real estate with partners is a perfectly legitimate solution for the cash-strapped beginner, but you don't need to pay thousands of dollars for a weekend seminar to figure this out.

As the new investor progresses through the courses and information, they soon learn how to put together more complicated deals. The type of arrangement we discussed where the seller refinances just prior to the sale is a technique that is sure to be covered. The catch is finding a seller willing to participate in such a strategy, not to mention those pesky due-on-sale clauses.

There are at least two reasons for promising seminar attendees that it is possible to buy real estate with no money and no credit. One is to prey on the hopes and ambitions of people who are broke. The other reason is to expand the pool of potential customers. One of the problems the gurus have is to keep people buying their information, seminars, and courses. To do so, they need to sell to people with poor credit and no extra money to be used as down payments. Therefore, they need to sell information that includes how to do the no money down deals.

Buyer Beware

Lying to a lender is loan fraud. It is a federal crime. Do not do it under any circumstance whatsoever!

Some of the techniques they teach are certainly unethical, if not illegal. For example, one of the techniques taught is to use a phantom second mortgage. This involves lying to the lender, telling them there is no second mortgage, but making one up after a closing. In effect, you hide the second mortgage. Another technique is to tell the lender you will be living in the property, when actually, you are buying it as a non-owner occupied property.

No guru is going to tell you to break the law. But unfortunately, many times what they tell you to do is something that can't be done unless you do break the law.

To make a no money down deal work, often you must take advantage of an unsophisticated seller. It is one reason so many FSBO properties are targeted by no money down dealmakers, hoping to make a deal with someone unprotected by the advice of a real estate agent.

Television gurus tell you to assume someone else's mortgage so there is no credit check. The problem is finding an assumable mortgage worth taking over. If you find one, it is probably years old and the balance is small compared to the actual value of the property. The gurus may omit this information.

A powerful sales force backs many of the companies selling real estate investing information via television infomercials. Once they sell you the initial package of information, expect repeated phone calls. You will be likely offered special seminar seats, mentoring services, and other unique offers. Buyer beware is perhaps the best advice to anyone considering purchasing expensive courses, seminars, boot camps, or mentoring services being hawked by the television infomercials.

Television is an enticing medium. It is easy to be lured into the trap of what is presented. You ask yourself how a couple of ordinary people can live in a beautiful mansion. Why can't you live like that? It is all designed to sell you on dialing that toll-free number.

Leverage, Flipping, and Cash Flow

As a real estate investor, you are primarily going to buy property to hold for cash flow, or to sell quickly at a higher price (flipping). If done correctly, both of these methods should produce profits for the real estate investor.

Leverage is the use of financial instruments or borrowed money to increase the return on the investment. In business, leverage is used to create wealth. Suppose, for example, that you had just $1,000. You could use that money to buy shares of Microsoft stock. If each share of stock costs $100, you would control 10 shares—and enjoy the value of the ownership. If the shares of stock rose in value to $120, you would have a return of $200 on your investment.

But suppose you used the same $1,000 to buy a stock option of 500 shares of Microsoft stock. Now you would control 500 shares. The return could be much larger. This is how leverage works.

In real estate, the same principles apply. If you have limited funds, how do you use that to get the maximum return? By borrowing additional funds to be able to employ additional financial leverage.

Another example of leverage at work is the condo flipping strategy you read about in Chapter 2. Because of rising real estate values, investors have been grabbing options on new high-rise condominiums. The plan is simple: they option the purchase of a condominium for a specified price by entering into a purchase agreement with a builder. The investor places a small deposit with the developer. Construction on the condominium begins. Prices appreciate during construction to a price higher than the agreed price on the builder's contract. As prices continue to rise for new units, the investor sells the contract to someone else, turning a quick profit.

As a real estate investor, you can do this type of speculative investing. On the other hand, you can buy properties to hold for cash flow.

Holding for cash flow can seem so unexciting when compared to fast money deals. When you buy and hold investment properties, each month you receive a rent check from the tenant. If your income exceeds your expenses, you will have cash flow.

Cash flow in the early years of ownership may be lean. However, as rents increase, your profit margin and cash flow are likely to increase. This is true because when you buy, you lock in the largest single cost of real estate ownership—the interest on the mortgage. Imagine if you could buy at prices from ten years ago but you could rent the property at today's rents. You'd really be in the money! Realize the property owner who has owned his or her building for that time period is enjoying exactly that equation. That could be you in a few years, if you get started now. Dave knows of plenty of wealthy retired landlords, but no wealthy retired property flippers.

If you could receive an average of $200 of positive cash flow each month from each of your rental units, look at what that means to you as monthly and yearly income:

1 unit = $200 per month = $2,400 per year

2 units = $400 per month = $4,800 per year

5 units = $1,000 per month = $12,000 per year

10 units = $2,000 per month = $24,000 per year

50 units = $10,000 per month = $120,000 per year

100 units = $20,000 per month = $240,000 per year

As you can see, the more units you have producing positive cash flow, the more money you make.

Another problem with flipping is that it does not take advantage of many tax preferences for real estate. Your property flip deals will at best be considered a short-term capital gain. However, if you start doing enough flip transactions, the IRS may view you as a dealer. The profits realized by dealers are ordinary income exposed to even more taxation.

When you buy and hold, your real estate loans are being paid off a little each month, and each year you own a bigger portion of the real estate. Forget about what your cash flow could be 10 years from now. Try figuring your cash flow with no mortgage payment. Suddenly, the buy, hold, and collect rent investment looks better, doesn't it?

Suppose you had only $10,000 to invest in real estate. Should you buy and hold for cash flow or find a property you can flip at a quick profit? More than likely, the nature of the deal will dictate which approach you take. If the property is a rare gem sure to appreciate over the years, buy and hold it. Alternatively, if the property is a fixer-upper, you have already made the repairs, and you don't see more than cost of living type of increases in your property value, maybe you should sell. You've made your money in this second deal. The final answer to this question may be dictated by the next deal you find. Maybe that gem you were planning to keep needs to be sold to raise the cash for the next deal that's just too good to pass up. You'll learn more about selling strategies like this one in Chapter 18.

Dealing Ethically with Sellers and Buyers

For a real estate investor, the most desirable properties …

- Are priced below fair market value.
- Need minimal cash to purchase.
- Can be resold quickly (if being purchased to flip).
- Can be rented so as to provide positive cash flow (if being bought to be held for rental income).

For most real estate investors, this means finding properties that are offered for sale by motivated sellers. Motivated sellers are individuals who have experienced some kind of change in their life that suddenly makes them not want to own real estate. It could be as simple as job relocation, to sudden, unexpected financial difficulties. For whatever reason, these sellers are looking for a buyer as quickly as possible because owning their property has become a burden.

Motivated sellers may agree to sell their property for less than the fair market value, or with favorable terms, or a combination of both. But in a hot seller's market, none of this is necessary. For example, if there is strong demand and a shortage of homes in the $175,000 price range, when an owner of a $175,000 property in a good location in excellent condition decides to sell, there will likely be a fast sale without any need to offer a discounted price or special terms, regardless of the seller's motivation.

Properties in declining areas, or in distressed condition, or that have been offered for sale for a period of time, may be available at terms favorable to a real estate investor.

Earlier in this book in Chapter 7, you learned about foreclosures and real estate owned (REO) properties. The owners and lenders are usually more than willing to negotiate deals with investors. Properties such as these are often available at below market pricing. The owners may be willing to structure a deal in a way that works for the buyer, just so they are relieved of the property.

Fortunately, readers of this book have one additional ace in the hole. You can develop your vision for seeing the value potential that others have missed. Change the use. Subdivide the large lot. Knock down the little house with the big yard. Add a garage. You learned about these kinds of opportunities in Chapter 6.

With so many opportunities, there is no reason to stoop to making questionable deals. There is nothing wrong with buying a property for the least amount possible. There is nothing wrong with asking for special terms—whether it be closing costs assistance or seller financing. It is up to the seller to agree.

But there is something wrong with taking advantage of people, stealing their equity, and putting them deliberately into a bad position. It just isn't right, ethically or morally. Consider these examples:

1. A person is in foreclosure. An investor goes in and offers the property owner a loan to bring the mortgage current. The owner agrees. The investor slaps a second mortgage on the property. Six months later, the owner is again in trouble—because if he could not pay the first mortgage, he can't pay the second, either. Now the investor swoops in, as planned all along, forecloses, and takes the property—including the equity—from the property owner.

2. An investor offers a lease purchase option to someone selling his or her property. To make the deal legally binding, the investor gives the property owner $20. The investor then gets someone to move into the property after giving him a $2,000 down payment. After six months, the property is trashed. It costs far too much to repair. The investor defaults, losing the $20 to the original property owner, who gets back the property—and all the damage.

3. An investor buys a property with a lease purchase option from someone who has to move because of a job transfer. The person moves to another state, rents for a year, and now wants to buy a house. When they apply, they can't qualify for a loan. The reason: they still have the other mortgage open and are liable to pay it. The investor never told the owner of this when offering a lease purchase option.

4. An investor buys a property to flip. He does cosmetic repairs, covering up structural damage that needs repaired. He sells the property at a profit without disclosing the defect. The new property owners, buying their first property, are just able to qualify. After living in the property for six months, they realize the property needs major repairs, and can't possibly afford to repair it.

5. An investor buys a property with 15 percent down. The investor gets the property owner to agree to give back the 15 percent after settlement. The investor gives the seller a second mortgage—without the lender knowing about any of this.

These are just some examples of unethical or illegal acts relating to real estate investing. Don't do it. It isn't worth it. There are plenty of legitimate, honest ways to make a fortune in real estate investing. Yes, it takes a lot of hard work. No, it can't happen overnight. There's no reason to be involved in shady dealings that could cost you everything—from losing your investments to ending up in jail.

If you want to be a real estate investor but have your own financial problems (such as weak credit or no cash), do not despair. You can still be a real estate investor, and you do not need to resort to seedy transactions. Here are some things to do to get you on the right track:

- Start working on your credit report. Get it back into shape. (See Chapter 11 for more information.)
- Consider being a bird dog for other investors in your area. Find properties for them for a finder's fee. Save the money you use from these transactions to be used as your funds for your first investment property. (See Chapter 12 for more information.)
- Instead of bird-dogging a property, consider forming a partnership with other investors who do have cash and credit. This way, you are at least a part owner in the deal and maybe you can have an additional income by charging your partnership a management fee.
- Move into a multifamily property (a four unit is best) as your primary residence. Live in one of the units. Rent out the other three. Allow your tenants to pay for the building costs. Pay yourself the rent, and build up your savings account. Use that money to buy your next rental property.
- Search for properties to fix up. Buy them with private lenders' money (see Chapter 11).

Interest-Only Loans

A recent trend is to buy property with an interest-only loan. Rather than amortize the principal, you simply pay interest payments only for a portion of the loan period. With an interest-only mortgage loan, most often you pay only the interest on the mortgage in monthly payments for a fixed term. After the end of that term, usually five to seven years, you start paying off the principal, in which case the payments increase substantially. Alternatively, you could refinance, paying the balance of your interest-only loan in a lump sum.

As a real estate investor, an interest-only loan might make sense, particularly if you are planning to sell the property before you must begin paying the principal. For example, an interest-only $200,000 loan at 7 percent saves about $164 a month over a loan amortized over 30 years. This would increase your monthly cash flow.

An interest-only loan probably does not make sense for long-term investment and ownership of a property. Once the loan converts from interest-only to paying interest and the principal, the payment adjusts upward. That same $200,000 loan would increase approximately $300 per month if amortization begins in the seventh year of a 30-year loan.

For regular homebuyers, the advantage of an interest-only mortgage is that it allows them to qualify for the purchase of a larger or more expensive house. For most people, this strategy would allow borrowers to dig a bigger debt-laden hole for themselves. The biggest risk, for both the homebuyer and real estate investor, is that if the property loses value, the debt could become greater than what the property is worth. There is additional risk in that even if the home does not lose value, the borrower may not be able to afford the higher payments once the interest-only period expires.

The Least You Need to Know

- You can buy properties with no down payment.
- Some creative financing strategies hawked by some real estate gurus are questionable.
- You can start as a real estate investor with weak credit and little money.
- Leverage may be in conflict with cash flow.
- Always deal ethically with sellers and buyers.
- An interest-only loan might make sense for real estate investors not planning to hold a property more than five to seven years.

Part 4 Managing the Property

As you have learned, one of the unique characteristics of owning real estate is that it requires your attention. If the investment property is to produce cash flow, then tenants' needs become part of the management equation. In this part, you will learn about managing your investment properties.

Chapter 14

Getting and Managing Tenants

In This Chapter

- Understanding landlord/tenant law
- Selecting good tenants
- Complying with fair housing laws
- The rights of property owners and tenants
- Handling disputes

Tenants are important to real estate investors. For the buy and hold property investor, tenants become their customers. Each month, tenants deliver rent payments to the property owner for the right to occupy the property for another month.

Real estate investors who flip properties must often deal with tenants as well. Sometimes, they inherit tenants with the property they just bought. Even investors who plan to buy and flip could be in search of tenants, if for some reason the flip does not work out.

It is important to be able to work with tenants, and this chapter will help you to do just that.

Finding Tenants

Finding tenants should not be hard. Approximately 30 percent of the population rents their housing. Tenants are everywhere. But before you start advertising for tenants, you need to know something about fair housing and smart pricing.

Fair Housing

Before screening your first prospective tenant, you should have a clear understanding of all applicable fair housing laws. Title VIII of the Civil Rights Act of 1968 (Fair Housing Act), as amended, prohibits discrimination in the sale, rental, and financing of dwellings, and in other housing-related transactions, based on race, color, national origin, religion, sex, familial status (including children under the age of 18 living with parents or legal custodians, pregnant women, and people securing custody of children under the age of 18), and handicap (disability). The law requires that you offer your property for rent without discrimination. For fair housing purposes, the groups listed previously are all protected classes.

You must make reasonable accommodations for someone with a disability, and may not discriminate against them. For example, if your building has a no pets policy, you must allow a visually impaired person to keep a guide dog.

For more information about fair housing and equal opportunity, check www.hud.gov/fairhousing.

You may find that there are additional fair housing laws unique to your state, county, or municipality. Your local apartment association or local municipal fair housing council can help inform you of any additional requirements.

def•i•ni•tion

Steering is when the landlord decides which unit protected class tenants can have instead of allowing the tenants to choose for themselves. Steering a protected class tenant is a fair housing violation.

One area of potential confusion in fair housing involves *steering*.

Some steering examples will help illuminate the point. Say you have two rental units available for rent, an upper unit and a lower unit. The prospect who comes to see the unit is in a wheel chair. Without further thought or comment, you logically show this prospect only the lower unit. You have just engaged in steering. Steering is a violation when you make the decision which rental unit a protected class prospect can have instead of letting the prospect decide for themselves. Steering itself isn't necessarily a violation. It only becomes a violation if the person is in a protected class. For example, you can have a policy of not allowing dog owners in upper apartments. Pet owners aren't a protected class. But having a policy of steering families with small children away from upper apartments would be a fair housing violation.

Other areas of potential fair housing violations include offering senior citizen discounts, which would be age discrimination, or attempting to limit the number of children in a rental unit. You can limit the number of occupants, but not the number of children. Two occupants per bedroom is a good standard for occupancy limitations. Therefore, a two-bedroom apartment could accommodate a single parent and three children.

Real Deal

Violations of the Fair Housing and Equal Housing Opportunity Laws are serious. These laws are enforced, and each month, new cases of violations are posted on HUD's website.

Rental Criteria

The key to avoiding fair housing violations is to have clear, written rental criteria that you follow and apply consistently. Some guidelines for points to keep on a good policy are found below:

- **Minimum Income.** A good policy for minimum income is that all adult occupants combined should have monthly gross income of not less than three times the rent. Therefore, for a unit renting for $800, minimum monthly income would be $2,400. If two adults applied together where one earned $1,000 per month and the other earned $1,400 per month, these applicants would qualify according to the minimum income standard.

- **Landlord Reference.** The landlord reference is the most important. You should ask the current and previous landlord these four yes or no questions: Did you rent your property to the applicant from the date of ___ to ____? Was the rent _____? Did they pay on time? Would you rent to them again? Note that the current landlord might lie to get rid of a bad tenant. The previous landlord would have no such incentive.

- **Employment Reference.** The employment reference should verify start date of employment, wages claimed, and outlook for continuing employment. If possible, speak to the individual's supervisor, not the personnel department.

Increasingly, many employers have adopted privacy policies to prohibit this kind of information from being disclosed without authorization from the employee. For that reason, your application should contain language to the effect that by signing the application, the applicant is granting the landlord permission to investigate the entire application, including running credit and criminal checks and wage verifications. If all else fails, an applicant's payroll check stub can also help to verify employment.

- **Maximum Occupancy.** Occupancy should be set at reasonable limits. A good standard is two people per bedroom. Less then that and you may be found to have policies that are discriminatory toward families. You already discovered that the key words here are "occupants" or "people," not adults and children.
- **Credit Check.** The credit check is used to confirm the applicant's current and previous addresses, social security number, employment, and payment habits. The credit report should not show record of any evictions in the last three years. A rigid minimum credit score is probably not a practical standard.
- **Criminal Check.** Criminal checks should be performed on all applicants. Your local apartment association or law enforcement can help you perform such checks quickly and conveniently. The way to market this check to prospective tenants is to tell them that the check is performed for their safety, so they can know that their neighbors have been similarly screened. Of course, such reasoning is less effective if the property is a single family home.
- **Pets.** Decide what your pet policy is in advance and stick to it. That way you won't have to agonize over the seemingly perfect applicant with the rottweiler they promise you is nothing but cute and cuddly. Some landlords hate any pets, while others see them as a profit opportunity by charging a higher monthly rent for the privilege of having a pet. This is purely a business decision you have to make, but once made, stick to it.

Once you have established your rental criteria, summarize them and make them available to each applicant as they apply. The following is an example of a Rental Criteria Form:

AB Properties - An Equal Housing Opportunity

Thank you for your interest in AB Properties. AB properties evaluates all rental applications according to the following criteria:

1. *The combined gross monthly income from all adults living in the unit must be equal to three times one month of rent.*

2. *Your current and/or previous landlord will be contacted to verify dates of tenancy, amount of rent paid, and timeliness of rent payments. These landlords will be asked if they would rent to you again if they had the opportunity.*
3. *Your current and/or previous employer will be contacted to verify wages claimed, start dates of employment, and outlook for continuing employment.*
4. *The maximum occupancy limits are two people per bedroom.*
5. *A credit report will be obtained and evaluated on all adult applicants.*
6. *A criminal background check will be performed on all applicants.*
7. *The pet policy includes the following pets: Cats allowed if front paws declawed and fixed, $25 per month extra. Dogs 25 lb. or less only, $35 per month extra.*

Smart Pricing

Once you know something about fair housing and you have established your rental criteria, you are ready to place a price tag on your rental. Smart pricing dictates that you do some homework. Before you advertise for tenants, you need to know what to charge for rent.

One way to answer this dilemma is to do a rent survey of comparable rental housing. Be advised that if you have a waiting list for your apartments or if there are people breaking down your door to rent your units, it's probably not because you are such a nice landlord. It's more likely that your rents are too low. Similarly, if your units sit vacant while everyone else is reasonably full, maybe your rent is too high.

Of course, you can only reach the conclusion that your rent is too high if the property is in excellent condition. There are three "P's" for renting properties. They are …

- Property
- Price
- People

The property should be in rent-ready condition, which is to say the unit should be clean and in an excellent state of repair both inside and out. The price should be right. The P for people means you. You should convey enthusiasm and take appropriate steps to sell your rental housing. If you execute the three Ps, your housing will rent. If you aren't renting, you must identify the error in one of the three Ps.

Having mastered fair housing and having established a smart price, you are at last ready to begin the hunt for tenants. Finding tenants will probably involve some kind of advertising. Placing an advertisement in the newspaper, or erecting a "for rent" sign usually will generate sufficient calls to find a tenant.

The purpose of these phone calls is to schedule a showing of the available rental unit. Your goal is to find a good tenant willing to rent in as few showings as possible. To meet this goal and for your own safety, you should screen tenant prospects over the phone and then properly schedule the showings.

Screening Tenants

Once you have a concrete understanding of fair housing law, you are ready to screen tenants over the phone by going over your rental criteria with them. You should practice your criteria questions so you can present them to the prospect as a benefit. For example, you are sharing the criteria out of respect for their valuable time and so that they can know in advance that they are qualified. For criminal background checks, the benefit to the prospect is that they know their neighbors will not be a criminal element. With each positive response to your criteria, you should display greater enthusiasm and anticipation. Soft peddle the criteria by beginning your questions with "do you mind if I ask …."

Properly Scheduled Showings

Assuming the prospect meets your rental criteria, you are ready to schedule a showing. But this isn't going to be any showing that you schedule. This is going to be a Properly Scheduled Showing (PSS).

The goal of a PSS is to maximize the number of on-time appointments and minimize the number of time-wasting no-shows. Therefore, a PSS is a showing where the prospect has clear directions on how to get to the property, and you have their full name and home, work, and cellular phone numbers. By having their name and numbers, they are more likely to show up.

Tell them to bring their checkbook. You want to get a deposit with the application to ferret out the tire kickers from the serious applicants. You also want the applicant to be psychologically and financially committed to the dwelling.

This deposit can be as little as $25 and should not be more than the entire security deposit. The higher the deposit, the greater the possibility of making the deposit a stumbling block to renting. Usually a deposit of $100 is more than enough.

You want a deposit so that you don't waste time and money processing applications for prospects who are still looking. Make sure your applicant understands that you will refund in full any deposits on applications you can't accept. For accepted applications, apply the deposit in full toward the rent and security deposit. That way, it does not really cost anything to apply.

The PSS should be set for a specific time. Don't tell them you will be there all day so they can come by any time, or the prospect will feel that a no-show is of little inconvenience to you. Don't hesitate to schedule several showings at once. The competition favors you and saves time.

The further in the future the showing is scheduled, the less likely that the prospect will keep the appointment. The best time to show the unit is later the same day you receive the call or as soon as possible after that. Confirm the appointment one hour beforehand. Remind them to bring their checkbook. Go over the directions again.

Never ask the prospect if they know how to get to your property. Tell them. Find out which way they are coming from, give directions, and spell out landmarks. Sometimes people think they know where something is, only to find out later they were mistaken. Don't let a lost prospect add to your no-shows.

Don't be afraid to schedule showings close together, or even at the same time. Any crowds will lend a sense of urgency and increase interest in your property and any no-shows will waste less of your time.

After their inspection, ask if they are interested in completing a rental application (a sample rental application is included in Appendix B). If they express an interest, give them an application. Have them fill it out on the spot if you can; otherwise, let them take the application with them.

Once you receive a completed application, begin qualifying the applicant according to your rental criteria. Unfortunately, in today's world, you must be skeptical of everything the applicant writes on a rental application. With identity theft running rampant, you must check everything.

Know that a Properly Scheduled Showing doesn't end after the showing unless the prospect fills out an application on the spot. Follow up in the next 24 hours. Any later than that and you are taking a serious risk of the applicant renting something else. Be ready with intelligent follow-up questions; don't just ask if they are still interested.

Ask them questions like these:

Did I remember to show you the …?

I'm showing the unit again on _____, did you want to take another look?

How does this unit compare to others that you have seen?

What can I do to help you make a decision?

Don't bad-mouth the competition, but don't be modest about your offering either. Go over the benefits of your unit again. You will be amazed by how applicants forget or get things mixed up. If they have rented something else, ask them for candid feedback as to why.

Author's Advice

If the applicant has provided false information, reject them immediately. It is easier to get rid of them before they actually take possession of your property.

If you must reject an applicant who has completed an application, make notes on the application as to why you turned it down and save denied applications for three years as further documentation against any kind of fair housing charge. The best way to reject an application is in writing. The following is a sample rejection letter:

Declining to Rent a Property to an Applicant

Dear Mr. X,

Thank you for your interest in AB Properties.

Your application to AB Properties has been reviewed, and unfortunately, we must decline renting our property to you.

Thank you for again for your interest and good luck in your house hunt.

Very truly yours,
AB Properties

Inevitably, you will wind up fielding a phone call from a prospect whom you have to deny or has received your rejection letter. They will want to know why they were rejected. The reason they were rejected is because they did not meet your rental criteria. Do not be more specific. If you are, you will only be drawn into an argument. Go over the general rental criteria again if you need to. Thank them again and apologize that you have to abide by "company policy."

If you follow these steps diligently, you will soon have a great applicant who you will want to accept.

Accepting the Application

Congratulations on finding that great applicant! However, the battle isn't over until the applicant has signed a lease, and the security deposit and first month's rent have been collected. Until then, continue to show the unit. Too many applicants back out before signing the lease, leaving you high, dry, and vacant.

Managing Tenants

The good news is that 90 percent of the battle of managing tenants is won by the screening and selecting process. If you have carefully screened the applicants and held out for at least the good if not the best, the job of managing your tenants will be easier.

There are five essential principles to success in tenant relations. Have a good lease, follow prudent collection procedures, resolve tenant disputes, keep good records, and know the law.

Leases

Always use a written lease or rental agreement. It can be for a year or month-to-month, but either way, it should be in writing. Never allow anyone to move into your property without first signing a lease or rental agreement.

A sample lease agreement is included in Appendix B. This is only a sample, and should not be used except as a learning example. You need a lease that complies with all of your local laws. The best source for a lease is to get one from your real estate attorney. He or she should already have a boilerplate form that can be made available to you at a reasonable cost. Alternatively, your local apartment association could help you in obtaining an appropriate lease.

Author's Advice

Do not fall into the trap of using a boilerplate lease from a stationary store. Make sure your lease complies with all local laws. A lease prepared by your attorney is best.

The lease or rental agreement will clearly state your rights. Make sure you understand them as well as everything else in the lease. If you do not, ask your attorney to explain any part that is unclear.

The lease or rental agreement will clearly state the legal rights of the tenant. Have your tenant read the lease, and understand its terms and conditions. You should also understand the tenant's rights.

Buyer Beware

Never give the keys to your property until the tenant has placed the utilities in their name, and you have received the signed lease, security deposit, and first month's rent.

You can't just enter the property to look around. The tenant has the right of privacy and the right to enjoy the quiet use of the property. Know how and when you can enter, and what kind of notice to enter you must give the tenant. Make sure they understand how you will need access for maintenance, and how you will give notice when you plan on entering. It is important that your tenant knows how to contact you to report any problems and maintenance requests.

You should have a clearly written set of rules that are attached to the lease and signed by the tenant. The rules should be unambiguous. No rule should be created that is unenforceable. For example, don't make a rule that says, "Tenants should be not be too loud." That, in reality, means nothing, and is unenforceable. Rather, create rules that are specific so that they are enforceable. For example, "No electronic device shall be played with the volume so loud that it can be heard out of the residential unit at any time."

You should be polite but firm and consistent in enforcing your rules. It should be a matter of black and white, and no gray. If a tenant is guilty of repeated noise violations and has not responded to verbal correction, write a warning letter. An example follows:

Sample Rule Violation Letter

Dear Mr. X:

We want all of the residents to be able to enjoy their homes in peace and quiet. Right now, in order to ensure the peace and quiet of your neighbors, I need your cooperation.

It has come to our attention that you have installed outside speakers at our property at 1212 Main Street. This is a violation of our rules, which you agreed to follow when you signed a lease to rent the property. (See Rule Number 31.)

Please remove these speakers within the next five days.

Thank you in advance for your anticipated cooperation.

Rent Collections

Establishing a prudent collections policy now will save hours of agonizing decision making later. Having a policy already in place will save you from having to decide something like, "should I really begin eviction proceedings on poor old widow Jones?"

Your policy should follow guidelines similar to the following. Rent should be due on the first of the month. You may want to allow a grace period of up to five days. During this time, payment can still be made without incurring a late fee. After the fifth day, a reminder notice can be distributed and a late fee of $5 per day applies.

It is better to use a daily rate so that the tenant still has an incentive to pay to avoid further late fees. Cap the late fee at a maximum amount for one month, say $25. However, if you find this amount to be too low to be a deterrent, increase it accordingly. Make sure that you do not violate any state or local ordinances in setting a late fee that is too high.

On the eighth day of the month, a quit or pay or equivalent notice is served to the tenant. By the fifteenth of the month, file in court on any unpaid tenants. The goal is to never allow a tenant to get more than 30 days behind in rent. If the tenant gets more than 30 days behind in rent, it becomes more economical for the tenant just to move to another rental than to try to catch up on the back rent.

Check the laws in your jurisdiction. You may want to amend the dates and deadlines in these procedures depending on how things work in your area.

Tenant Disputes

Work to resolve tenant disputes. Most can be resolved quickly and quietly. If you become angered with your tenant, walk away. Do not do anything rash or precipitous. Take your time before deciding what to do.

Most of the time, the disputes are minor, and only escalate because of personality conflicts. Tenants aren't always going to do what you want. They will, many times, do exactly what you do not want.

If you tell them no pets, they will get one, and hide it from you. If they have a cat, they might try to dispose of the kitty litter by pouring it down the commode, only to hide the fact they have a cat from you. How you learn about it is when you receive a $195 repair bill from the plumber. Give yourself a cool-down period before confronting the tenant.

It is always better to put your dispute in writing (giving yourself a paper trail). Sometimes, slowing down to write the grievance automatically provides a good cooling-down period.

Keeping Records

One area where real estate investors can run into problems is in the area of simple administrative failure. They ignore the necessity of proper paperwork. Just as buying a property requires a written contract (as well as many other pieces of paper), so does the management of a property. From the application to the lease, from simple rules to collection letters, real estate investors must be ready with a toolkit of forms to manage their property.

Author's Advice

Put everything in writing! When dealing with tenants, always reduce all agreements to writing.

Maintain good records. Keep a file on each of your tenants. Make sure you keep accurate and updated records. You should place a copy of all correspondences in the tenant's file (and not simply stored on your computer). Keep meticulous records, including records of rental payments.

Maintain other files on the property. Keep records of repairs, and items that will need maintenance. All of your files should speak for themselves. That means that anyone could pick them up and see what you have—or have not done.

Because we live in a litigious society, and landlords can be a favorite target for lawsuits, it is important that you be ready to defend yourself. Without a paper trail, you may lose in court. Maintaining records is your best defense—and it shows that you have done what is required of you.

Fortunately, there are a number of landlord software programs that can help you manage your properties without getting buried in a blizzard of paperwork. Simple electronic checkbook programs can also be extremely helpful. Some sample landlord software programs are listed in Appendix C.

Knowing the Law

You must comply with all local laws and regulations. Many towns and municipalities have passed laws designed to protect tenants against unscrupulous property owners.

All states have some type of landlord/tenant laws. The laws enacted give each party—the landlord and tenant—certain and specific rights, and places duties or responsibilities on the other.

Unfortunately, landlord and tenant disputes are too common. Most likely, your state's Attorney General's office, or county District Attorney's office has information available about the applicable laws. Local municipalities will also likely have free information. So may your local apartment association.

Buyer Beware

It is important that you seek out and know the legal information about being a landlord in your area.

Most laws have these common elements:

- Two types of agreements between landlords and tenants are defined: a month-to-month agreement, or a fixed-period lease.
- A month-to-month agreement continues until either party gives proper notice to the other to end the agreement.
- A month-to-month agreement can be either oral or written.
- With a month-to-month agreement, the rules can be changed or rent raised at any time with proper notice.
- The tenant or landlord can cancel the agreement and the tenant has 30 days to move out under a month-to-month agreement.
- A lease requires the tenant to stay for a specific period of time and restricts the landlord's ability to change the terms of the rental agreement during the time period described in the lease.
- A lease must be in writing to be valid.
- During the term of the lease, the rent can't be raised or the rules changed unless both landlord and tenant agree.
- Deposits are refundable.
- Fees charged must be stated as fees, and may not be called deposits. For example, a carpet-cleaning fee—a charge the tenant must pay when vacating the premises—must be described as a fee, and not a deposit.

The states (and some local municipalities) have passed laws that prohibit a landlord from taking certain actions against a tenant. These illegal actions include …

- **Lockouts.** The law usually prohibits landlords from changing locks, adding new locks, or otherwise making it impossible for the tenant to use the normal locks and keys. Even if a tenant is behind in rent, such lockouts are illegal. A tenant who is locked out can file a lawsuit to regain entry.
- **Utility Shutoffs.** The landlord may not shut off utilities because the tenant is behind in rent, or to force a tenant to move out. The landlord may only shut off utilities so that repairs may be made, and only for a reasonable amount of time. If a landlord is responsible for providing utilities but does not pay the bills and the service gets turned off, that could be considered an illegal shutoff.
- **Confiscation of the tenant's property.** The law usually allows a landlord to take a tenant's property only in the case of abandonment.
- **Renting condemned property.** The landlord may not rent units which are condemned or unlawful to occupy because of existing uncorrected code violations.
- **Retaliatory actions.** If a tenant exercises rights under the law, such as complaining to a government authority or deducting from rent for repairs as provided by statute, the law prohibits the landlord from taking retaliatory action. Examples of retaliatory actions are raising the rent, reducing services, or evicting the tenant.

If the matter is taken to court and the judge finds in favor of the tenant, the landlord can be ordered to reverse his or her actions, as well as pay for any harm done to the tenant, and possibly pay the tenant's attorney's fees. Sometimes, even double damages apply.

State laws specify how evictions must be handled. When a landlord wants a tenant to move out of the rental unit, certain procedures must be followed …

- **For not paying rent.** If the tenant is behind in rent, the landlord can issue a notice to pay or move out. If the tenant pays all the rent due within a specified time (usually less than a week), the landlord must accept it and can't evict the tenant. In most jurisdictions, a landlord isn't required to accept a partial payment.
- **For not complying with the terms of the rental agreement.** If a tenant isn't complying with the rental agreement (for example, keeping a dog when the agreement specifies "no pets"), the landlord can give a notice to comply or move out. (The amount of time varies in different states.) If the tenant remedies the situation within that time, the landlord can't continue the eviction process.

- **For creating "waste or nuisance."** If a tenant destroys the landlord's property; uses the premises for unlawful activity including gang or drug-related activities; damages the value of the property; interferes with other tenants' use of the property; the landlord can issue a notice to move out. The tenant must move out after receiving this type of notice. There is no option to stay and correct the problem.
- **For no cause.** Landlords can terminate tenancy with proper notice at the end of the lease term or with proper notice anytime in a month-to-month agreement without having or stating a particular reason.

State laws usually uphold the tenant's rights when the property is transferred. The sale of the property does not automatically end a lease or month-to-month rental agreement.

Under most state laws, the landlord must …

- Maintain the dwelling so it does not violate state and local codes in ways that would endanger the tenant's health and safety.
- Maintain structural components, such as roofs, floors, and chimneys, in reasonably good repair.
- Maintain the dwelling in reasonably weather-tight condition.
- Provide reasonably adequate locks and keys.
- Provide the necessary facilities to supply heat, electricity, and hot and cold water.
- Provide garbage cans and arrange for removal of garbage.
- Keep common areas, such as lobbies, stairways, and halls, reasonably clean and free from hazards.
- Control pests before the tenant moves in. The landlord must continue to control infestations except when the infestation was caused by the tenant.
- Make repairs to keep the unit in the same condition as when the tenant moved in (except for normal wear and tear).
- Keep electrical, plumbing, and heating systems in good repair.
- Maintain any appliances that are provided with the rental.
- Inform the tenant of the name and address of the landlord or landlord's agent.
- Provide working smoke detectors.

A landlord isn't responsible for the cost of correcting problems that were caused by the tenant.

There are usually other provisions in landlord and tenant laws. These include such things as abandonment of the premises or personal property, return of security deposits, damages, and proper notice when moving out.

As you can see, it is important to understand the landlord and tenant laws for the area where you own property. Failing to comply with the laws could be costly with fines and other damages.

Offering a Tenant a Lease Option

If you are going to offer your tenant a lease option, make sure your tenant understands what a lease option is, and be sure your tenant is able to qualify for a loan from a legitimate lender.

You and your lease-option tenant should schedule a meeting with your lender to determine the viability of your lease option program. The lender will be able to coach your tenant on what they may need to do to clear up their credit or otherwise prepare to take out a mortgage in the future. You already read about lease options and renting to own in Chapter 12.

It is grossly unfair to take a renter's money for a purchase option knowing that they will never be able to qualify for a mortgage. Do not use a lease purchase option as a way to rent a marginal property.

Determining what to charge for rent takes some consideration for the real estate investor. Tenants can be quite fickle over what they are charged to pay for rent. While to you, the difference of $10 a month relates to only $120 a year, to a renter, that makes a huge difference. Why? It's just the way some people think.

Some renters will move quickly if you raise the rent by just $10. Even though it might cost them $500 to move (the costs of reestablishing cable, telephone, and other services, plus a moving van, etc.), they would rather leave than pay an extra $10 a month.

Keep this in mind. One real estate investor bought a fixer-upper to keep and rent. He acquired the property for only $3,000, but it cost him about $14,000 to make it livable (it would cost anyone else a lot more, but he is a professional contractor). He was able to rent the property to a tenant for $400 a month. The tenant is far less than a tidy person. But every month, for the last nine years, she has made her $400 a month payment faithfully (she only called this investor once, to tell him her rent payment would be late by five days because she fell at work and could not work for one week). Insofar as paying her rent, she is a perfect tenant. She never calls the property owner to fix or repair a thing—as she does not want him to spend any money, in fear he will raise the rent. And he has no plans to raise the rent. If he did, she would move. He would then have thousands of dollars of repairs to do to the property. In other words, they are both happy with the current situation. And each month, the real estate investor receives his $400 rent.

Does that make sense to you? It may not, but that is how one investor handles one of his properties. You can handle yours as you please, but be aware of the sensitivity people have to the cost of rent.

Use your best judgment when setting rent, and think carefully when you raise it for a current tenant.

One way to set the rent is to conduct a rent survey. Contact other property owners and find out what they are charging for rent on comparable properties. They should be close by, and offer similar features (for example, two bedrooms, one bath, second floor unit, free heat.)

Author's Advice

Be sure to compare apples to apples—do not use comparable properties that are unrelated. You can't compare a three bedroom, two bath to a one bedroom, one bath unit.

The Least You Need to Know

- The key to smooth management is to carefully screen tenants.
- Understanding fair housing is essential.
- Use a written lease and establish rental rules.
- Develop a rental collection policy and follow it diligently.
- Learn your local landlord and tenant laws.

Chapter 15

Controlling Expenses

In This Chapter

- Operating your business
- Handling emergency repairs
- Saving money in daily operations
- Routine maintenance of your investment property
- Understanding your insurance needs
- Buying contracted services

The moment you purchase your first investment property, you become a small business owner. You may think of yourself as just a real estate investor, but an individual who is just an investor would be a person who retains a professional property management company to run his or her property. This individual isn't involved in the day-to-day operation of the property. Each month, this investor receives a statement and hopefully a check reflecting the month's profits. This is the picture of real estate investing. Anyone actively involved in the day-to-day management of his or her property has gone beyond just being an investor to being in the property management business. This is the situation that describes most owners of investment real estate and it probably describes you.

This chapter will show you that it's time to start thinking and acting as a small businessperson. The more you do, the more likely you will be successful investing in real estate.

Avoiding Unnecessary Costs

One of the best things you can do is to avoid unnecessary costs. For example, suppose you could save $10,000 a year in expenses. Saving $10,000 in expenses is the same as an equal increase in income. You have $10,000 more in your pocket. You could use it to invest in another rental property. What you do with it is up to you, because it is your money. Consider this simple strategy: one investor took two hours to shop for property insurance. By doing so, he saved $100 a year. He could have accepted the first quote, and been done with his search for insurance. Instead, he persevered, and found the same insurance for $100 less than his first quote. Another way to look at this is to say he earned $50 an hour. That isn't a bad return on two hours worth of time. Saving a $100 here and there adds up.

When purchasing insurance, consider a higher deductible. Check the difference of premium with a $500 or a $1,000 deductible. If you can afford a $1,000 loss, consider the savings on the yearly premium.

Apply your skills at sniffing out a bargain piece of real estate to every expense you may incur. Shop around. Think out of the box. Go beyond just buying items on sale. Maybe you pick up some deals at a rummage sale. Better yet, can an expense be eliminated entirely? For example, does your investment property have one furnace for the entire building? If it does, you are probably paying to heat the building and heat is included in the rent each of your tenants pay. Such a situation invites waste. You may be able to at reasonable cost install individual meters so the tenants can be billed for the utility, eliminating this expense entirely. You can install flow meters on boilers, and individual gas meters on forced air furnaces.

At a minimum, be sure to install an outside thermostat governing the temperature of any boiler that you have to pay to operate. This thermostat helps regulate the maximum temperature that can be achieved in any of the apartments, thereby reducing the opportunity for waste.

David purchased a building a number of years ago where 11 individual forced-air furnaces were on the same natural gas meter. He had individual meters installed so the tenants would be responsible for natural gas consumption for their own furnace.

One step better than buying something on sale is to avoid buying it at all. Sometimes a complicated repair may require expensive specialty tools. If you are attempting this repair yourself, think about renting the tool instead of buying it, particularly if you do not anticipate needing the tool often. Remember once you own a piece of equipment, you also need to find a place to store it when not in use. If the equipment has a small gasoline engine, then you will also need to perform maintenance on the equipment to keep it in working order. Consider the full cost of owning something and think about renting such equipment when it makes sense.

Preventative maintenance always makes sense and saves money in the long run. An oil change for your automobile is cheap. While it is possible to never change your oil and filter, eventually you are going to pay for this lack of maintenance.

Maintenance of your real estate also makes total sense. New filters in the heating/cooling system are cheap. So are batteries in the smoke detectors. Keep your property in an excellent state of repair.

Real Deal

The term "slum landlord" came about by unscrupulous property owners who rented their real estate and refused to do any repairs. Their strategy was to suck every cent from the property, and never fix anything. In today's competitive rental market this is a foolish strategy that would lead to a building with high vacancy and bad tenants.

Some things you can do to maintain your property include …

- Make it easy for your tenants to report problems. You should be accessible by phone. Some landlords prefer that maintenance requests be in writing. If you elect to go this route, create a simple form to report nonemergency items. Make sure there are several forms on the property. Better still, give tenants your e-mail address.
- Conduct a thorough, once-a-year inspection of the property. Exterior and common area inspections should be ongoing. But once a year, you should go inside the rental units themselves. Make this a part of your lease or rental agreement. Tell your tenants about this when they rent. Assure them that you aren't trying to invade their privacy, but it is your desire to maintain the property. Seek their assistance in telling you what defects they see. At a minimum, you will need to exchange the batteries in the smoke detectors at this time. You'll be surprised by the dripping faucets, missing smoke detector batteries, and other maintenance items that your tenants didn't bother to tell you about.

- Remove hazards from the property. For example, if a tree is leaning toward your building, take it down before a storm does.
- Fix leaks quickly. Whether it is the roof or a pipe, leaking water causes damage. Prevent additional damage by getting all leaks repaired.
- Develop a maintenance plan for each property. For example, you might consider that within three years, you will need to replace the water heater, within five years the kitchen appliances, and ten years, the roof. Having a plan of action will allow you to better plan for maintenance and repairs.
- Make seasonal maintenance plans. Make sure outside water spigots are turned off inside the building before winter. Arrange for snow removal. Have the furnaces tuned and cleaned. Make sure gutters are free of fallen leaves and other debris. In the spring, check air conditioning equipment.
- Set up pest control service. Some tenants always need this, while others do not. It's unfortunately true, but some people just cause pests, because of the way they live. In some parts of the country, pest control is a necessity. You may require your tenants to pay for it, or you might provide this as part of the rent.

Working With Contractors

As part of your real estate investing business, you need to develop a list of qualified, reputable contractors who can do work for you. Obviously, any work you can do yourself will save you money. A thing like replacing batteries in a smoke detector only makes sense for you to do. Although you could employ an electrician to do this service for you, it makes little sense to pay $100 to unplug an old battery and replace it with a new one.

> **Author's Advice**
>
> For nonemergency jobs, always get bids from three different contractors. You are always looking for the best deal, and you want your service providers to offer their best price.

Bigger jobs call for the services of reliable and dependable contractors. For example, repairing a gas-fired furnace usually requires a professional. You have to decide what work you can do and what needs handed off to a professional.

Even if you have good experience with one contractor, seek other estimates. You want all of your contractors to know that they must not pad their estimates in order to get your work. Perhaps this strategy isn't important for small jobs of less than $100, but for bigger jobs, ask for estimates, and let your contractors know they are bidding against others.

Many times, it makes sense to bundle several small jobs into one larger one. For example, if you are seeking a plumber to replace a hot water heater, and next year you plan to replace the bathroom vanity, it might make economic sense to have both projects done at the same time. Remember, this is only business, and there is nothing wrong with asking for the best deal a contractor can give you.

Always remain on the lookout for good contractors and tradesmen. Just as you learned earlier, if you can get the same quality work done for $500 less, there is no reason not to do so. Make sure that your contractors are licensed (if required to be so), and that they are properly insured. Proper insurance includes business liability and workmens' compensation insurance. Contractors who have this insurance are used to providing it to their customers.

Often, knowing a handyman who can handle a wide range of repairs is money-saving knowledge. A handyman may be every bit as capable for many minor repairs as a licensed plumber or electrician, and much cheaper. The handyman will probably be able to perform a much wider range of work at one time than the specialty contractors. Your plumber isn't going to hang a light fixture for you while he or she is fixing the plumbing leak, but a handyman would.

If the repairs you need done require a permit, then your handyman will not be able to help. Further, the handyman probably will not have the proper insurance. Anyone who ever works at your property should be covered by Workmens' Compensation Insurance. If your handyman doesn't have such insurance, you should carry it. This chapter covers such insurance needs in a later section.

Making Emergency Repairs

All real estate investors with tenants will experience emergency repairs eventually. The types of emergencies that call for immediate action include no heat, burst pipes, or lockouts. You should have a plan of action in advance to handle such problems.

Today, with the popularity of cellular telephones, it is much easier to be reached in the event of an emergency. Make sure that your tenants can contact you without difficulty. You can't rely on a telephone answering system that you turn on Friday afternoon and only check on Monday mornings. A tenant without heat all weekend can become a major issue for you.

A lockout—where the tenant locks himself or herself out of the property—is easily handled. Water gushing from broken pipes requires the water to be shut off and an emergency repair made. Loss of electricity also calls for immediate action.

You need to develop contingency plans. Consider installing dead-bolt locks with passive doorknobs on all entry doors. This requires a key to lock the door and makes it impossible for tenants to lock their keys in their unit. Of course, they could still lock their door, leave, and lose their keys later.

Be sure to take care of your tenants in these types of situations. One landlord, in the middle of a sweltering heat wave, put the tenants in a hotel for three days when the air conditioning broke. It took all weekend until the compressor could be replaced. The landlord also gave a few dinner gift certificates, just because of the inconvenience. This type of outstanding customer service paid off: the tenants renewed their lease for two years. Knowing they could trust their landlord to take care of them was the only incentive they needed to re-sign their lease.

Locate plumbing shutoffs now. Show them to new tenants so that they can turn off the water themselves in an emergency. You should have 24-hour heating/cooling contractors available, as well as plumbers and electricians. Those firms that you would use in such an emergency should be readily available to you. Store their telephone numbers in your cell phone. Add their numbers to your Rolodex.

Providing Routine Maintenance

The earlier discussion on how to control costs largely dictates how you will provide routine maintenance. Your maintenance plan should include routine inspection, care, and fixes. Who will do this is up to you.

Remember the old saying, "a stitch in time saves nine." The message is that a little preventative maintenance can eliminate the need for major repairs later. You may also have heard that "an ounce of prevention is worth a pound of cure." For the real estate investor, both of these sayings make sense. For example, repairing and painting exterior wood trim could prevent wood from rotting and rain from being driven into the house. Plan your routine maintenance.

Make minor repairs yourself when you can. Hire a handyman for repairs beyond your time or ability. Rely on licensed and expensive contractors only as a last resort.

As mentioned earlier, twice a year properties have to be readied for the coming seasons. In most locales, this is done in the spring and the fall. Service heating and air conditioning equipment seasonally. Cover air conditioning units and prune trees and shrubbery. Your property could require other outside work, from simple cleanup to painting.

Each property is unique. You must stay involved, and do whatever routine maintenance is required. Do not overlook these simple property-management requirements.

Acquiring Proper Service Contracts

There are several services that you are likely to need on an ongoing basis. They include pest control, snow removal, lawn maintenance, waste hauling, fuel oil delivery, coin laundry appliance leases, water softener rental, salt delivery, and more. Some of the specifics of these service agreements are covered in the next section.

The first decision to make is which services to contract and which to try to do on your own or to delegate to tenants. Delegating to tenants will risk the work being done improperly or not at all. Additionally, what happens if the tenant is injured while doing the work? The message isn't that you shouldn't delegate any work to tenants. Just know the pitfalls. Alternatively, you can do the work yourself or hire a service provider.

Shop around for any service you decide to contract. Because you may be paying monthly for any particular service for years, small cost disparities can add up. However, cost should not be your only guide. Poor service can increase potential liability for you, particularly in the area of snow removal, for example.

Be careful to pay attention to the fine print on these service agreements. Pay close attention to the term of the service contract. Many of these agreements are multiyear contracts that renew automatically. You are unable to cancel the service, but the vendor can still pass along price increases, even while providing mediocre service. Don't be intimidated by the standard language in these agreements. Cross out these provisions and change the contract term to month-to-month with no more than 30-days written notice required to cancel.

Author's Advice

Amend any multiyear service contracts with automatic renewal clauses to 30-day agreements that may be canceled at any time.

Other Necessary Contractual Services

As a real estate investor, among the gamut of services that you may need, the services in this section are the most common. These services include snow removal, lawn care, waste hauling, and coin laundry leases.

Snow Removal

If your property is located in an area that receives winter snowfalls, you may need to arrange for the removal of snow and ice accumulation. Some areas have local ordinances that require snow removal from sidewalks. Local officials are often quick to issue citations and levy fines against property owners who do not remove snow accumulation.

It is also important to remove snow from your property for the safety of your tenants and visitors. Failing to do so could expose you to injury claims.

If your rental property is a single-family home, you may be able to delegate this responsibility to the tenant. Your lease should clearly spell out who is going to be responsible.

In most areas of the country where snow accumulates, local businesses have sprung up to provide this service. The time to contract for snow removal is before winter. Shop for the best rates and ask for references.

Often, snow removal contractors are only interested in clearing the snow from the parking lot and other areas that can be cleared using a snow plow truck. They do not want to have to exit their vehicle or carry additional equipment like a snow blower to remove snow from a sidewalk. You may find that you need to make separate arrangements for sidewalk snow removal. Usually, a tenant can be compensated for removing snow from these areas.

Lawn Maintenance

Another service required to maintain the property is lawn maintenance. From cutting the grass to fertilizing, from pruning to adding mulch, lawn maintenance can become costly. Yet it is one thing that you must provide. The range of solutions includes delegating the work to the tenant of a single-family home or an on-site manager, to doing the work yourself or hiring a service provider.

Properties with Homeowner Associations include this service. For one monthly fee, these services are provided.

Taking Care of Waste Hauling

In some areas, waste removal is provided by the local municipality. In other areas, you hire your own waste-hauling contractor to remove garbage and recyclable materials from your property.

If the municipality is providing the waste hauling, all you can do is pay the bill for the service. If you can hire your own hauler, you can shop around for the best price and service. This is one area where the contractors like to use multiyear automatically renewing agreements. Remain on guard.

Make sure you are complying with all recycling requirements and regulations. Provide recycling bins, and provide your tenants with information required by your local authorities.

Garbage trucks are extremely heavy. The weight of these vehicles can destroy the paving. Therefore, locate waste collection areas so that the trucks drive on the least amount of pavement on your property as possible. Maintain sufficient waste capacity that these vehicles do not have to service your site any more than once per week if possible.

Coin Laundry Leases

If your investment property has four units or more, it probably makes sense to provide coin-operated laundry appliances. You can buy, install, and maintain the machines yourself, or you can retain a service provider. If you decide to retain a contractor, take extra care to work with a reputable firm, as there are so many opportunities for you to be shorted on the revenue.

Most coin laundry leases allow for a 50/50 split of revenue between you and the contractor. You are responsible for providing the room and the utilities for the machines and the contractor provides the equipment and any needed service, including collecting the coins.

To get a contract to install new equipment in your building, you will probably need to make at least a three-year commitment, allowing the vendor exclusive rights to operate the coin concession. However, these service agreements are notorious for having automatic renewal clauses that are difficult to avoid or cancel. Insist after the initial period (of hopefully no more than three years), the agreement becomes month-to-month with cancellation possible at any time.

Buyer Beware

Don't fall victim to dishonest laundry contractors. Check out any vendor carefully, limit any contract to three years or less, and do not accept any kind of automatic renewal clause. Or just buy your own equipment.

Unscrupulous contractors plague the coin appliance industry. David acquired a building with a coin laundry lease already in effect. The lease ran with the land, so David was still bound by the terms of the lease. The initial lease period was for ten years. After the first ten years, the lease was renewable for ten more years at the vendor's option. In effect, the lease was really a twenty-year lease. The lease also contained an automatic renewal clause allowing only a 90-day window, twenty-years in the future, where the lease could be canceled before it renewed automatically for another ten years. And the coin laundry split was 85 percent for the vendor, 15 percent for the landlord! Need David tell you that their service was lousy besides?

Extended Warranties and Service Agreements

When you purchase new appliances, you are often presented with the option of buying an extended warranty or a service agreement. These agreements and warranties are usually a bad idea.

These agreements are driven by actuarial science. In other words, the vendor must calculate expected failure rates and the resulting costs of repairs or replacements, and then factor in overhead and profit. In at least some industries, these extended warranty programs are a high margin business because the products being covered are actually highly reliable. Electric stoves are one example of appliances that rarely fail. You can recapture the profit and overhead portion of this service by taking your chances and paying for service only when and if it is needed.

Extended warranties and service agreements are essentially an unregulated form of pseudoinsurance. You should only insure that which you can't afford to lose. Hopefully, you can afford the impact of a failed appliance like a refrigerator. Find a handyman who knows something about small gasoline engines and appliance repair and take your chances.

If you do decide to get the extended warranty or service agreement, remember that a brochure isn't a contract. Always read the contract to determine what additional warranty or service you might receive for your money. Be sure you understand how to file a claim, and how you are reimbursed.

Check for things like the length of the warranty period, the items covered, and other contract details. For example, is service provided locally or do you have to ship to a repair center? If shipping is involved, who pays for it?

Ask questions. If a tenant's child were to jump up and down on an oven door, would the extended warranty cover the cost of a replacement door, and the service call to have it replaced? Often these service agreements apply to home personal use only. Commercial applications such as a rental setting sometimes void these agreements.

Consider the reputation of the company offering the extended warranty agreement. If the firm has been in business for years, you are probably okay. But a vendor who has gone out of business is worthless to you, no matter how much your contract says things are covered.

Understanding Insurance

Without insurance, you could not invest in real estate. If you wanted to buy a property for $250,000, could you afford a total loss and start over? A lender would not loan money if they could not insure their collateral.

In the simplest terms, insurance is the transfer of risk. By the payment of a premium, the insurer establishes a pool of money to pay probable claims. If your $250,000 property becomes a total loss, the insurer pays $250,000 to you and your lender. You have transferred the risk of such a total loss—and the financial burden caused by that loss—to the insurer. Always think of insurance as way of transferring risk from you to the insurance company.

Insurance is more complicated than stated here, but here are the basics of insurance offered for protection of your property. As a real estate investor, you are concerned about four types of insurance:

- **Property Insurance.** This provides protection against hazards such as fire, wind, or storm.
- **Liability Insurance.** This provides protection against claims of negligence on your part.
- **Title Insurance.** This provides protection against claims of others saying they have an interest in your property.
- **Workmens' Compensation Insurance.** This provides protection against claims of workplace injuries on your property.

Real Deal

Many times, insurers combine property and liability coverage together into one policy. It does not matter if your insurance company issues one or two policies. What does matter is the coverage provided.

def•i•ni•tion

Exclusions of coverage is exactly what it says—specific items are excluded from any insurance coverage. One common exclusion in a liability policy is contractual obligations. No matter what you agree to contractually, you might be legally obligated to pay, but your insurer would not—they have excluded any contractual liability from your policy.

One big fallacy of most insurance buyers is thinking that they are covered for all losses. Nothing could be further from the truth. All insurance policies include *exclusions of coverage*. One common exclusion is that no coverage is provided for damage caused by "an act of war." Any damage your property suffers would not be covered.

Other common exclusions include no coverage from flood damage, mold, or intentional damage. There are many others, which vary from things like nuclear accidents to damage caused by freezing pipes in unoccupied buildings. Coverage and exclusions vary from state to state.

You will also be amazed at what is covered with insurance. If a careening car becomes airborne and lands in your living room, expect your claim to be promptly paid. If a wayward skunk wonders into the property, becomes agitated and sprays the walls and carpet, your policy will pay for the damage.

Many people wrongly call property insurance, "fire insurance." The last thing you want is only fire insurance. You want your property covered (and you protected) against as many hazards as possible.

For investment properties, you can't purchase regular homeowner's insurance. Rather, you need an insurance policy that protects the property against damage caused by tenants. Commonly called Owners, Landlord, and Tenant coverage (OLT), this type of policy provides protection against claims made against you during the operation of the property as an investment.

Liability coverage protects you against legal action. The types of claims that are covered include slip and fall accidents on your property. For example, if someone falls on the sidewalk and claims the accident was your fault because you negligently failed to remove snow and ice on a timely basis, your liability insurance would provide protection. The insurer would pay a settlement to the claimant, up to the limits of your policy.

Most important, liability coverage includes the payment of your legal fees. This means that the insurer would hire and pay for an attorney on your behalf. In today's litigious society, this is an absolute necessity for any real estate investor. With lawyers advertising for injured clients, you must have this coverage. You do not get to pick your defense lawyer, but rather your insurer does. They routinely hire experienced defense law firms with expertise defending insurance company policyholders.

When it comes to insurance, you should always shop around. Not all insurers are created equal. Many provide extra coverage, and often offer coverage at differing rates.

Some things to consider when considering purchasing insurance include …

- Get a price quote from an independent insurance agent. Independent agents represent multiple insurers, and have various rates available from different companies.
- Meet with the agent you select. Let the agent know what you are doing as a real estate investor. In addition to being good for networking contacts, ask the agent to explain what coverage you have purchased, and in particular, what isn't covered.
- Request as high a deductible as you can afford. If you can purchase insurance with a $100, $250, or $500 deductible, consider the $500 deductible. Place $500 in an account and leave it there for any small claims if you must. Use insurance for those claims that you can't pay yourself. While you can't afford a $250,000 loss, you could handle a $300 loss. If you bought the $250 deductible coverage, you would only be paid $50.
- As your assets and net worth increase, consider purchasing an umbrella liability policy. This provides excess liability coverage. A good rule of thumb is to carry liability coverage of at least one million dollars, or an amount equal to your net worth, whichever is higher.
- Buy sufficient coverage. Do not be underinsured, either with property or liability coverage. Discuss your coverage with your agent and update your policy coverage once per year.
- Do not try to hide the fact you are using a property as a real estate investment. If you represent that the property is owner-occupied when it isn't, while you might get the insurance, it is useless if you make a claim. All policies include an exclusion called "material misrepresentation." This means the insurer does not have to pay any claims if you have made significant misrepresentations about the property.
- Always buy your insurance from a local agent.
- Seek premium discounts by purchasing all needed insurance from one company.

As discussed earlier, title insurance, bought at the time you purchase the property, provides protection from title defects. Should the legal description be faulty, or someone else claim to have an interest in the property, your title insurance would provide protection against such claims.

One type of insurance that many new investors overlook is workmens' compensation insurance. This insurance pays for any claim related to any employee workplace injury. You may not think that you have any employees, but the government sees it differently.

If you have an on-site manager that cuts the grass for you, that person may be regarded as your employee for workmens' compensation purposes. What happens to this individual if there is an accident? You could be held responsible for any medical care and disability payments, in addition to probable fines, if you do not have workmens' compensation insurance. The impact could be ruinous.

Rest assured that anyone doing work for you at any investment property you own must be covered by workmens' compensation insurance. Either the contractor must carry it or you must carry it. When bidding work, make submitting proof of insurance part of the bid requirements.

Your insurance agent will be able to help you with the details of your workmens' compensation insurance needs.

The Least You Need to Know

- As a real estate investor, you are operating a small business.
- Control your expenses as much as possible.
- Develop a plan to handle emergency repairs, a team of reliable contractors, and a plan to complete routine maintenance on your properties.
- Avoid multiyear, automatically renewing service contracts.
- Buy the right insurance with the proper coverage, including Workmens' Compensation Insurance.

Chapter 16

Problem Tenants

In This Chapter

- Handling problem tenants
- Understanding the eviction process
- What to do when rent is unpaid
- Building a paper trail

Inevitably, someday you are going to come across a problem tenant. Perhaps more irritating than fingernails scraped across a chalkboard, the problem tenant will cause you numerous troubles. Nothing will make you happier than the day your problem tenant moves from your property.

You're going to find that it isn't always easy being a landowner. Collecting rent can sometimes be as easy as holding down a lion and giving it a root canal—without anesthesia.

Every single problem tenant you encounter can make your life miserable. In this chapter, you will learn some techniques for dealing with your problem tenants.

Problem Tenants Defined

A good tenant is a tenant who pays the rent on time, does not abuse the property, and gets along with the neighbors. A good tenant may have hobbies and habits that you don't agree with, but that doesn't matter. To be a landlord, you will need to develop a little bit of a laissez-faire, live and let live demeanor.

So what is a bad tenant? A bad tenant is anyone who doesn't pay their rent on time, abuses the property, or agitates the neighbors. What about good old widow Jones? She keeps her home as neat as a pin. She always has fresh baked goods to share with you whenever you're at the property. She's always kind and neighborly. She's also three months behind in rent. Ms. Jones is a bad tenant.

Widow Jones is also a fictional character. Most problem tenants don't just have one problem. It seems like real-world bad tenants have problems that at least come in threes. The same tenant who can't make the rent is the same tenant who litters cigarette butts everywhere and stores his motorcycle in his living room (and Dave wishes he were making that up).

Bad tenants are loud, they litter, they live in filth, and they intimidate the good tenants. Bad tenants have unauthorized pets and ill-mannered children. Bad tenants move their ex-con cousin or recently released relative right in to your freshly scrubbed housing.

Before we fill you in on how to cure the bad-tenant blues, first understand who is to blame for this mess. Is it just bad luck? Is it the sinful nature of man? Just one of those things? No, it's none of the above. Every bad tenant was selected by a landlord. You probably inherited your bad tenants when you bought your property. Always remember that prevention is the best cure for bad tenants.

Author's Advice

The more you bend the rules to fill a vacancy, the greater the odds of disaster. Probably 90 percent of problem tenants occur because you were faced with the dilemma of a vacant housing unit versus accepting a less than perfect applicant.

In Chapter 14, you learned some important steps in managing your properties. The first rules of working with tenants are to first screen carefully and then put everything in writing. The moment you overlook these simple details, be prepared for problems to develop quickly. A marginal tenant can blossom into a real problem if you give him or her the opportunity.

For many real estate investors, the problem tenant is the one who does not pay rent. There are many others. Tenants who have substance abuse problems can turn any property into a drug den. Tenants who can't live peacefully in their rented space become police problems. In a multifamily property, problem tenants can influence your other good tenants to leave.

Nonpayment of Rent

In your lease, you should specify the date the rent is due, usually the first of each month. You should also specify when the rent is late, and should assess a late fee. Make sure you hold all of your tenants strictly to the terms of your lease. This policy should be black and white, with no shades of gray. Either your tenant pays the rent on time, when due, or they are on their way out of your property. Be tough when you need to be.

Record all late rent payments, just as you would all on-time rent payments. Note the date the money was received and even the check number. You need to establish a paper trail, especially if you need to evict a tenant. Going to court and proving to the judge that your tenant has not paid rent on time for the past five months is going to help your case.

Buyer Beware

Judges love paper trails. If you want to win your case, always be in a position to produce a well-documented file.

The key to rent collections is to have a policy and to stick with it. You can't allow each delinquency to become an agonizing personal decision about what to do about this particular tenant based upon the strength of your relationship with them. If your collection efforts are haphazard, you may even find yourself inadvertently committing fair housing violations.

A good policy specifies all rents are due on the first of the month. Allow a five-day grace period where rent can still be paid without incurring a late fee or other collection effort. On the fifth of the month, distribute a reminder notice to any tenants as yet unpaid. Late fees would now apply. On the eighth day, file an eviction in the proper court having jurisdiction on any tenant that remains unpaid. (Jurisdictions may differ when you can actually file the eviction notice. Whatever the minimum day is, that is the day you should file.) While this timeline may seem harsh, it is necessary to remove a nonpaying tenant by the end of a month.

Note that should the tenant come forward with the rent anytime prior to the eviction being completed, you could accept their money and reinstate their tenancy. Most security deposits are equal to one month of rent. If the tenant gets more than 30 days behind in rent, your odds of incurring uncollectible losses escalate. Never allow a tenant to get more than 30 days behind in rent.

There are exceptions to this timeline, of course. If a delinquent tenant who has been otherwise reliable in the past reports a problem, you may want to work out a repayment plan with them. But the same thinking applies. You still do not want to allow them to get more than 30 days behind. You will learn more about repayment plans later in this chapter.

To be successful in your collection efforts, you will need to understand the local laws governing evictions. Again, your local apartment association can be of great help. More than likely, there are special forms applicable to your state for use in collections and evictions. Stock these in advance of ever needing them.

An eviction can be expensive for you. Depending on the jurisdiction, it will probably take at least 30 days or longer to discover the delinquency, file for an eviction, and recover the rental unit. Evicted tenants often leave their apartment completely trashed. You will likely incur more rental loss and repair and cleaning charges prior to being able to rent the apartment. Naturally, there will be the added expense of advertising and your time.

Of course, you can expect to get a money judgment against the evicted tenant, but good luck collecting it. You should docket the judgment so that any future creditors will be put on notice of the existence of your judgment. You can also pursue an earnings garnishment if you know where your tenant is working. But understand this: posteviction collection efforts are a losing game. You would be better off and money ahead by spending your limited time screening future tenants more thoroughly and by pursuing the next real estate deal.

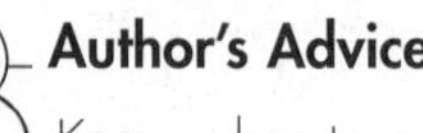

Author's Advice

Know when to cut your losses, both when filing for an eviction and when trying to collect on a judgment after the tenant is out.

Other Lease Violations

Not every bad tenant is guilty of nonpayment of rent. David had a tenant perfectly capable of paying the rent because she made plenty of money as a prostitute working out of her apartment. Listen to your other tenants and the neighbors. These people are living there with your tenant. If they say there is a never-ending stream of visitors every Friday night from 11 P.M. to 3 A.M., they are right. Do not dismiss what they are telling you. You want to know about any strange or illegal activity.

Some tenants are slobs and create pest control problems. David has had tenants who kept the entire apartment covered in several feet of rotting, stinking trash. Only a narrow path wound its way around the garbage to the various rooms. Flypaper was distributed throughout the unit to keep the bugs down. David does not get angry with tenants like this. Circumstances like these reflect a mental health situation.

Some real estate investors physically pick up the rent each month at their properties. It is often convenient for the tenant, and it allows the investor to check out their property. This may not be an option in all cases, but it does help to collect rent due, and to keep an eye on the property.

Other tenants live with you in peace for years before moving in a new boyfriend or taking in a troubled adult child or relative. Then the trouble starts.

It would be impossible to catalogue every problem that you could face as a landlord. All of these problems have one thing in common. No matter who your tenant was before, they have now become a bad tenant. You'd better take action before they cause the good tenants to move away.

Nonpayment of rent is easy to prove, but these other lease violations are more difficult. There are three requirements for success. You must first have a lease with well-drafted rules that prohibit these kinds of behaviors. You must then have a paper trail of thoroughly documented lease violations. Finally, you must know landlord-tenant law.

When your bad tenant commits a lease violation, make careful notes. Details speak to truth. If your tenant had a wild, loud, late-night party, try to get all the details that you can. Try to count the number of people in attendance, even getting names. Additionally, noting the name of the song that was blasting over the stereo is helpful. Take photographs of any damage.

If you wind up in court over the matter, you will have all the details, all the facts. Your bad tenant will almost certainly not be as well prepared if they show up at all. They will probably say something like, "well, I didn't think it was that loud …."

Obviously, before the matter gets to this point, you should try to resolve the matter by both verbal and written warnings. Working from the assumption that your tenant is hopefully a good tenant and whatever incident that occurred was a one-time aberration, begin the process by simply calling to tell the offending tenant that you have received a complaint that you feel you must investigate. Document the call by making some notes that you place in the tenant's file.

If problems persist, employ the kind of warning statement that you read about in Chapter 14. If the problem is still not resolved, inform the tenant that further violations will lead to a termination of tenancy. A sample letter follows:

Termination of Tenancy

Dear Tenant X:

Enclosed please find an additional copy of my letter, dated ________, sent to you about the noise level in your apartment. I am disappointed at having to write you again about this same subject. However, on the night of ________, additional complaints were received from a number of neighbors regarding at least nine individuals congregating in your apartment with loud music, voices, slamming of doors, etc. from about 10:00 P.M. to 3:00 A.M.

Such conduct is a violation of your lease. I will not be writing to you on a matter of this nature again. Instead, if there is a repeat of this situation, an action will be filed in small claims court to terminate your tenancy and to seek appropriate money damages.

If you believe you will not be able to comply with the provisions of your lease, please contact me now so that we may arrange a mutually agreeable date for you to move out.

Thank you for your cooperation.

Sincerely,
AB Properties

Be sure that you never bluff, but always back up any warnings with appropriate actions should there be further violations. In all interactions with the bad tenant, written or verbal, maintain a tone of detachment. Never allow the situation to degrade into a shouting match, nor should you ever engage in anything that could be construed as a personal attack.

If you can't gain the tenant's cooperation, you are going to have to proceed to an eviction. In order to be successful, you will need to correctly fill out a legally enforceable eviction notice and have it properly served on your tenant. You must be certain the portions of your lease that were violated are indeed legally enforceable provisions. In other words, you have to know the law.

Author's Advice

Take the time to learn the local laws. It will help you resolve disputes, and make you a better landlord.

As mentioned earlier, knowing the law dictates that your lease be drafted to address the laws unique to the jurisdiction where you are operating. If the eviction notice is properly filed with the court and served on the tenant, then and only then can you get your day in court to state your case and present your evidence about why this tenant should be removed.

Just as you would send a notice for nonpayment of rent, be efficient demanding that all other terms and conditions of the lease be observed. For example, your lease agreement might require that no junked automobiles are allowed to be stored on the property. When one appears, send a letter demanding the vehicle be removed within a specific, reasonable length of time.

Who Isn't a Problem Tenant

Bad things can happen to good people. There are automobile accidents, serious illnesses, and sudden job losses. If you have a tenant who has always paid the rent on time in the past, and suddenly can't pay because of a major uncontrollable event, you probably want to do what you can to collect the rent and keep the tenant. A tenant who calls you and explains what has happened, and asks for some additional time to pay, is probably not a problem tenant.

If this happens to you, tell the tenant that you must still send the notices. Work out a payment plan, and put that plan in writing. In the letter, thank the tenant for calling and working out a plan of payment. The following presents a sample letter for your review.

Sample Letter Working Out Payment Plan

Mr. Thomas Jones
123 Main Street
Anytown, WI 53403

Dear Mr. Jones:

Thank you for your telephone call of this date explaining your unfortunate accident.

You have asked for two additional weeks to pay your June rent. You indicated that you will, by that time, be able to return to work.

Accordingly, as we agreed, you will pay, on or before June 17, a total of $835. This represents the June rent payment of $810, and a late fee of $25.

I will not commence eviction action against you if your payment is received as agreed. Should your payment not be received on June 17, I will have no choice but to proceed with the eviction, as described in the attached notice.

I wish you a speedy recovery from your injuries.

Sincerely,
Kenneth C. Knight
Knight Properties, LLC

Include with the payment plan letter the appropriate notice to initiate an eviction such that if the tenant fails to comply with the payment agreement, you can immediately file for an eviction.

Work with tenants when you can, but don't become the local charity, or you will quickly enough be a candidate for charity yourself. Realize that accepting partial payments can be tricky. Depending on your locality, the acceptance of a partial rent payment may cause you to start the eviction process from the beginning. In this case, there may be a legal form that you can use that will allow the receipt of a partial payment without having to start the eviction process over. Check with your local attorney for advice on accepting partial rent payments.

You are protecting your interests by putting your agreement in writing. Should the tenant not pay the rent, you have a strong argument showing a judge that you tried to assist your tenant by making an agreement to accept the rent at a later time.

In your written agreement, be friendly and businesslike. Always keep in mind that whatever you write in a payment arrangement letter could be introduced in court as evidence.

Handling Very Bad Tenants

Some tenants are terrible. Each day they are in your property is another day of aggravation. It could be a day where they are loud, slamming doors, yelling, and partying. On another day, it seems like their children are hosting every other kid within a three-block radius on your property. They are hanging from trees, and bicycles are everywhere. Bushes are dying, and while you do not know the exact reason, you must assume it is from something the tenants are doing. The kids are dirty. They are playing with a mangy dog, even though you have a no pets policy. Of course, this dog is a stray—and not your tenant's dog.

The past New Year's Eve, a shotgun blast was heard from the back porch—all in the spirit of celebration. The recycling bin overflows each week with an abundance of beer bottles. One of the dependable neighbors tells you that at night they cower in their living room, afraid to look out through tightly closed window blinds.

Let's call our fictional fright family the Get-Thee-Gones, so that you'll recognize their name later.

One of your real problems with such tenants may be that they do pay the rent—on time, and as agreed. You can't evict them for nonpayment of rent—if they paid it.

What do you do?

You need the full power of the bad tenant remedies mixed with a healthy dose of the creative solutions that we are about to explore now.

Real Deal

Eviction for other than nonpayment of rent is often harder to prove. But that does not mean it is impossible.

Problem Tenant Remedies

The obvious solution for unpaid rent is to receive the rent payment from the tenant. Your demand for payment must remain clear and show no signs of wavering.

Other problems can often be handled with written notices. If there is a violation of the lease or your rental rules, send a letter, identifying the violation and expecting full compliance. Do not allow things to slide. If you show that you don't care about loud noises or accumulating garbage, you are sending a powerful message to a tenant. You probably will not care about rent payments, either.

For violations of your rules that are obvious, take a photograph (such as accumulating trash). Make notes of the time and date the photograph was taken, and keep it in your files.

Evictions

Evicting tenants is never a pleasurable experience, but sometimes, it is the only way to handle the problem tenant. Each jurisdiction has established its own manner and procedures to evict a tenant.

The standard procedure is for the landlord to file an eviction action in the proper court after notices were delivered to the tenant, and the tenant failed to comply. After the tenant received notification of the court action, the tenant responds to the complaint filed by the landlord. A hearing is scheduled, where both sides have the opportunity to present their case. The judge decides who wins.

If the landlord wins, the tenant is ordered to pay any unpaid rent and other damages, and is ordered to vacate the premises. If the tenant refuses to do so, the court will order a sheriff (or other law enforcement agency) to *evict* the tenant. With that court order, the proper authority will enter the premises, and physically

def•i•ni•tion

Eviction is a legal process, and legal remedy, where rented property is returned to the property owner. Both the landlord and the tenant must follow the law.

Real Deal

Never try to evict a tenant yourself. Doing so is illegal. Turn this unpleasant work over to the proper legal authority.

remove the tenant. What happens to their personal property depends on the laws of each jurisdiction. Following the eviction, the landlord has control of his or her property again.

As stated, this procedure varies throughout the country. The important point to note is that the landlord does not physically evict the tenant, but rather the proper legal authority, under court order, does.

Other Creative Remedies

Some potentially problematic tenants can be handled with an incentive. One technique that has worked for other real estate investors is to offer a rent discount to any tenant who pays their rent on or before the day it is due. It works this way: you rent a property for $715. However, if a tenant pays the rent on or before the twenty-fifth of each month, they are entitled to a $25 discount. In other words, they rent the property for $690. Their rent check can't bounce, and it must be in your hands on the 25th to qualify. Property owners who use this technique are often amazed at what a tenant will do to enjoy a rent reduction.

This incentive need not actually cost you anything. You could build a late fee into the base rent. By paying on or before the first, the tenant gets a "discount," or they avoid the late fee, depending on your perspective. Of course, if rent remains unpaid, additional late fees could apply.

Sometimes, when you are handling the very worst tenants, you need out-of-the-box solutions. Remember the Get-Thee-Gones? What do you do with tenants like this?

One emergency solution employed successfully in the past to easily and quickly remove the worst tenants is to simply pay them to leave. Such an offer should be accompanied by a throw-the-book-at-them eviction notice so that you have the benefit of both a carrot and a stick. The offer for them to move should have some immediacy to it and no payments are to be made by you until they are actually out. You may also need to forgive some or all of any back rent. Make the best deal that you can. But it may be better to spend your money on the bad tenant before they cause good tenants to move, even if the thought of rewarding their bad behavior seems disgusting. Be pragmatic about cutting this cancer out of your building.

Even Worse Neighbors

Sometimes, the worst problems aren't caused by your tenants, but rather, by the neighbors of your property. It should not need to be said that before involving the authorities, you try to work things out with your neighbors on a friendly basis. But if the problem persists or if you can't gain cooperation, documentation again is the answer to your problem.

Take photographs, maintain accurate records, and promptly complain to authorities of any violations of ordinances or laws. Find out if your problem neighbors are owners or tenants. More than likely they will be tenants. If they are tenants, find out who owns the property and have a frank discussion with this landlord about his or her tenant's behavior.

This could indeed be an interesting discussion. The result could range from your problem neighbors being properly controlled all the way to you acquiring another property at bargain-basement prices from a landlord fed up the tenant problems.

View your problem neighbors as an opportunity.

Protecting Your Investment

Real estate is expensive to buy and maintain, and above all, you made the purchase as an investment. You need to protect your investment. By purchasing casualty insurance, you are protecting it against fire, wind, and other accidental damage. You need to protect it by following the local laws when dealing with tenant problems.

Being lazy or lax is never the solution. You must actively protect your investment by properly managing your property.

The Least You Need to Know

- Establish and follow reasonable rental-collection procedures.
- Carefully document all lease violations, be they for nonpayment of rent or for other violations.
- Learn and follow the local laws to evict a tenant.
- Never try to evict a tenant yourself.
- Employ creative remedies to induce the worst tenants to move.

Chapter 17

Property Problems

In This Chapter

- Handling rent increases
- Managing repair requests
- Preparing for unexpected repairs
- Fighting your tax assessment

Increasing your rent is not just about creating additional cash flow. As the cost of operating and maintaining your rental property increases over time, you need to raise the rent that you charge. Additionally, since real estate values are at least partly determined by the income-producing ability of the real estate, raising the rent is crucial to adding value. Before you raise the rent, consider first whether or not you are allowed to do so. This chapter will explain how to raise rents and manage your property properly.

Raising Rents

Most likely, any lease in effect prohibits the landlord from increasing the rent before the lease expires. This is a contract, and you should honor it, just as you expect the tenant to do.

Buyer Beware

Raising rent is a big concern for new landlords who purchased an existing rental property. As the new owner, you are required to honor the terms of the current lease for your tenants, even if the present rent does not cover your operating expenses.

Some states and cities have enacted rent control measures. These laws are designed to prevent landlords from supposedly overcharging their tenants. Regardless of the intent, if your state or city has a rent control law, the amount of rent you may legally charge your tenants is limited.

If you live in a community that has a rent control law, then you can't raise the rent unless the rent control law permits you to do so. Most rent control laws allow property owners to raise rents once a year. The amount of the increase is usually a specified percentage set by the local rent control board. Before getting yourself embroiled in a legal battle that you can't win, be certain that you are complying with all applicable rent control laws.

If you have a month-to-month rental agreement with your tenant (either oral or written), you may raise the rent as often as you like. All you must do is give proper notice of the rent increase ahead of time. State law often specifies the minimum amount of time required before the new rent increase can take effect.

You should provide your existing tenants with enough notice that a rent increase is forthcoming. Usually laws require 30 days written notice before the rent increase takes effect. Written notice is best, even if you have a verbal rental agreement. The actual time requirement may differ according to state or local law.

Rent increases are an important reality in the real estate business. Without regular increases, your cash flow will eventually be eroded by increasing costs. There are two kinds of rent increases: cost of living adjustments and repositioning adjustments.

A cost of living adjustment is just what it sounds like. This is an increase designed to help you keep pace with increasing costs such as utilities, insurance, and property taxes. This increase type reflects the impact of inflation and is usually a small increase, just 2 to 3 percent.

Repositioning adjustments are much larger increases that reflect that the property is different from what it was before. Low-income housing units may become middle-income or even high-income units. This adjustment reflects more than just increased cost of operations like utilities, taxes, or insurance. This adjustment reflects upgrades—anything from new flooring and appliances to extensive remodeling. In any case, the product has fundamentally changed.

Whatever increase you may be proposing, there is one common requirement. The increase must be sold to your tenant.

When you rented to your tenant, you were marketing the property. You were doing everything possible to make your offering attractive to induce a tenant to rent from you. The same thinking applies to rent increases. You must again market the property to persuade your tenant to continue renting at a higher price. Just as you did before, you will need to do some homework.

Before increasing the rent, make sure that the local housing market will support your higher rental rate. Research other rental properties in your area before making your final decision about raising the rent. If the majority of the other properties are charging less for rent, you probably will not attract new tenants—or even retain your existing tenants.

When interest rates are down, it is often harder to find tenants (they are buying houses instead). When interest rates increase, people can't afford to purchase a home and will often rent, increasing the demand for rental housing. Everything depends on your local market area.

The bottom line is that you need to determine the market for rent before you send out the increase notice. Having made a decision about the amount of increase you are going to require, you are now ready to draft an increase notice.

Think of the notice of increase as a sales letter. This letter should never be a bare recitation of the facts surrounding the increase. Instead, your sales pitch should be a reminder of all of the great things you have done around the property in the last year, the great service you have rendered, the late fees you forgave, the prompt repairs or improvements that you made inside of the tenant's unit, and anything else you can possibly think of to justify your increase. Share with your tenant any recent increases in property taxes, fuel costs, insurance expenses, or any other increases you have had to pay. Share the results of your rent survey in at least a general way, stating that the apartment is still priced at or below the competition.

Use proper language. Your increase is not an increase, it is an adjustment or a change. If the change in rent can be correctly expressed as an adjustment of just a percentage point or two, say so. Sometimes it is helpful to break down the adjustment in terms of the cost per day instead of the cost per month. For example, an adjustment of $25 per month is less than $1 per day. Are you really going to move over less than $1 per day?

Obviously, if you have not been keeping precise records, then a letter like this one is going to be hard to write. Your sales letter may start life as a form letter, but each letter will eventually be customized to remind each tenant of the unique benefits and services provided to them in the last year. Does such a letter sound like a lot of work? It is. But writing letters is less work and a lot cheaper than renting vacated apartments. A sample increase letter is as follows:

Rent Increase

Dear Mr./Ms. Tenant's Name

Thank you for your continued tenancy at the ABC Apartments. We are hoping that you will continue to make your home with us for many years to come.

AB Properties is committed to improving and maintaining your home. That is why in the last year, we engaged in a comprehensive upgrade to the landscaping of your building. New mulch beds were installed with new plantings and flowerbed accents. In all, $15,000 was spent on these upgrades. I hope you have been able to enjoy these new improvements the last several months.

Our concern for the building generally extends all the way to our concern for you personally. I am glad that we were able to replace your range this year as evidence of that concern.

Our commitment to maintaining and improving your building includes a commitment to control costs. This year, despite all of our efforts, property taxes increased over 6%. With the unusual snowfall last winter, snow removal was 23% higher than the previous year.

Accordingly, I hope you would agree that a cost of living adjustment for your rent is reasonable. Therefore, effective September 1, 2006, your rent will change from $810 to $835. This change reflects an adjustment of about 3%. The change is less than $1 per day. Even after this modification, I am sure that you will find that your apartment remains a competitive bargain in the marketplace, particularly considering the prompt service you have enjoyed.

To continue your tenancy for another year, please sign and return one copy of the enclosed Lease Extension Agreement by July 1, 2006. You would be assured of no further changes to your rent during this time.

Unfortunately, if you do not return a copy of the signed Lease Extension Agreement, then it must be assumed that you intend to continue in your old lease under a month-to-month tenancy with 60 days written notice required to vacate. In that case, due to the high cost of turning over apartments, please consider this letter as written notice that your rent will become $860 instead of $835 effective September 1, 2006.

I hope you will choose the savings of a one-year renewal and return a signed copy of the Lease Extension Agreement. A stamped, self-addressed envelope is enclosed for your convenience. Please call me if you have any questions.

I look forward to continuing to provide the highest housing services to you for many years to come.

Sincerely,
AB Properties

There are several features worth noting about the rent increase letter. First, note that the tenant is addressed by name and never as merely, "Dear Tenant." The notice includes reminders about upgrades to the building generally and to the tenant's unit specifically. An itemization of some increased costs is also related. The tenant is invited to extend the lease for another year with the assurance of no further increases. Failure to return the extension results in another increase for the privilege of having a month-to-month tenancy.

The month-to-month tenancy option has three benefits. First, it is an inducement to encourage the tenant to return the extension agreement promptly. Second, the month-to-month option is a revenue opportunity if the tenant doesn't extend. Third, presented this way, the yearly renewal option can be called a savings opportunity.

Author's Advice

Always charge extra for a month-to-month tenancy option. Generally, your posture should be to reward long-term tenancy and discourage short-term tenancies. Charge extra for short-term leases too, if you decide to offer them at all. You'll be surprised by the number of tenants who pay extra for a month-to-month option and yet continue to reside in the same apartment for years.

As we mentioned before, there are two kinds of increases—cost of living adjustments and repositioning adjustments. For either one, even a modest increase, you should fully document and justify the increase as set out in the rent increase letter. Cost of living adjustments are the easiest kind of rent increase.

Cost of Living Adjustments

Most of your rent increases will be cost of living adjustments. When you purchase an investment property, you may make dramatic repairs and improvements to maximize rent income. But once you have increased rents to market, from that point on you will more than likely be just passing on small, modest increases. Stay abreast of the market by doing rental surveys to make sure your proposed increase is neither too little nor too much.

Note that the best rent survey possible is your own experience renting your apartments. It may be that your rents are already higher than the competition. But if tenants are still beating down your door to get one of your units, you can still afford to increase rents. You should always struggle a little to rent an apartment and you should occasionally suffer a vacancy. Otherwise your rents are probably too low.

Repositioning Adjustments

Often when you buy a property, particularly if you are exercising your vision for spotting hidden value, you will find yourself repositioning the property. What was once a low-income, run-down rental becomes a shiny new middle-income unit with a large corresponding rent increase. For example, if you have improved your building to the point that you believe a $100 per month increase in rent is justified, how should you go about phasing in this change?

The best way is to just make the increase all at once. Big, repositioning rent increases are when the sales letter really comes into play. You can amend the letter to indicate that the tenant will not face this dramatic kind of rent increase again. Your tenants will know that what you have done to the building changes its value and justifies an increase. Phasing in a large rent increase takes too long and just annoys the tenants, and the length of time to phase in the increase costs you money.

Understand that no matter how sharp your sales letter may be, when you introduce a large, repositioning rent increase, you are going to lose some of the tenant population no matter what you do. This was a requirement anyway, since repositioning a property inevitably involves changing the customer or tenant base as well. Repositioning rent increases are an excellent tool for getting rid of the poor quality tenants that would have been a stumbling block to your plans had they stayed.

Pending Repairs

In Chapter 15, emergency repairs and preventive maintenance were discussed. Properties also need regular repairs. Sometimes, you might also need to make improvements.

As repairs are scheduled, you should notify your tenants in writing of the work to be done. This is good for not only the craftspeople doing the work, but for the tenant, and you. The last thing you want is workers standing outside your property because the tenant refuses access.

The following is a simple notice:

Tenant Notice

Dear Resident:

On Wednesday, September 7, a work crew will be at your building installing a new cement walkway from the drive to the back porch. We apologize for any inconvenience this work might cause you. If you have any questions, please call my office.

Sincerely,
Judy Franklin
JF Properties, Ltd.

Making repairs is an opportunity for you to either demonstrate your service excellence or prove your approach is more slothful. Customer surveys show that the happiest customer and the most loyal customer is not the individual who buys a product and never has a problem with it. The most satisfied customer is one who buys the product, has a problem, and that problem is resolved promptly and conscientiously. People do not expect perfection. They realize that things break down or go wrong. When this happens to you, recognize that this is your opportunity to shine.

In a perfect world, all repair requests would be satisfied as soon as they become known. However, many landlords who are only part-time investors can't hope to attain this standard. Interestingly, you do not have to achieve this kind of response to earn a glowing report from your tenants. You can still expect to win accolades from your tenants if you take the following approach to maintenance requests. These maintenance requests may be made through a phone call, a letter, an e-mail, or by a note included with a rent payment.

You may have a procedure for reporting maintenance requests, such as requiring non-emergency repairs to be made in writing on your request form. If you have such a procedure, understand that your tenants may not always follow it. Should the request be not made according to your procedures, you would still be better served by responding promptly anyway. You can go over the nuances of the request procedure with the tenant again once the repairs are made.

Upon receipt of a request, first decide whether the repair represents an emergency. Emergencies such as a no heat call require immediate attention. If it's just a failed garbage disposal, that could wait. If the problem reported is not an emergency, then you should acknowledge the request as soon as possible, certainly within 24 hours of receipt of the request. While acknowledging receipt of the request, you set an appointment for making the repair. That appointment might be several days away.

You will find that usually, your tenant will be completely satisfied waiting a few days for a repair if you have an excellent record of accomplishment for keeping repair promises. If something goes wrong, preventing you from keeping your promise, keep the tenant fully informed and reschedule the service. If you are sending a contractor to do the work, inform the tenant who the contractor is, when they are expected, when the tenant can expect the work to be done, and that the tenant can expect the contractors to clean up after themselves when finished. Ask the tenant to contact you immediately if the contractor deviates from any of the standards that you just outlined.

Real Deal

Prompt, complete communication with tenants is key to managing repair requests properly.

Government-Mandated Repairs and Improvements

The government, in its wisdom and work for the public good, may mandate certain repairs or improvements to your property. The list of what they might want you to do is long and varied, and often depends on your location. You could be forced to connect to a public sewerage or water system, install or repair sidewalks, or comply with landscape restrictions.

Such notices from the local authorities can't be ignored. Usually there is a window of opportunity to complete the work. If at the end of that time you have not made the mandated repairs or improvements, legal action can be commenced against you. Either way, it is going to get a lot more expensive in a short time.

You should be maintaining your property in such a way that government should never have to insist that you take care of obvious problems. However, many municipalities have annual inspections of elevators, boilers, and other complicated equipment that might reveal a need for a repair that many laymen landlords might not have realized on their own. You should welcome such inspections and make required repairs promptly.

When city officials, such as a building inspector, require that certain repairs be made, realize that you have little negotiating leverage. What leverage you gain will come from the typically excellent state of repair that consistently exists at your properties and your enthusiastic, cooperative attitude with trying to satisfy the inspector's concerns.

Major and Unexpected Repairs

It would be impossible to catalog every possible disaster that could happen to your property. A storm could tear off the roof. A municipal water main break could flood your basement. The furnace breaks, the building catches fire. The list goes on.

Thankfully, many of these kinds of repairs will be an insured loss. Insurance would probably recover the roof damage and the fire damage. Other damage might be someone else's fault, meaning that their insurance will pay for your damage. This would probably be the case in the example of the municipal plumbing main break.

However, not every disaster will be an insured loss or someone else's fault. The example of the broken furnace would be one of these. While a furnace replacement is not inexpensive, you should really not be caught by surprise by the failure. If you are performing any kind of regular maintenance, you would know about the condition of the furnace and if it was near the end of its life, you should have been setting aside funds or making other plans for its replacement.

> **Real Deal**
>
> Sharp landlords who take good care of their properties are rarely surprised by sudden repair needs.

One option you should not consider in resolving your repair problem is selling the property. You should only sell your property when the building is standing tall, in an excellent state of repair. Doing anything less may turn you into a motivated seller.

For instance, assume that your property experienced a failure in the foundation and now requires $30,000 in repairs. The property would otherwise be worth $300,000, but given the need for the repair, you price it at $270,000.

Many buyers will be intimidated by the need for this repair and will have no further interest. Buyers who are still interested will be thinking, "the property is available for $270,000 but needs a $30,000 repair—I'll offer $240,000."

You may not have to literally pay twice for the repair, but the need for the repair will cost you more in a lower sale price than if you had fixed the problem and then sold the property.

Chapter 22 includes refinancing strategies to make improvements that can help get you out of a jam.

Even when you are on top of your game, there can still be surprises. The rain falls equally on the evil and the good. It still pays to set aside some emergency repair dollars for those rainy days.

Property Tax Assessments

If your property is in a location where municipalities assess taxes against it, each year you need to pay the taxes. Some locales have multiple government entities levying taxes against the property. For example, you might have to pay a tax to the local school board, to the county, and the local municipality (town, township, city).

In such areas where property taxes are assessed, each year an assessment is made on the probable value of your property. It is from that assessment that the taxes are levied. Although each area is different, there is some type of appeal period where you can contest the amount of the assessment.

By requesting an appeal, you usually have to appear before someone and tell why you believe the assessment is inaccurate. This is often an informal meeting. You state your case as to why your assessment is too high. The best case is when you can show other similar properties with lower assessments, or recent sales. (Refer to Chapter 5 for more information about determining the value of properties.) After that meeting, a notice is sent with an adjustment, if any. If you disagree with those findings, you can usually appeal to a court for a final judgment as to the amount of the assessment.

Real Deal

If you believe your assessment is too high, appeal it.

Appraisal theory is the tool you will use to contest your assessment. Complaining about high taxes generally or government waste is not going to persuade anyone to reduce your assessment. Do your homework and present your findings calmly. The tax assessor office is often at a disadvantage, owing to the volume of work they have to do. They have to assign an assessed value to every nongovernment-owned property within their jurisdiction. The assessor may have made an error or overlooked information favorable to you purely out of the size of the task.

Other Problems to Solve

If you own real estate long enough, you will eventually run into some interesting situations. David has owned buildings where there were rumors that tenants were trying to organize a rent strike. At another building, a woman drove her car into the living room of one of the units. David's properties have been invaded by everything from skunks to squirrels. He has seen insect infestations by everything from ladybugs to critters he has never heard of and can't remember.

Before long, you will have your own war stories. Just about every problem can be solved cost effectively. Keep an emergency fund. Never panic. Network with other landlords. Whatever may happen to you has probably happened to someone else before.

The Least You Need to Know

- Keep marketing your property to your existing tenants when it is time for a rent increase.
- Big, repositioning rent increases are best handled when the increase takes effect all at once.
- Communicate properly and promptly with tenants about maintenance requests to ensure high customer satisfaction.
- Maintain an emergency fund for handling larger, unanticipated repairs.
- Fight an unfair tax assessment using the appraisal theory.

Part 5

Beyond the Basics

As you build your success investing in real estate, as you gain knowledge and experience, you will want to branch out into other areas.

Once you have perfected your methods of finding, buying, fixing, holding, or selling the property, you can begin to focus on other important issues affecting your real estate investing. This part of the book will take you beyond the basics of investing.

Chapter 18

When to Sell Your Investment Properties

In This Chapter

- Knowing when to sell
- Getting ready to sell
- Selling yourself or using an agent

The time to think about selling your real estate is when you buy it. Even if it was your intention to own the property for the long-term, you should still have an exit strategy for getting out. You need this exit strategy just in case a need to get out should arise unexpectedly.

Remember that motivated seller you found who enabled you to get such a great deal? That individual did not have a proper exit strategy. This chapter discusses the timing and strategies for selling your property.

Planning the sale of your property makes sense. Rather than sell under pressure, it is always better to plan the sale, and methodically offer your investment properties to others under the best terms for you.

Not All Properties Should Be Held Forever

Earlier in this book, you learned various techniques of buying property and then selling it quickly. Flipping properties is one strategy that real estate investors use to make money. When flipping, a quick sale is part of the plan.

Properties purchased to be held for speculative price increases (raw land, building lots, etc.) are sold when their value has significantly increased. Properties purchased for rental income can also be sold for profit.

Knowing When It Is Time to Sell

There are many reasons you might want to sell your real estate. Despite all the reasons, they could be summarized as:

- You want your money out of the property.
- You no longer want the responsibility of owning the property.

Only you can decide when it is time to sell properties that you have acquired. It is usually difficult for a real estate investor to sacrifice their cash cows. Properties that have become regular sources of income each month aren't easy to sell.

Some of the sure-tell signs that you should probably sell your investment property are …

- You do not enjoy owning the property any longer.
- You are becoming more lax in maintaining the property.
- The neighborhood is deteriorating.
- Major repairs will be needed soon, and you do not have the desire to oversee those repairs being made.
- Managing the building is just taking too much time.
- You do not want to answer the phone because it might be another call from a tenant.

Real Deal

Most investment properties purchased to produce rent become more profitable the longer you hold them.

Selling an investment property takes much preparation. The best time to sell is when you are ready to sell, not when you are forced to sell.

Timing is everything when it comes to selling real estate. You want to sell when your local economy is strong. You want to sell your investment properties in a seller's market.

Consider, too, that there may be solutions to your problems without needing to sell the property. For example, if managing the tenants and the property has become an issue, consider hiring a property manager. By retaining professional property management, you might be able to stop a worsening situation, eliminating your frustrations. It may be a good interim step, and give you some time to decide whether you want to or should sell the property.

Another alternative to consider if you need the money is refinancing the property. You can often pull cash out of a property with refinancing. This might solve the problem, and when done, may be a better alternative than selling. If you still own the property, and if the cash flow covers the loan and expenses, that property can easily help you buy your next investment. You will learn more about refinancing strategies in Chapter 22.

When You Have Made Your Money

One of the best justifications for selling any investment property is that you have made your money. Perhaps you used your newly developed vision for value and spotted an opportunity. You bought the property, made major changes and improvements, and repositioned the building, or even changed its use. The rent commanded by the property and the cash flow are similarly higher today, reflecting the changes you have made. What happens now?

Moving into the future, you will probably be only passing along small, cost of living rent adjustments. The days of passing along huge repositioning rent increases are gone. In other words, you have made your money. You have already done everything possible to squeeze value into this deal. The future looks bright and your cash flow is likely to continue.

This seemingly happy situation may have an unanticipated downside—you could get bored. Once you get bit by the real estate bug, you may want to go out and do deals like this again and again. While the cash flow provided by the equity in the property you have now is nice, by harvesting that equity and again employing your vision, you might be able to increase that cash flow even more in the next deal.

When Your Goals Change

Sometimes, your investment goals will change. One investor bought a series of single-family homes. They were what would be best described as starter homes. Each one produced positive cash flow. However, they were scattered around a two county area. He decided that he was taking too much time traveling between properties. It was costing too much and taking too long to drive to each of the properties as needed.

He opted to begin investing in multifamily units. It took nearly three years, but he sold all of his single-family investment properties, and used the cash he received to buy multifamily properties. He now owns more rental units, but at fewer locations. Clearly, his investment goals changed, and it made sense to sell those properties that did not fit in his long-range plans.

You may find your investment goals changing in different phases of your investing career. Residential investment properties can provide great cash flow with reasonable risk. However, they are more management intensive. One day, you may want to scale back your management responsibilities and acquire commercial real estate that is more management friendly, such as a single-tenant retail store. You can learn more about commercial real estate in Chapter 23.

When There Is a New Deal You Just Can't Pass Up

Sometimes, there are new deals that you believe you must buy. The only way to do it is to sell other properties so you can get involved in the new deal. This obviously makes sense.

For example, you might have the opportunity to develop several larger buildings, returning them to vital use in a downtown area. You are excited about rehabbing, designing, remodeling, and bringing them back to life. However, you would have no time to manage your other investment properties, or you might need the equity in them to do this new deal. These would be good reasons to sell those properties.

Author's Advice

There is never a better time than now to rid yourself of a negative cash-flow property.

When Buying Was a Mistake

Sometimes, it is best to admit you have made a mistake, and get yourself out of the situation. Unfortunately, not every investment property is profitable. If you can't make money with the property, or if it is just plain driving you nuts, it is always time to sell it.

Getting Your Property Ready For Sale

Remember that great deal you got from that motivated seller? You want to make sure that you never join the ranks of the motivated seller yourself. That means that there is only one way to own property, and that is to own the property in "for sale" condition all the time.

You never know what may happen. You may be the one with the illness or the job transfer and suddenly and unexpectedly, you need to sell your property. Or more fortunately, perhaps the deal of a lifetime comes along and you need to sell an existing property quickly to seize this new opportunity. Be prepared. Keep your property in an excellent state of repair so you can sell on a moment's notice.

Properties age slowly. The changes might be so subtle that you miss the slow decline that will inevitably occur with all of your properties. David has met many long-term owners who were proud of the run-down properties they owned!

Sometimes it is helpful to have a trusted friend in the business or an experienced real estate agent to periodically take a fresh look at your property and critique its readiness for resale. You may be surprised by their comments.

As you plan to sell your investment property, consider the costs associated with disposing of the property. They include …

- **Repair expenses.** As you get the property ready, you need to think about what repairs might be necessary to attract the right kind of buyer. For example, if you are selling a single-family rental home and you believe you might command the highest price through a sale to an owner-occupant, you might complete a different set of repairs and improvements than if you were intending to sell the home to another investor.

- **Closing costs.** Determine what closing costs must be paid. Minimally, you will need to transfer any security deposits to the new owner. There may also be a substantial transfer tax in your area. You may have to pay for title insurance.

- **Sales commission.** If you list the property with a real estate agent, you need to pay the sales commission (usually 6 to 7 percent of the selling price).

If your property is occupied by tenants, it is always a bit more difficult to sell. The tenants must be notified prior to any showings to prospective buyers. Tenants aren't always the neatest people. Their sloppiness may make the property less appealing to a potential buyer. Nor may your tenant be cooperative if the sale of the dwelling might force him or her to move.

Nonetheless, it is probably a mistake to wait until the property is empty before selling. Empty rooms look smaller and reveal every flaw. Vacant homes attract vandalism. Litter and free newspapers will accumulate on the property. In the meantime, your cash flow goes down and it may take longer to sell than you thought. If your tenant is a slob that who inhibit a sale, then get rid of the tenant, but don't leave the unit vacant.

Buyer Beware

Never obligate yourself to notify a tenant to vacate before a sale until the buyer has removed all contingencies from the purchase contract. Otherwise, if the deal falls apart, you could be left with no deal and no tenant.

If you do have a tenant and you are thinking about selling, allow the lease to become a month-to-month tenancy so that you will have the most options. For example, if you are selling a single-family rental home, and you are selling to another investor, your buyer will already have a tenant. If you are selling to an owner-occupant, you can always offer to take it on yourself to notify the tenant and deliver an unoccupied home by closing.

When you prepare to sell, you need to do some of the same homework as when you were buying. You should perform a rental survey to make sure the rents you are charging are as high as they could be. Even if you do not want to disturb your tenants with a rent increase, or if they are in a lease and you can't pass along an increase right now, you still need to be able to show prospective buyers meaningful data about market rents. That way, your claim about projected rents will not just be the same empty promise that every other seller is making.

Selling It Yourself or Retaining an Agent

One of the selling decisions you must make is whether to sell the property yourself, or list it with an agent. The largest portion of your sale transaction costs will be the agent's commission. There may be a temptation to try to save this expense by selling the property yourself. However, if you save the commission at the expense of a substantially reduced sale price, or if there is no sale at all, then such a decision would be a poor one.

When It Is Best to Retain an Agent

Depending on market conditions, selling a piece of real estate may not be easy. Even in a seller's market when properties are moving briskly, a minor pricing mistake could make the agent's commission look like a bargain.

Any intelligent decision about selling requires a review of recent comparable sales. Remember when you were buying, you relied on real estate agents to provide this information or you researched sales through your local property-taxing authority.

The problem with the data from the taxing authority is that the information is often not as timely as the information you would be able to obtain from an agent. The taxing authority gets their information from the register of deeds or other government agency that is responsible for maintaining real estate records. The paperwork processing time involved means that when the taxing authority becomes aware of the sale, the sale is often several months old. There may be an additional delay before the taxing authority updates the information they make available to the public.

Another problem with taxing authority data is that the information is likely to be less complete than information obtained by your agent through the Multiple Listing Service (MLS). The MLS file will include pictures, room sizes, lists of recent improvements, personal property included in the sale, the number of days on the market, and the listing price as well as the selling price. The taxing authority will provide only a fraction of this data.

It may be possible to obtain information directly from the register of deeds or equivalent government agency. However, these agencies are typically maintaining records for an entire county. They aren't usually set up to make meaningful reports available to the public. If you knew about the sale of a particular property, the register of deeds would be able to give you the details. If you wanted to know about all the recent sales in a particular area, this agency probably would not be able to help.

In contrast, the Multiple Listing Service available to most real estate agents has up-to-the-minute accurate sales data, which is more complete than most other data available. Further, this computerized database can be searched in sophisticated ways to provide the best information. For example, you can search only three-bedroom, one and a half bath dwellings with a one-car garage that sold in a ten-block radius in the last six months.

The two sources of data may be summarized by saying the taxing authority will have more comprehensive data because they will have a record of every sale. But the data is less accessible and not as complete. MLS will have more recent, more readily accessible, complete data, but the data isn't comprehensive. Despite the limitations of MLS, this data is by far more valuable.

Herein lies the quandary for the property seller. In a brisk seller's market, it may seem like an agent is unnecessary. However, one of the characteristics of a seller's market is that properties are appreciating rapidly. Without access to MLS, the seller is making a pricing decision without having the best available information. It would be easy for a seller acting alone to make a pricing mistake that would exceed the cost of a real estate commission.

Think of it this way. What are the techniques that you use to find a bargain? Isn't one of them having superior market information? Think carefully before you become someone else's property bargain.

A compelling argument will always be able to be made for using a real estate agent. In a brisk seller's market, you need the agent for accurate pricing. In a buyer's market, you need the agent to maximize your property's exposure to the market.

If you are determined to proceed without an agent, one alternative to consider is obtaining an appraisal on your property. The appraisal won't be free, but you will avoid a costly pricing mistake. Most appraisers have access to MLS and rely heavily on it. The appraisal you obtain will be a strong argument in your favor if you price your property according to the appraised value. The appraiser's opinion of value is more relevant than any listing agent's opinion.

Author's Advice

One way to get free valuation help is to invite various real estate agents to perform a market analysis of your property under the guise of giving one of these agents a listing. With several free value opinions in hand, you then sell the property yourself. This strategy goes by several names, but the most accurate one is called stealing.

There are other benefits attributable to a good agent beyond good sales data, accurate pricing, and market exposure. A good agent should serve as your negotiating go-between. The agent owes his or her first loyalties to you and should do everything in their power to obtain the highest possible price for you.

Good agents are used to prequalifying buyers to make sure no one's time is wasted on buyers who can't close. The agent should be able to assist in having proper contracts filled out. Once an offer is accepted, the agent will be able to assist the buyer in obtaining financing and will help in the other details of closing a real estate transaction, including ordering title insurance.

It's nice to have an agent handle any inspections required as a part of the contract. The owner is better served by not attending any of these inspections. With the owner present, it's far too easy for a buyer to put the seller on the spot with every minor defect that may be discovered.

As each torn screen, drippy faucet, or loose doorknob is found, it's so simple for the buyer to say, "would you mind taking care of that?" It is difficult to say no in this situation. However, if the seller isn't there, then the buyer has no choice but to compile a list of needed repairs. The agent should be challenging the buyer, asking whether the buyer wants to erect a potential stumbling block to a deal over such minor repairs.

Sometimes negotiations can be contentious. Without an agent involved, not only may there be no sale, there might be murder instead! Everyone in the real estate business thinks they are a great negotiator. Some of these people are wrong. One thing you know for sure is every successful agent is, in fact, a good negotiator or they would not be successful.

A good agent is well-connected in the real estate industry. The agent may be able to obtain title insurance for less than it would cost you to get it on your own. Your agent can help with many other things as well; for example, he or she might have a lead on a handyman who can help you with a repair.

Many agents engage in direct-mail campaigns with their listings. Practically speaking, this approach is probably not available to the seller trying to market a property alone.

The Pitfalls of Selling Your Property Yourself

There is really only one good reason for selling your property yourself, and that is to save the expense of a real estate commission. A real estate commission is the largest portion of the transaction cost associated with selling, so it is understandable that an investor would want to save this fee if possible.

Because the decision to sell yourself is a decision driven by the economics, this section deals mostly with the additional costs you will incur by trying to sell on your own. Some of the costs are obvious. You will have to pay for your own advertising and any signs. There may be some minor stationary costs associated with developing and mailing, faxing, or e-mailing pertinent information to interested buyers.

You may have the added cost of an appraisal if you seek this help in making a pricing decision. You will certainly need to retain a real estate attorney to make sure that contracts and closing documents are prepared properly.

You will also incur the added cost of your time. You will be the one meeting with buyers and holding open houses. Be sure to prequalify potential buyers before scheduling a showing, or you will waste your time showing your property to individuals with no hope of ever being able to close.

Good qualifying questions would include whether the potential buyer owns any investment real estate already. At some point, you need to inquire if the prospect has sufficient funds available for a down payment. This awkward question can be softened by asking, "would you feel comfortable committing $XXX,XXX to a real estate transaction right now?"

Selling your investment properties is an important part of your overall real estate investing strategy. There are times when selling makes sense, for any number of reasons. Never reject the notion of selling any property you own. Always consider the possibilities of selling, and what it could do for you.

The Least You Need to Know

- Plan an exit strategy when you buy and know when it is time to sell.
- Always be ready to sell so that you can maximize your profit and meet or exceed your real estate investing goals.
- A real estate agent can help avoid a costly pricing mistake and enable the widest exposure reasonably possible to sell your property.
- If you forgo using an agent when you sell, make sure your property is still priced accurately.

Chapter 19

Going to the Next Level

In This Chapter

- Learn how to move up from beginner status
- Becoming smarter with your investments
- Avoiding costly errors
- Building your cash flow
- Developing a niche as a real estate investor

As a real estate investor, the sky is the limit. You can purchase as many investment properties as you can find and you can afford. With ever-growing experience, your deals will make more sense. You know exactly what kind of real estate investment to make, and what to avoid.

You are probably still a part-time real estate investor, but you are finding that your investments are taking more of your time. That is bound to happen—getting to the next level is the question. The answers are in this chapter.

Setting Goals

Before you can decide what the next level is, you need to stop and figure out where you are. Probably by this point, you have purchased several properties. Maybe they were flips, or buy and holds for cash flow, or a combination of both investment types. Congratulations on your deals, but it's time to make an assessment of where you are, and where you plan to go.

The best tool is paper and pencil. Get away from the computer, the television, and find a quiet place to think and write down your thoughts. Ask yourself the following:

- How many properties have you acquired?
- How much cash do you have in the bank?
- What has been your degree of success?
- Are you enjoying the entire experience of real estate investing?
- What are your goals for the next year, the following year, and the third year?
- What do you want to be doing five years from now?
- What do you want to be doing ten years from now?

Author's Advice

A real estate investor without a written business plan has no plan to be successful.

At first, this might seem like a foolish exercise. It isn't. This is the beginning of the development of your own business plan. By forcing yourself to write your thoughts on paper, you develop a clear direction and objective.

Start thinking about where you want to go. Some investors want to make a specific amount, and save their money. Others want to invest in properties for the long term, planning to pass them on to their heirs. Still others invest for retirement, planning to sell properties at their retirement age and live off the proceeds. There is nothing wrong with any of these plans. The important thing is to develop a plan, and move forward based on that plan.

Suppose you have acquired a few cash flow rental properties. When you first bought them, they required additional investment as repairs and improvements were made. Today they provide a steady income stream. If your average cash flow is $150 per unit per month, you can begin to outline how many more investment properties you need to acquire to reach your income goals. For example, if you desire cash flow of $5,000 per month and your average cash flow is $150 per unit per month, then you need to acquire about 33 units to achieve this goal. Practically, as your investments mature, cash flow will increase and you may not need 33 units to realize this income goal.

Only you know if these goals are realistic. If your goals seem out of reach, break down the task to its smallest steps. Continuing the same example, if acquiring a total of 33 rental units seems daunting, focus just on acquiring the next property. You could even further break down this task to the individual actions required to make the next deal. For example, "this week I am going to find out who owns that run-down duplex and call them and see if they want to sell" or, "I am going to have lunch with that agent who found that last deal for me to see if she has any more great opportunities like that for me."

By now, you should have developed an investment strategy that works for you. You should be able to extrapolate the effort required to achieve your goals. You ought to be capable of breaking down this effort into a weekly or even daily action plan. As you move forward and gain experience, you will gain momentum. The first deal is always the hardest. Subsequent deals will get easier. They will be easier to find, easier to finance, and easier to fix up or reposition.

Until you reduce your goals to writing, and identify what needs done to reach those goals, you can't see where you are going. When your plan and goals are refined, it's time to launch them.

A written business plan is a powerful tool for any real estate investor. Most err by not creating one. Instead they keep such thoughts in their head. This is neither wise nor proper.

How Many Properties Are Enough?

No one except you can decide how many properties you should buy. You know the work it takes to invest. By now, you realize that much of the work is finding the property and making the deal. Once that is over, it becomes routine to close the properties.

You realize that you can do this over and over, as often or as little as you want. But as you ponder this, you have to question yourself.

"Why don't I do this again?"

When you stop and think about it, there is no reason not to continue investing in real estate. You may need to slow down here and there, only because of other commitments or cash flow issues (for example, you can't purchase a particular property because the down payment and closing costs are more than you have available. Your extra cash was just used for repairs or another purchase).

Because you have successfully purchased several properties and are receiving monthly cash flow from your tenants, you probably have the time to purchase several more properties. Only you can determine how far you want to go with your real estate investing. How many properties you acquire is ultimately a personal decision.

The real goal isn't to acquire an unlimited number of properties. Rather, you only want to buy profitable properties.

How Much Cash Flow Is Enough?

One old adage is you can never have too much money. As a real estate investor, you can never have too much cash flow. If you have six rental units, and each produces $200 per month positive cash flow, it only makes sense to acquire more rental units.

When setting goals, instead of establishing a number of rental units as your objective, think in terms of cash flow. Thinking strictly in terms of the number of rental units you need to acquire will tend to blind you to other opportunities. Instead, you will think mainly in terms of duplicating the same kind of deals that you have already completed successfully. While sticking to a proven strategy can be prudent, you may fail to discover better prospects.

You can also increase cash flow in other ways. You don't always need to acquire more property to increase your cash flow. You could …

- Increase rents.
- Decrease expenses.
- Change your real estate investment strategies.

Increasing the rent is a fast way to improve your monthly cash flow. Any increase must remain within what the market will bear or your property will sit vacant.

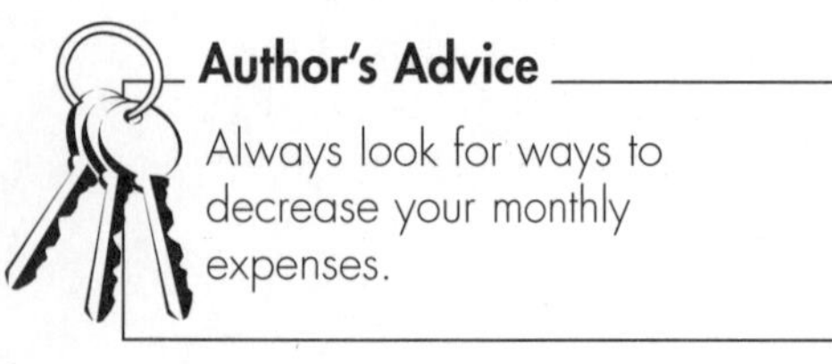

Decreasing expenses is always a good idea. If you can contract for a cheaper waste removal service, or purchase lower cost property insurance, your cash flow can increase. As you learned earlier, the best way to decrease expenses is to eliminate expense items entirely, perhaps by delegating them to your tenants, as you would by billing back utility charges.

Changing your real estate investing strategies could vastly improve your cash flow. For example, suppose you have never flipped a property. Rather, all of your properties have been bought with the idea of buying and holding for cash flow. Adding just one or two flips over the next year could have a positive influence on your cash flow.

Moving from single-family residences to multifamily residences can also have a positive effect on your monthly cash flow. Often, your cash flow can move to a higher percentage for each owned unit with multifamily units.

If your goal is to have a $5,000 a month positive cash flow from your real estate investments, then you need to have made enough investments to achieve that amount of income. Of course, this type of income is available from one property (for example, see Chapter 23 for more information about investing in commercial properties).

Once you have decided how much positive cash flow you need each month, you can set a plan into motion that will assure your desired cash flow.

Getting Help

One often-experienced symptom of growth is growing pains. You already observed the term "real estate investor" is a misnomer. The better description would be to say the investor is an entrepreneur engaged in the real estate business. And being in your own business can be time-consuming.

You may have started out enjoying the pride of ownership associated with maintaining your investment properties, but the day may come when that which was a delight becomes drudgery. It could be the repetitive nature of the work or the volume of work as you acquire more properties, but either way, owning real estate can become a chore. That's when you know it is time to bring in some help.

A good *on-site manager* can be like the cavalry riding in to your rescue. This individual can assist with some of the more mundane property management duties. The key is to know where to find them and to know how they can help you.

def•i•ni•tion

On-site managers may also be called apartment managers or caretakers. Property managers are your eyes and ears, and can often keep your property operating smoothly. From noticing problems that need corrected to watching out for questionable actions of tenants, the on-site manager can make the difference between a profitable property or one that is nothing but an ongoing headache.

Finding Good On-Site Managers

Here's a little secret about finding a great on-site manager. He or she may already be living in your building! And maybe they can help put out the fire! You can probably imagine the type. Their apartment is always immaculate and their rent is always paid on time. They may be a little fussy. If anything is wrong at your property, they are usually the first one to call you.

These kinds of individuals clearly take pride in their homes, and that's just what you want in helping run your property. The best caretakers will also be gregarious, outgoing, and enjoy people.

Of course, not every apartment building has one of these potential manager candidates already living there. In that case, you can work your network of landlords and other contacts to try to find a manager. As you inquire with your peers about potential caretaker candidates, be sure to ask about the going rate for managers in your area.

Think out of the box and expand your network. Stop at the local coffee shop or restaurant closest to your building and chat with the staff. Let them know you're looking for some help. Inquire at local churches for candidates.

If your network ultimately does not produce a manager, you can always advertise. Regardless of how you find your candidate, check them out carefully. You don't want to turn over a set of building keys to a criminal.

Apply all your usual rental criteria in evaluating any manager prospect. Make sure your candidate has no record of any kind of theft, drug use, or violent crime. When you perform the landlord verification, tell the landlord that you are contemplating hiring the individual as an apartment manager and ask if the owner would recommend them. Ask specifically about the applicant's housekeeping.

When hiring a manager, complete a home visit. A home visit is the best way to discern how well the applicants maintain their own home and how well they will likely maintain your building.

If you are going to rely on your manager to help with repairs, during the home visit you can ask to see any work they may have done around their own home. Ask to see their tools. Don't accept the claim that they can borrow any needed tools. Individuals experienced at repairs usually have their own equipment.

On-Site Manager Duties

Well-trained, motivated, conscientious on-site managers can be the key to trouble-free property management. A manager should be able to maintain common hallways and basements and care for the lawn and remove snow from sidewalks.

Managers should be available to help with showings. Managers with a cellular phone can be fielding rental calls even when they're not home.

A skilled caretaker can also help with minor repairs. Painting, cleaning, drywall repair, minor electrical work, and light plumbing are fair game for a manager.

Working With Your On-Site Manager

Housing provided as a contingency of employment isn't subject to income tax withholding. Therefore, a good way to compensate a manager is by allowing a rent discount for services.

Develop a simple written job description for your manager. Show them the location of any water and gas shut-offs. Educate them about fair housing if they are going to participate in leasing. Make sure that your caretaker has a clear understanding of your expectations.

Once the manager understands what is expected, keep an eye on them, particularly a new manager. Warn a new caretaker that you may have them "shopped," which is to say that you might ask a friend to call them posing as a rental prospect.

Don't get in the business of providing a caretaker with many tools. They should have their own. The ones you provide are likely to get lost or broken.

If you have a caretaker, your state may view this individual as your employee. Therefore, you should have a workmen's compensation insurance policy in the event of an injury.

Finding Your Niche

As you have learned from reading this book, there are many different niches for you to gravitate toward and become active as an investor. The different niches can be loosely grouped two ways, by location or by property type.

If your niche is defined by location, then you will become an expert within that location. It does not matter what kind of property is involved, you know what it should rent for, how much the properties are selling for, and what is for sale. This kind of investor will need to draw a smaller investment circle. It would be impossible to have the depth of knowledge required for this strategy over a wide geographical area.

Some investors limit themselves to a radius of just a few miles or even just a few blocks. This strategy has a number of advantages. This plan allows you to be centralized. Obviously, there is less travel time, but there are other benefits as well.

For example, if you have multiple properties in proximity to one another and you are responsible for lawn care, you could use just one set of equipment to service every building. If you owned properties that were each 30 minutes away in all different directions, you may find yourself relying on individual on-site managers, all of whom will need a separate set of equipment. The same contractors and service people will also be able to help you if your properties are close together.

The second kind of niche is to specialize in one kind of property. You may buy only single-family rental homes, or perhaps you may find yourself one day buying only gasoline stations. This niche may enable you to combine both strategies. For example, if your niche is to buy only single-family rental homes, there are enough of these that you could focus on buying within only a single neighborhood. However, the more unique and specialized your niche properties are, the more likely that you will have to expand geographically.

Part of finding and working a niche is that it should become enjoyable work for you. Yes, it is still work to be an active real estate investor, but investing in the types of properties that work best for you makes the most sense.

One niche investor was a real estate agent for years. After nearly 25 years of sitting in open houses on weekends, answering phone calls until midnight, and chasing buyers and sellers, he had enough. Although he maintained his license, he left what he considered the rat race and became a full-time investor.

He developed a niche where he bought only the worst properties he could find. From burnouts to the dilapidated, he bought the worst of the worst. With an old pickup truck for his tools and building supplies, this former real estate agent drives to his just acquired properties. Wearing his blue-bib coveralls, he happily works away, sawing wood, rebuilding kitchens, and bringing dead properties back to life.

He buys properties for $2,000 or less. Many of the properties were abandoned by their owners and confiscated for unpaid taxes. Within a month or so, they are like new. He transforms them from near death to the best-looking properties on the block. He sells them for 40 times what he paid for them. After deducting his expenses, he is making about $20,000 a month.

What a niche! It works well for him (and pays well, too). He'd rather be covered in sawdust and pounding nails than selling real estate. Not everyone is geared for this lifestyle. But he enjoys taking off weekends, and spending that time with his grandchildren.

Real Deal

A real estate niche is what you make it. Specializing in specific property types increases your knowledge and profitability.

Find your niche as a real estate investor, and work it for all that it is worth. You will be rewarded both financially and emotionally.

Staying in Your Investment Circle

By staying within your investment circle, you are working a geographical niche. You should consider all different property types within your area. By staying in familiar territory, you will be better equipped to service your properties and you will be better able to compete for the best deals. You are more likely to spot the best deals as they come available for sale, or even before they become available for sale. This is an excellent way to begin.

Growing Beyond Your Investment Circle

As you concentrate within your investment circle, you may find yourself becoming an expert in a particular property type. For example, you may have begun with a few rental houses. As you expanded, you traded some of your homes into an eight-unit apartment building.

Things have gone so well with the eight-family building that you would like to trade your remaining smaller properties for even larger apartment buildings. You will find that twelve-unit and sixteen-unit and larger apartment buildings aren't congregated on every block. You will have to go further afield to find them. You may have to expand your investment circle or go outside of it in order to continue your investing activities.

Becoming a Smarter Investor

As a person involved in real estate investing, you need to continue to learn about real estate law, investing, and financing techniques. Additional knowledge is always good.

Keep yourself in the learning loop. Attend seminars, read books, subscribe to financial magazines. Never stop acquiring additional knowledge.

The same way that you will gravitate toward one particular niche over time, you may discover that you have different investing strengths. This may help you further define your niche. For example, if you get bored with the day-to-day details of property management, but you delight in the process of fixing up a run-down building, these characteristics should direct your path.

Playing to Your Strengths

We all have special skills and things we like to do, as well as things we'd prefer not to do. The sooner you recognize your strengths, you should focus on them and use them to your best advantage.

For example, you might enjoy negotiating. Haggling over price and terms is a natural talent for you. It is part of what you describe as the game. There is nothing wrong with this. You believe, because of your ability to make offers and close deals with favorable terms, this is your main strength. Use it. Spend your time acquiring properties. If that is what you have discovered you do best, then do it.

Delegating Your Weaknesses

It's hard to admit that you aren't good at something, or fall down on the job here or there. The sooner you do, the better off you will be.

For example, let's assume that you hate bookkeeping. For whatever reason, keeping track of expenses and receipts is your least favorite thing to do. You would rather sit in a dentist's chair and get a root canal than work on your books.

The answer is simple. Admit your shortfall, and find a solution. In this example, the solution might be as close as a telephone call away. From scanning advertisements, you find someone offering services as a bookkeeper. They operate a small home-based business. You negotiate a monthly fee, and turn all the unpleasant work over to someone else. Now your bills are paid on time, and rent is collected as agreed (and if not, your bookkeeper sends the collection notices).

Your life as a real estate investor has become easier. With this help, you are able to spend more time searching for additional properties to acquire. It only makes sense to delegate such chores to others.

Avoiding Mistakes

While being an active real estate investor, it is easy to make mistakes. The mistakes may be as small as the wrong approach to the right deal or as large as getting involved in the wrong deal. One error too many, and you could be down and out of the real estate business.

Buying the wrong building could become a huge and costly problem. Failing to follow the basics, including a thorough title search, or maintaining proper insurance coverage, could mark the end of your real estate investing career.

Learn from some great American corporations to avoid costly errors. Stick to what you know how to do best. Look at AT&T. In the 1980s and 1990s, AT&T jumped into the personal computer business. The launch unveiled new products and gained much fanfare, but they never made it. AT&T put plenty of money behind the venture, but it was just not their core business. Smaller, passionate companies outsold and outmaneuvered AT&T, one of America's largest corporations. A kid in Texas, Michael Dell, easily passed AT&T in the computer business. How could a kid outperform a giant corporation?

Railroad companies can't run airlines, even though they have the experience in moving people. Bank corporations do not get into the oil refinery business. Food companies can't sell electronics … the list goes on.

Closer to home, you should think hard about what could become the wrong deal for you. For instance, hotels involve real estate, but hotels aren't real estate investments. Operating a hotel is a unique business. If you have training or experience in the hospitality industry, then fine. If not, stick to what you know. The same thinking applies to resorts and even seasonal rentals. Many investors have made the mistake of getting into a new business thinking they were experts because the venture involved real estate. Don't let this be you.

Buyer Beware

Avoid getting involved with businesses that you don't understand or aren't comfortable with. Stick with what you know, and what you do well.

The Least You Need to Know

- Establish goals for your real estate investing because before you can decide what the next level is, you need to stop and figure out where you are.
- Until you reduce your investment goals to writing, and identify what needs to be done to reach those goals, you can't see where you are going.
- Find a real estate investment niche and work it.
- Avoid costly mistakes by sticking with what works for you and what you know and understand.

Chapter 20

Becoming a Full-Time Investor

In This Chapter

- Learn about switching from employee to self-employed
- Understand the self-employment tax
- Health insurance and other benefits
- Other careers in real estate
- The importance of establishing a budget

It is the dream of many real estate investors—leave your job and become a full-time investor. It can be done, and you will learn how in this chapter.

The good news is the path to full-time investing is well worn. Many have preceded you and blazed a trail. Like any journey, you need to make certain provisions to be certain of reaching your destination.

There are many things to consider before handing in your notice to your boss. There is nothing wrong with dreaming about leaving your job to work full-time as an investor. Your dream can soon become a reality.

Interim Steps to Going It Alone

Moving from being someone's employee to becoming self-employed is a big step. Moving from the security of a job with weekly wages earned and benefits provided, to the lonely, scary ranks of the self-employed is a leap into a different world.

As an employee, you have that weekly paycheck. You can count on it, month after month. As long as you show up on time and do your work, the paychecks keep coming.

Suddenly need hospitalization? You reach into your wallet and pull out an identification card. The insurance, provided by your employer, includes payment for all of your services, except perhaps a few dollars for a co-payment.

You receive paid holidays, some sick leave, and a couple weeks of paid vacation. Maybe you even get some life insurance and disability insurance coverage.

Are you sure you want to give all that up for a career as a real estate investor? Your job sounds almost too good to give up, especially when you look at your salary and benefits.

Before making the leap to self-employment, you should know what it will cost to duplicate or replace the benefits that you have now. The greatest cost will be health insurance. Tips on obtaining insurance appear later in this chapter.

One benefit often missed by novices contemplating self-employment is the employer's contribution to payroll taxes. Employees pay 7.65% of their gross wages in Social Security and Medicare taxes.

What you may not have known is that your employer also contributes 7.65% toward these taxes. Together, employer and employee pay 15.3% of the employee's gross wages in Social Security and Medicare taxes. The self-employed person pays the entire 15.3% tax on his or her own.

The following is a summary of costs you should consider:

- Self-employment tax (currently 15.3%)
- Health Insurance
- Disability Insurance
- Unemployment Insurance
- Workers' Compensation Insurance
- Time off (holidays and vacations)

All of these items cost money. Your employer has been paying for them. Now it will be you.

> **Real Deal**
>
> Before deciding to make the leap, consider the true cost of replacing your current wages and benefits.

As you plan to move to the ranks of the self-employed, start gathering information. Find out what it will cost for own health insurance, dental care, and other coverage such as disability insurance.

You should also build a war chest of cash—for up to six months. This should be liquid cash—in a savings account or some other easy-to-withdraw reserve. This is more important for the real estate investor working flips—as you could go longer periods before finding and closing your next deals. For real estate investors with established positive cash flow from multiple rental units, a lower cash reserve may work.

After assessing your true requirements for going full-time, you may discover the goal is more distant than anticipated. Don't become frustrated. There are a number of interim steps available to help bridge the gap between where you are now and where you need to be to go full-time.

Become a Property Manager

A property manager maintains a client's property in order to produce the highest possible financial return over the longest time. They are responsible for protecting the owner's investment. Managed commercial properties are likely to be large office buildings and shopping centers. Residential properties might be apartment buildings, apartment developments, condominiums, or groups of homes owned by a single investor.

Becoming a property manager is a strategy that could be played out either as a career change or as an interim step toward full-time investing. You could simply go to work for an existing property management company. True, this isn't full-time investing, but this step would allow you to get further experience and connections in the real estate industry while you add to your own portfolio.

Another way to employ this strategy is to take on property management clients yourself, essentially becoming your own property management company. This isn't as complicated as it sounds. You already are a property management company, by virtue of managing your own real estate. You can extend your skills and talents to other investors who may be struggling.

Finding property management clients isn't complex either. Remember those dilapidated buildings you called on, hoping to buy them? Not every one of those owners was willing to sell, were they? Say hello to your new property management client!

Acquiring real estate is capital intensive. Building a portfolio of real estate with sufficient cash flow to enable you to become a full-time real estate investor could take years. However, it may be possible for you to attain a stable of property management clients in order to speed you toward your goals.

Another benefit to property management is that you will be perfectly positioned to buy these properties when the owner decides to sell.

Become a Real Estate Agent

Some investors are good at sniffing out deals. So good, in fact, that they can sniff out more deals than they can ever hope to buy for themselves. Have you already been referring your surplus deals to your friends? It may be time for you to become a real estate agent.

Each state has their own requirements for licensure, but after completing the required education and passing the examination, you are ready to work as a real estate agent.

A job as a real estate agent is one of the easiest jobs in the world to get. Assuming you have your license, you will probably even get solicitations in the mail from different agencies encouraging you to work for them. The reason this is so is that as an agent, you will be working on 100 percent commission.

As an agent, be prepared to work long and irregular hours for a sporadic income. You can almost be assured that as a newly licensed agent, you will work many Saturdays and Sundays.

One way to beat the evening and weekend working responsibilities of a residential agent is to specialize in commercial real estate. Logically, you should become an agent specializing in the type of property that fits the niche you have been or would like to be investing in.

Author's Advice

Think about becoming a licensed real estate agent. The benefits of working as an agent could help your real estate investing goals.

Training you to be ready for all the nuances of life as a real estate agent is beyond the scope of this book. The main point is that if you have been successful in identifying a steady stream of good real estate deals while working part-time as an investor, you may be able to build your real estate empire faster while earning a living as an agent.

Other Real Estate Career Opportunities

There are other real estate careers you could consider as a bridge from your current employer. You could work for a title company, learning to search courthouse records.

Another possibility is to work as a loan officer for a lender or mortgage broker. Often these are commission-only positions, but might include some benefits.

A great but little-known real estate career opportunity is to be involved in the building trades. Many real estate millionaires started out as electricians, plumbers, or painters. By learning principles of construction and through connections gained at work, some individuals have gone on to acquire huge real estate portfolios, both by buying existing properties and by building new.

Dave knows of one investor who started out as a humble building supervisor for an office building. Today he is a super office building investor and owns an empire of properties.

Some Self-Employment Pitfalls

As you further consider moving into self-employment, consider some the problems you will face:

- No one will buy your equipment, tools, supplies, or other necessities. If you need a new computer, you buy it when you are self-employed. The tools your employer provides will no longer be available. This includes monthly expenses, like telephone, Internet service, cell phone service, etc. It is up to you to purchase everything. You must pay your expenses before you can pay yourself.
- You will need to pay for your health insurances. Besides writing the monthly check, one of your real problems is finding a place to buy it.
- You must make quarterly estimated tax payments. Employees have taxes withheld automatically. The self-employed have to do this on their own. Each month, you must save money to send to the IRS, your state revenue department, and perhaps to a local taxing authority, when quarterly returns are due. Your payments are due in January, April, July, and October.
- If you don't work, you make no money. Without a supervisor, you must be self-disciplined enough to get up every day and get your work done.
- As a self-employed individual, you are responsible for completing multiple tax forms. You must maintain acceptable recordkeeping to comply with tax laws.

- You do not have worker's compensation coverage when you are a self-employed individual. If you are injured on the job, you receive no disability benefits or medical coverage unless you carry personal health insurance.

Self-Employment Tax

> **Real Deal**
>
> You can deduct half of your self-employment tax in figuring your adjusted gross income. Wage earners can't deduct Social Security and Medicare taxes.

As you read earlier, employees contribute 7.65% of their gross income under the present tax code for Social Security and Medicare taxes. The employer also contributes an equal 7.65% of the employee's gross income in payroll taxes. Because the self-employed have no employer, self-employed individuals must pay the entire 15.3% tax on their own.

The tax is computed and reported on IRS Schedule SE (Form 1040).

Isolation

Another issue a self-employed individual faces each workday is isolation. Most self-employed real estate investors work from a home office. This is one of the benefits, but it is also one of the detriments.

Working in isolation is a change. There are no friendly meetings at the water cooler, no one to talk to about Sunday's football scores, and no one to bounce ideas off when you get a sudden brainstorm.

It takes an adjustment. Sure, you can work in your pajamas, and you can get coffee whenever you want. That independence is the lure of the self-employment dreams that are tugging at your heartstrings. But be prepared for the cold, harsh reality of working alone on your own.

Isolation isn't only a matter of inconvenience in working conditions. There is a real danger of losing touch with breaking trends or developments in real estate investing. You should plan on networking with fellow investors, bankers, real estate agents, and others in order to keep a fresh perspective.

Maintaining Health Insurance and Other Benefits

One option available to many employed persons moving into self-employment status is to continue their healthcare coverage under the Consolidated Omnibus Budget

Reconciliation Act, better known as COBRA. This law gives workers and their families who lose their health benefits the right to choose to continue group health benefits provided by their group health plan for limited periods under certain circumstances, such as voluntary job loss.

You are required to pay the entire premium for coverage up to 102 percent of the cost of the plan. Many times, this coverage is less expensive than what you can find on your own.

COBRA requires that group health plans sponsored by employers with 20 or more employees in the prior year offer employees and their families the opportunity for a temporary extension of health coverage. COBRA defines how employees and family members may elect continuation coverage. It also requires employers and the health plans to provide notice of available continued coverage. COBRA may not be your cheapest alternative. Often the plans provided by employer coverage are more extensive, and offers more benefits. You may not need all the extras, and might be able to find less expensive health insurance coverage on your own.

Another way to continue coverage is to find it through your local Chamber of Commerce. Many times, because the Chamber is supported by small local businesses, group health insurance is offered. This source is often less expensive than an individual policy. You might also find reasonably priced insurance from a local insurance agent.

It is often a matter of shopping, and not giving up. Before making the leap into self-employment, get quotes for your insurance coverage.

Author's Advice

You can't afford to be without health insurance. Never allow it to lapse.

You should check with your accountant to determine if you should consider forming a corporation, and then become an employee of your own company. While you will be required to file more tax returns, it is often beneficial for self-employed persons to use this strategy. Often, there are tax savings to gain. Only a competent tax professional can analyze your individual situation. Seek assistance to determine if this is a viable option for you.

Remaining Part-Time

Before making the jump to self-employment, you may want to experiment by going part-time. Although it may seem like you already have one part-time job managing your own real estate, you may want to consider starting part-time, if you are contemplating one of the career-change options. For instance, if you are thinking of becoming a real estate agent or getting involved in property management, these are both career moves that you could try part-time. Many agents have started this way and there are plenty of weekend or evening leasing agent positions available in property management.

Another way to experience self-employment is to take vacation time working in your new self-employed capacity or to arrange a leave of absence from your current position.

Making the Leap

The day you make the decision to leave your employment for the great unknown is a big day for you. You give your notice, work until your last day, clean out your personal property, and officially enter the world of the self-employed. It's scary out there!

Make sure you leave your present employer under positive circumstances. You may need to go back if things don't work out. If you have planned properly, making the switch will not be a leap into the unknown but a confident stride into an already thriving business plan.

The main reasons you should become self-employed are that you can be happier and at least eventually make a lot more money working for yourself than working for someone else.

No boss is holding you back. It's up to you to make your first dollar, or as many of them as you can. And so, now it's up to you—from emptying your trash can to making all the executive decisions.

Establishing a Budget

One of the biggest problems you will face is developing a budget and sticking to it. Too many small business owners overlook this important issue.

Using a simple spreadsheet, identify your ongoing monthly expenses. These include such things as your business telephone lines, Internet service, accounting service, etc.

Also determine what your major expenses are likely to be over the next three years, and plan for them. This does not include real estate you will acquire, but rather items of $500 or more that you need for your business. In a three-year period, you will probably experience at least one hardware and software computer upgrade.

Developing a budget is tricky. Most beginners greatly underestimate the costs of running their own office. Entire expense categories can be omitted. For instance, you should probably budget something for continuing education, seminars, or conferences. What about the travel expenses to attend these conferences? Then there are professional dues, extra phone lines, perhaps a pager for emergencies, auto expenses, office supplies, subscription services, and more.

Review your budget against your actual expenditures. Common accounting software programs can help make these comparisons with just a few simple clicks.

By now, you realize the importance of properly handling money. Budgeting allows you to keep track of what you are spending, and where you are spending it. Becoming self-employed, you will have additional expenses that need to be paid each month, such as health insurance premiums. If you are going to control your expenses, you will need to track them carefully.

Maintaining a Cash Reserve

You must maintain sufficient cash reserves when you are self-employed. Money management is an essential skill. Being able to maintain a cash reserve is important for your survival.

You should have several bank accounts, one for your operational funds. You should also have another account to deposit your quarterly estimated tax payments—the money you need to send to the taxing authorities.

You should have another account—one for your emergency reserve cash. This should have three to six months of your monthly personal expenses (your home mortgage, utilities, food, etc.), as well as your regularly monthly business expenses. It is okay if this account fluctuates from month to month. Always maintain a minimum of three months of funds in your reserve funds.

Buyer Beware

Without a reserve fund, you are living dangerously as a self-employed person.

Your emergency reserve cash does not include additional funds you should set aside in anticipation of needed capital improvements at your properties. If the furnace or the roof looks like they are at the end of their effective life, begin saving now. Remember, sometimes even newer equipment fails unexpectedly.

If it is a matter of passing up a deal versus taking money out of your reserve funds, pass up the deal. This money is your lifeline. Protect it and keep it sacred. It will also allow you to sleep at night. You need this money when nothing goes right—for whatever reason. You can't afford to skip payments insurance or other important expenditures.

Actions to Take Before You Leave Your Job

Before you leave your job, there are several things you need to do. Here is a list:

- Carefully analyze whether you are ready to become self-employed.
- Make plans to continue all necessary insurance coverages.
- Consult with your tax advisor to see if you should operate as a sole proprietor, or if you should form a corporation.
- Comply with all regulatory agencies.
- Establish reserve funds.
- Plan for your departure from your job.
- Develop a budget for your business.

The Least You Need to Know

- You need to earn more than your current salary to break even as a self-employed person.
- Before deciding to make the leap, consider the true cost of replacing your current wages and benefits, because finding suitable benefits might be difficult.
- Self-employment tax must be paid quarterly: April 15, June 15, September 15, and January 15.
- Switching from someone's employee to self-employment takes planning.
- If you are going to control your expenses, you will need to track them carefully, and you will need to keep reserve funds for expenses.

Chapter 21

Real Estate Investing and Taxes

In This Chapter

- Understanding depreciation
- Other available write-offs
- Expensing versus capitalizing
- Section 42 and other government tax credit programs
- Taxes when you sell a property
- Legally minimizing taxes
- Taxation exit strategies

One of the greatest barriers to amassing wealth is the burden imposed by the tax code. Governments need revenue to pay for public infrastructure and public services that benefit nearly everyone. Billing end users is simply not practical, hence the taxing authority of government.

Taxes are a reality of life. The point of this book isn't to argue whether taxes are too low or too high, or fair or unfair. Paying them is our duty as citizens, regardless of how we feel about them. The point of this chapter is to explore opportunities presented by the tax code and to show you how to minimize your tax liability legally and appropriately.

The tax code isn't just about raising revenue. Taxes are additionally imposed to punish the "wrong" behaviors and encourage the "right" ones. For example, a package of cigarettes costs just a few cents to produce. The rest of the purchase price is comprised of taxes paid to various layers of government. Thankfully, the production of real estate is an activity the government wants to encourage and the tax code is written accordingly.

This chapter will explore the basics of real estate taxation. It would be impossible for one chapter of any book to provide everything you will ever need to know about the ever-changing complexities of the Internal Revenue Service Code. For that, you will need an accountant. But this chapter will outline general and specific areas of opportunity in the tax codes that have existed for decades and have been a boon to nearly every real estate investor.

Understanding Depreciation

One basic premise of this book is that if an investor follows the advice presented here, does his or her homework, buys carefully, and maintains the property faithfully, then that property is likely to increase in value. Yet this isn't the view assumed by the writers of the tax code.

The tax laws assume that nothing lasts forever. Things wear out or become so obsolete that they must be discarded. Every product or system has a certain life expectancy. At the expiration of that life expectancy, the item will have to be replaced if a continued benefit is desired.

In many ways, the point of view of the tax code is correct. For example, no matter how careful a property owner may be, nothing can be done to extend the life of a shingled roof beyond a certain period of time. The shingles, despite how high the original quality and no matter how careful the original installation and subsequent maintenance, are still going to be exposed to the vestiges of time. Baked by the sun and tortured by wind and storm, any roof will only last so long. In short, the value of this hypothetical roof is declining with time. In other words, the value is depreciating.

Recognizing that nothing lasts forever, the government has established various schedules of life expectancy for various asset classes, including real estate. Our government has additionally determined various mechanisms for recognizing depreciation. For example, for an asset with a seven-year life, depreciation rules might require the taxpayer to employ either a straight-line depreciation schedule or an accelerated depreciation schedule.

A straight-line schedule would allow the taxpayer to expense an equal seventh of the original cost of the asset every year for seven years. An accelerated schedule would allow the taxpayer to expense more of the original asset costs in the first years of the asset's life, with a lower deduction in the last year's of asset life. Most real estate depreciation deductions are made on a straight-line basis.

Currently, residential rental real estate enjoys a depreciation schedule of 27.5 years computed on a straight-line basis. What this means to you as investor is better described by an example.

Say that you purchased a residential rental property for $100,000 on January 1, 2006. This purchase consisted of two elements, land and improvements to the land. The tax code does not recognize land as a wearing item, and therefore, land isn't depreciable. The rest of the improvements are depreciable however, so a decision must be made about how much of the purchase price should be allocated to improvements and depreciated and how much of the purchase price should be recognized as land.

There is obvious incentive for the investor to declare as much as possible of the purchase as being improvements. This way, the greatest depreciation benefit is gained. However, the division between land and improvements must be grounded in reality, not grounded in greed, if you want to survive IRS scrutiny.

A good rule of thumb for establishing a breakdown between land and improvements is to apply the same percentages of land and improvements found in the property tax assessment to your purchase price.

Alternatively, if you have a recent appraisal that gives a clear indication of an estimated value of the land versus the improvements, you could use that number. The point is to use whatever outside expert opinion that might be available versus relying upon just your own opinion.

Author's Advice

Use an independent third-party expert, such as, a tax assessment or an appraisal to establish the breakdown of the purchase price between land and improvements for computing depreciation.

In this case, in your $100,000 purchase, 15 percent of the most recently available tax assessment for the property was recognized as being the value of the land. Using this information as a guide, you decide to value the land at $15,000 and the improvements at

$85,000. Therefore, you would generate depreciation expense of $3,090.91 each year for up to 27.5 years: $85,000 / 27.5 = $3,090.91.

How does depreciation benefit you? Continuing this same example, if this particular property generated positive cash flow of $4,000 after all expenses, you would otherwise have a tax liability on $4,000 of taxable income were it not for the depreciation expense. Depreciation reduces your taxable income to $909.09 as shown here: $4,000.00 – $3,090.91 = $909.09.

If you spend much time analyzing depreciable lives and depreciation mechanisms (straight-line versus accelerated) for different asset classes in the tax code, you may conclude that these asset lives and depreciation mechanisms are arbitrary. You would be correct in your thinking.

Remember, the government is allowing you to take expense deductions under the assumption the asset is wearing out, declining in value, when in reality, at least with real estate, the asset is increasing in value. While all this may seem like a boon to the investor, remember that what the government arbitrarily gives, it can just as arbitrarily take away.

When you make investment decisions based at least in part on the benefits available to you from the tax code, your equity could be adversely affected if the tax laws making those benefits possible are changed. This has already happened in recent history.

In the early 1980s, the Federal Government changed the depreciable life and the depreciation mechanism for real estate. Previously, real estate was depreciated on a straight-line basis over 30 years. The tax laws ushered in the early 1980s changed the life to 19 years and allowed accelerated depreciation.

Under the new provisions, investors who were writing off one thirtieth of their real estate were now allowed to write off nearly one tenth of any new real estate they bought after the new regulations went into effect. Not surprisingly, the marketplace responded to this incentive by producing tons of investment real estate.

Limited partnerships were formed to take advantage of the available tax write-offs. These limited partnerships were formed by business people adept at marketing shares in real estate ventures, but not necessarily sophisticated about running the real estate itself. However, real estate business acumen was not needed anyway. The chief benefit to many of these partnerships was that the losses that they would incur would provide a tax shelter for high-income, high-taxpaying individuals.

In short, it made some degree of sense to continue to create more developments regardless of the ability of the development to command enough rent to pay expenses. A glut of properties resulted. Then, to add insult to injury, perhaps in recognition of the overstimulation of real estate, the government changed the tax laws again.

Instead of an accelerated 19-year write off, the laws were changed in 1987 to reflect the 27.5-year straight-line depreciation that we know today. Some have blamed these changes for creating the crisis in the savings and loan industry that occurred in the 1980s. One way or another, the savings and loan industry disappeared and many financial institutions that did survive were bloated with REO properties.

The point is that you should pay close attention to any changes in the tax code. One change that is often batted about is eliminating the interest deduction allowed to homeowners. The likelihood of such a provision being passed into law seems remote. However, if it were, homes would become less affordable, perhaps depressing prices. Alternatively, rental housing may become more attractive as home ownership becomes less attractive.

One thing that you learned earlier in this book is that owning your own home can be one kind of real estate investment. However, for income tax reporting purposes, the present tax code does not recognize your home as an investment at all.

Accordingly, you may not deduct expenses associated with operating your home nor may you depreciate any part of your home unless you are using part of your home as a home office. In the past, home office deductions have been an invitation to a tax audit. If you feel like you have a legitimate deduction, you should take it, but be sure to consult with your accountant.

Other Available Write-Offs

Everything that you spend to manage your rental property is a tax-deductible item. Such tax-deductible expenses would include property taxes, insurance, utilities, mileage to and from your property, repairs, cleaning, painting, and more.

One further deduction is the remaining depreciable life of an asset that you replace prior to the end of its useful life. For example, according to present IRS regulations, appliances such as refrigerators and stoves have a seven-year life when new. If you for whatever reason have to replace the appliance again after five years, you are entitled to write off the remaining two years of life when the replacement with a new appliance is made.

Similarly, if you are amortizing the costs of obtaining financing but refinance and retire the old loan early, you should declare any remaining costs from the old loan in the year you take out the new loan.

Rather than trying to list all the possible tax deductions, it is actually much faster to discuss what isn't tax-deductible.

Author's Advice

Does all of this depreciation sound confusing? Your accountant will be able to explain all of this to you.

You already learned that the expenses associated with maintaining the home you live in aren't tax deductible. Other main nondeductible items include the principal portion of each loan payment, most of the costs associated with obtaining financing, and capital improvements.

Each loan payment that you make consists of at least two parts if you are amortizing the loan. Those two parts are principal and interest. Your loan might also include an escrow payment to pay for insurance premiums and property taxes when these expenses come due. Although the escrow payment isn't technically a tax deduction for the cash basis taxpayer, when these funds are used to pay the insurance and property taxes, these deductions can then be recognized.

However, the bulk of your loan payment will probably be principal and interest. Remember the interest portion of your payment is the "rent" you pay for the use of the lender's money and the principal portion is the amount of the loan that you pay back with each payment. You should know that the principal portion of your payment is never a tax-deductible item.

Also, the cost of obtaining financing typically can't be recognized as an expense in the year that you pay for it. To understand better why an item can be taken as an immediate deduction or not, you would benefit from the quick accounting primer in the next section.

Expensing Versus Capitalizing

Thankfully, within the complexity of the tax codes is an area of simplicity. Everything that you spend associated with your investment properties will be lumped into one of two categories, expense items or capitalization items.

What Can Be Expensed

You already learned that nearly every cost of operating a rental property can be taken as a tax deduction with few exceptions, like the principal portion of a loan payment. The question is whether the entire cost of an item can be taken as an expense immediately or if the taxpayer would have to amortize or depreciate the cost over a number of years.

What Should Be Capitalized

The answer is governed by the size of the cost and how the benefit from any particular item is realized. If the benefit is short term or the cost is small, the item should probably be expensed. However, if the cost is high or if the benefit has a duration of years, the item should probably be capitalized and depreciated or amortized.

Some examples will be helpful ....

If you repair a few missing roof shingles, the repair may last for many years, but the cost is low. The repair is an expense. However, if you replace the entire roof, that cost would have to be capitalized and depreciated.

Similarly, a repaired pothole in a driveway may again last several years, but since the cost is low, the repair is an expense. However, replacing the entire driveway would be capitalized.

Fixing a broken window is an expense. Replacing all the windows would be capitalized.

The cost of obtaining financing must be amortized over the life of the loan because the benefit of having the loan occurs over the same life.

Section 42 and Other Government Tax Credit Programs

Everything you have learned about taxation so far has been about the legally allowable tax deductions for the investor. Tax deductions reduce taxable income, resulting in a lower tax liability. The only thing better than a tax deduction is a tax credit. Tax credits are dollar for dollar reductions of tax liability. Tax credits reduce tax liability directly, compared with tax deductions that only reduce tax liability indirectly.

Earlier you learned that the government uses the tax code to punish or reward certain behavior. Tax credits are a reward on steroids.

Recognizing the need for quality low-income housing, the Federal Government has elected to build additional incentives in the form of tax credits into the tax code to reward real estate developers for producing new low-income housing opportunities.

State governments sometimes get on the bandwagon as well, offering various other incentives, such as below-market interest rate loans. Sometimes developers are able to tap into multiple programs to help facilitate their projects. It would be impossible to explore all the varying state and local programs available, but a brief summary of Federal Government programs follows.

One federal program employing tax credits for low-income residential developments is called Section 42. The Department of Housing and Urban Development (HUD) governs these programs. The basic premise of the program is that a certain allotment of tax credits will be made available for the developer in exchange for setting aside a certain percentage of the housing units, or even all the housing units, for low-income tenants.

The developer may sell these tax credits to investors to raise the down-payment funds necessary to launch a development. By selling the tax credits and borrowing the balance of the project costs, the developer may be able to finance 100 percent of the development's final cost.

Most beginning investors aren't going to embark on petitioning the government to obtain tax credits for a large low-income development. But you may find yourself competing against one of them for tenants. Therefore, the real point of this section is for you to know the weaknesses of your Section 42 competitor.

One obvious weakness is the stigma associated with living in low-income housing. A second, less known weakness is the intrusive nature of the application process required of tenants. Having given away all those tax credits, the government wants assurance that the tenants that ultimately get to rent the housing units are indeed low-income. To gain that assurance, the government requires the landlord to obtain third-party written verification of the tenant's income and assets.

The verification process is similar to what you would go through to obtain a mortgage, and is both time-consuming and intrusive. Tenants applying for an apartment today want to know immediately whether they are going to get the apartment. They aren't anticipating having to obtain written statements from banks and employers about their income and assets. The self-employed need to turn over two years of tax returns—to rent an apartment. Use these facts to your competitive advantage.

Real Deal

You will have to enter into the Section Eight rental agreement if you elect to rent to Section Eight tenants. Agreeing to use the Section Eight contract does not prohibit you from also using your own lease.

Other government housing programs include Section Eight subsidized housing. In this program, the government directly pays all or a portion of the tenant's rent. Sometimes these developments are restricted to elderly or handicapped tenants.

The small investor may find him or herself in competition with Section Eight, particularly if the tenant has a Section Eight housing voucher. The voucher allows the tenant to rent from any private landlord willing to accept the voucher.

Section Eight tenants are universally low-income tenants. Some landlords despise these kinds of tenants, others swear by them because at least the portion of the rent paid by the government is money in the bank.

Taxes When You Sell a Property

The same government that was so good to you about giving you those wonderful depreciation deductions while you owned the property isn't nearly so kind when you sell. If your property has gone up in value, the tax collector is going to want a piece of the action. Welcome to capital gains taxes.

Capital Gains Taxes

Capital gains taxes are just what they sound like: a tax on capital you have gained through appreciation of an asset. For example, if you bought an asset for $100,000 and later sold it for $150,000, you would have realized a capital gain of $50,000.

There are two kinds of capital gains, short-term and long-term. A long-term capital gain is the gain realized on any asset held for at least a year or longer. Short-term capital gains involve sales of assets held less than a year. Short-term capital gains are taxed similarly to ordinary income. Long-term capital gains are taxed at a lower rate than ordinary income.

In this example, had the asset been real estate and had the holding period been longer than one year, then the investor would have a long-term capital gain of $50,000, right? Wrong! There is the ugly matter of depreciation recapture.

Computing the Basis and Depreciation Recapture

Depreciation recapture is the depreciation party hangover. Remember all of those wonderful depreciation deductions you were able to take to shelter your cash flow all of those years? Now you have to give them back.

Using the same example, remember the asset was originally acquired for $100,000. You sold it for $150,000. But let's further assume that you held the property for five years and took total depreciation over those five years of $15,500. Your *tax basis* in the property is no

def•i•ni•tion

The **tax basis** of any property is equal to the acquisition cost plus any capital improvements minus total depreciation.

longer $100,000. Your basis declines according to the amount of depreciation you have taken. In this case, your basis is $100,000 – $15,500 = $84,500.

Your capital gain will be computed on the sale price of $150,000 less the basis in the property, $84,500. In this example, what would have been a long-term capital gain of $50,000 becomes a long-term capital gain of $65,500!

Is there any way to beat the taxman legally? There is, and you will learn more about it in the next section.

Legally Minimizing Taxes

You already learned that one of the greatest impediments to accumulating wealth is the tax code. Therefore, in order to be successful in real estate investing, you need to minimize potential tax liability while you own and when you sell your property.

Minimizing Taxes While You Own Investment Property

The key to minimizing taxes during your ownership is to have a good understanding of the tax code and to maintain good records. Think of the tax code as the set of rules that define how the game is played. You must know the rules if you want to come out a winner.

For most investors, the specifics of the tax code are sufficiently complex that you will need to retain a good, experienced accountant. But one idea that is simple to understand is that owning investment property is much like owning any other business. Just about every expense you incur in the operation of your property is usually tax-deductible in some way. Hence the need for keeping good records.

Fortunately, modern computer technology makes the job easier. In fact, there are a number of property management software packages that are available to small landlords at reasonable prices (see a list in Appendix C). At a minimum, you will need to develop a system for keeping track of rental income received and expenses incurred. Having a separate checking account and credit card for your investment properties is essential.

Buyer Beware

Never cheat on your taxes. Pay what you owe. But there is no reason not to minimize your tax liability by taking advantage of every available deduction authorized under the tax code.

Minimizing Taxes When You Sell Investment Property

Good record keeping is essential to minimizing capital gains taxes as well. You should take care to properly capitalize any item you aren't able to expense such that you may add to your property basis and thereby reduce the potential capital gains tax.

Further, unless you anticipate a decline in your property value, have urgent need for the money, or are getting eaten up by negative cash flow, always hang on to your properties for a year if you can to gain the advantage of the more favorable long-term capital gains tax rates.

Even after taking these prudent steps, there are still additional remedies to minimize your tax liability legally when you sell.

Taxation Exit Strategies

An exit strategy is a fancy name for the plans you will make in advance so that when you sell your property, you will have the lowest possible tax liability. There are a number of possibilities for you to learn about, including Tax-Deferred Exchanges, TIC Deals, and various trusts.

Tax-Deferred Exchanges

You may be beginning to think that our government is rather schizophrenic. First the government allows depreciation deductions while you own, but then the government takes them away when you sell. This position may seem inconsistent, but it really isn't.

Remember that one fundamental premise is the government is trying to encourage the production and ownership of real estate. Allowing depreciation is that encouragement. Depreciation recapture is a form of punishment for selling real estate.

However, if you are selling your real estate to use the money to buy even more real estate, then the government becomes your encouraging friend again. The tax code allows the investor to sell real estate at a profit (capital gain) and defer any tax payment if the money from the sale is used to buy more real estate. Such transactions are called tax-deferred exchanges.

There are three kinds of tax-deferred exchanges—simultaneous exchanges, delayed ("*Starker*") exchanges, and even reverse exchanges. The three kinds of exchanges differ from one another by virtue of timing and whether a third party is involved in the exchange. Otherwise they are the same.

def•i•ni•tion

The term **"Starker"** exchange comes from the court case precedent involving a man named Starker who was ultimately successful in persuading the court to allow a delayed exchange.

Every kind of exchange must meet the following criteria:

- It must be a like-kind exchange.
- The new property(s) must cost the same or more than the sale price of the property you sold.

A like-kind exchange sounds just like what it is. You are exchanging like for like, or one investment property for another investment property or properties. For example, if you sold a single-family rental home and properly used the proceeds to acquire a duplex, you have a like-kind exchange. A like-kind exchange would even include the acquisition of an office building, a retail store rental, industrial real estate, or any other type of investment real estate. Like-kind exchanges are investment real estate exchanged for other investment real estate. A like-kind exchange would not include any of the following:

- Using the proceeds to buy common stock, even the shares of a real estate investment trust (REIT).
- Using the proceeds to buy a vehicle, even if the vehicle is going to be used exclusively in your investment real estate business.
- Using the proceeds to buy a home for you to live in.

In addition to exchanging for a like-kind, you must also complete an exchange for the same amount or more real estate than you sold. For example, if you sold a property for $150,000, then the property you exchange must also cost $150,000 or more. Another alternative would be to acquire two or more properties so long as the total value of all the properties acquired is more than $150,000.

Assuming that you are ready to sell your property and you understand that you must buy at least the same or even more like-kind real estate, you are ready to explore the three different kinds of exchanges: simultaneous, delayed, and reverse exchanges.

The simplest exchange is a simultaneous exchange. You exchange the equity in your old property for a new property that costs the same or more than the old property you are selling. Consider the following illustration ….

Say you want to exchange a rental house you own that is worth $150,000. Your mortgage balance is $40,000, so your equity is $110,000. You have found a four-unit apartment building that you would like to buy. The owner is willing to sell for $400,000.

You would exchange the equity in your rental home, $110,000, plus $290,000 in extra cash for the four-unit building. You could take out a new mortgage on the four-unit for $290,000 to come up with the additional cash required. At the close of the transaction, you would own the $400,000 four-unit building and the previous owner would own your rental home subject to the $40,000 mortgage. The previous owner would also have the $290,000 in cash.

The problem with this type of simultaneous exchange is finding an owner willing to take your smaller single-family rental home in the exchange. This problem is so cumbersome that this kind of two-party simultaneous exchange rarely occurs. The solution is to bring in a third party to make this simultaneous exchange a three-way simultaneous exchange.

Going back to the same example, what would you do if the seller of the four-unit apartment was not interested in owning your single-family rental home? Bring in a third party buyer for the rental house. Now this third party buys the house for $150,000, you pay off the mortgage of $40,000, and you take the remaining $110,000 to use as a down payment to buy the four-unit.

Closing on all the properties occurs simultaneously. Everyone is happy. But there is still one practical problem. The owner of the four-unit may not be willing to wait while you find a buyer for your rental home. What to do now? The remedy is the delayed exchange, also called a Starker exchange.

In a Starker exchange, you sell your property, place the proceeds on deposit with a qualified escrow intermediary like a title company, and then find and close on the same or more real estate later. This is by far the most frequently employed exchange remedy.

First, do not be intimidated by any of the complexities or terminology. An escrow intermediary is just the name for someone who holds the proceeds of the sale from the smaller property that you are exchanging. Just about any title company can act as a qualified escrow intermediary. Besides, you are going to have an attorney helping you navigate the exchange minefield, right? Even if you ignored our advice earlier about using attorneys, do not ignore it here.

If you are going the Starker route, you will have up to 45 days from the day of closing of the property you sold to identify up to three properties that you would like to buy. Having made the identification, you then have six months in which to close on one or all the three of the properties that you identified earlier.

Starker exchanges have two problems. The first problem is that you could become a motivated buyer. Faced with an enormous capital gains tax that you were not intending to have to pay, you may become motivated to overpay for a property to avoid the tax consequences of an outright sale.

The second problem with the delayed exchange is that you may have already found the property you want to buy but you do not have a third party buyer for the property you need to sell.

The solution to both of these problems is a reverse exchange. In the reverse exchange you actually acquire the new, larger building first, then you sell your smaller building later. The problem with the reverse exchange is that you will not have the proceeds of the sale from the smaller building available for the down payment on the larger building. The answer to this problem is to refinance the smaller building before you sell.

Returning to the example of the $150,000 sale of your single-family rental home that you want to exchange for the $400,000 four-unit, let us assume that you have decided that a reverse exchange is the best way to proceed. You decide to refinance the $150,000 home and obtain a new mortgage of $120,000. The old mortgage of $40,000 had to be paid back, so you are left with $80,000. The $80,000 is sufficient for a down payment on the four-unit, so you are able to buy the new property. You then have up to six months to sell your single family home.

The reverse exchange is the most complex of all, and it is somewhat new. Not many attorneys have done these. Make sure that you are using a lawyer who has experience in reverse exchanges if you think this is your remedy.

If the complexities of completing an exchange are giving you a nervous tic, them maybe you should seek the simplicity of a TIC deal.

TIC Deals

TIC is an acronym for Tenants in Common. Therefore, a TIC is really defining a method of owning real estate. In some ways, TICs are modern-day incarnations of the limited partnerships discussed earlier that were thriving in the 1980s. There are a number of companies specializing in doing TIC deals. Examples of these companies are identified in Appendix C. Theoretically, any kind of investment real estate can be owned by a TIC.

In a TIC deal, a party or an entity identifies a piece of real estate that would be suitable for TIC ownership. Once identified, the TIC dealer offers fraction ownership positions available for sale to the buying public. The TIC dealer may also serve as the property manager and collect a fee accordingly. After closing, the TIC owners meet regularly to decide two things: first, whether to change to keep the present TIC property-management firm and second, whether the TIC should be sold. TICs qualify as a like-kind exchange.

The problem with TICs is that they are relatively new. An IRS ruling could negate the like-kind status of these investments, resulting in an unplanned tax liability. Similarly, if the majority of the TIC owners decide to sell, you could again be faced with an unplanned tax liability. Finally, should you wish to sell but be unable to gain a majority vote with the other TIC members, there may not be much of a secondary market for your TIC interests.

Trusts

Another viable exit strategy is to place your properties into a trust. There are a number of different trust vehicles available, such as private annuity trusts and charitable remainder trusts, to name just two. The different trusts allow you to stretch out a tax liability over time or to diminish tax liability by designating a charity of your choice among other options.

Explaining the nuances of these trust opportunities is beyond the scope of this book. If you think that a trust may be the right exit strategy for you, you should seek the advice of a financial planner, CPA, and attorney who specialize in this field.

Seller Financing and Taxes

One way to manage your capital gains tax liability is to carry the financing on the property when you sell, for example, by selling on a land contract. Instead of owing the tax all at once, your tax liability is paid over a number of years and you would receive interest income from whatever debt instrument you create. The disadvantage is that when you finance your own sale, you have not completely divorced yourself from the property. Should the buyer fail to make payments as agreed, you may need to foreclose and take the property back, probably in a deteriorated condition.

Paying the Taxes

The decision to sell real estate outright is nearly always a life-style decision, never an investment decision. Typically, a successful real estate investor discovers that there is no other alternative investment offering the return available from real estate investing. But there comes a time when the investor no longer wants the responsibilities of real estate ownership.

There are alternative real estate investments that are less management intensive, or the investor could hire a property management firm to handle the day-to-day obligations. But for many investors there comes a day when they have enough and it is time to cash out.

They no longer want the worries associated with mortgage debt or the hassles associated with tenants. The alternative real estate investments that are less management intensive may be foreign to the investor. Foreign and new sometimes translate to worry.

In the end, there is nothing wrong with paying the taxes and just getting out at the end of a successful real estate investment or career. Remember the tax that you owe reflects the profits that you made. Sometimes a big tax bill is a nice problem to have.

The Least You Need to Know

- The government encourages investment property ownership by allowing depreciation and tax-deferred exchanges.
- Successful real estate investing requires careful tax planning, record keeping, and management both during ownership and when you sell.
- There are a number of exit strategies to help minimize capital gains taxes when you sell.
- The complexities of tax-deferred exchanges require an experienced attorney and CPA.

Chapter 22

Refinancing Strategies

In This Chapter

- Learning to manage your debt
- Refinancing to make improvements
- Refinancing for expansion

Congratulations! You have moved from a beginning real estate investor to a seasoned pro. You are continuing down the path of success. You are buying, selling, and holding. You are in a position that you only dreamed of a few years ago.

There is yet another important principal for you to tackle: refinancing your real estate investment properties. Once you learn the techniques, you can easily change your whole outlook on real estate investing. You might find yourself thinking differently about buying and holding.

The good news is that refinancing isn't brain surgery, and you can learn this easily. By the end of this chapter, you will change the way you look at mortgage lenders.

Managing Your Debt

There are good reasons for wanting a refinance of your property. A purchase money mortgage can be a hard thing to get. You have to convince a lender to back an inexperienced investor such as yourself on a loan placed against an unfamiliar property. That property may be more than just unfamiliar. It may be a future gem in your imagination, but in real-time reality, the property might be a dump. Isn't that how you got such a good deal on it?

Therefore, the lender you chose might not necessarily have been the lender offering the best deal. Your choice of lenders may not have been a choice at all. Chances are, you searched frantically to find anyone crazy enough to give you a loan and once you found them, you probably didn't quibble about the details. In the most extreme cases, you may have even gone to a nontraditional lending source such as a private individual for a loan. If so, then you wound up paying far more in interest as well as other less favorable terms.

Besides all your other troubles, the loan you took out to buy the property was probably found under some time pressure. The financing contingency in most offers is rarely more than 60 days and is usually far less. That may not be much time, particularly when you consider that you are also involved in inspecting the property, arranging insurance, setting up filing systems, and taking all the other steps necessary to acquire the property.

By comparison, refinancing is much easier. The time pressure is gone. If your efforts to refinance fail, you don't lose a deal, you just have to live with the loan you already have. When you apply to refinance, you are no longer an unknown investor seeking a loan on a tired-out property. By now, that property has become the gem that you imagined. Further, both it and you have a verifiable track record. As a result, you are in a much better position to make a fresh start with a new loan.

Real Deal

The terms mortgagor and mortgagee are often confused. Most people think that since the lender grants the mortgage, the lender must be the mortgagor. But a mortgage is a lien against property. Therefore, while the lender makes the loan, the borrower gives the lender a lien called a mortgage on the property. This makes the borrower the mortgagor. The lender who received the borrower's mortgage and holds it is the mortgagee.

By far the largest expense of owning investment property is the interest on the mortgage. Therefore, you want to do everything you can to prudently manage your biggest expense. That means managing your debt.

You may want to refinance to take advantage of a lower interest rate, or to lock in a fixed interest rate if your old loan is adjustable. You may want to seek a refinance to pay off a second mortgage that has a higher interest rate, shorter amortization, or large balloon payments coming due.

Refinancing for a Lower Interest Rate

Everyone knows they should refinance debt at a lower interest rate, whenever possible. If you are paying 8 percent interest, and you can move the debt to a 6 percent rate, of course you refinance. That only makes sense.

On a $200,000, 30-year loan, the difference of a monthly payment between an 8% and 6% rate is substantial. The 8% payment is $1,467.53 and the 6% payment is $1,199.10, a difference of $268.43 per month. There is no logical reason not to refinance.

You don't have to wait until the mortgage interest rates drop by two percentage points before you consider refinancing a mortgage. The decision to refinance your investment properties is dependent on many things, including …

- How much lower the interest rate is on the new loan.
- What the costs are for the new loan.
- What your equity position is in the property.
- How long you plan to own your property.

Shopping for a refinance loan takes some time, and you have much to consider. One thing to consider is your anticipated holding period. If you are thinking of selling in the near term, you might want to consider an adjustable rate mortgage (ARM) when refinancing. Suppose your plan is to refinance, pulling enough cash out to upgrade the property, and sell it, all within the next two years. Suddenly, a three year adjustable ARM makes sense. Getting a lower interest rate over the next two years of ownership becomes a good strategy.

To take advantage of a lower rate mortgage, you'll have to close on the new loan and pay the closing costs associated with that loan. That's true even if you apply for a no-cost or low-cost closing. With a no-cost or low-cost closing, the costs still need to be paid. It is just that they are paid for either with a higher interest rate or are added to the principal balance of the loan. (As you know by now, there's no such thing as a free lunch.)

Whenever you refinance for any reason, you should at least consider refinancing with your current lender. You may be able to make a better deal with the existing lender than you would be able to make with a new lender. For example, consider the case where you want to retire an $80,000 loan to get a new loan of $100,000. The going rate for loan origination fees in your market is 1% of the loan amount. Your existing lender would have the opportunity to earn $1,000 (1% of the new loan), but would only have to come up with $20,000 of new money to make the $100,000 loan. For the existing lender, the 1% fee looks like a 5% fee. That's a lucrative deal for the lender. Maybe you can talk the lender down to a fee of 1% on the new money only ($200).

A refinance for a lower rate is almost certain to be approved if you have made your payments as agreed on the old loan. For instance if you paid $1,000 a month perfectly for the last 24 months, why wouldn't the lender make a loan at a lower rate with an $850 a month payment? It is a no-brainer, even for a loan officer working the second day on the job.

Refinancing for Better Loan Terms

Probably the most important loan term is the interest charged, but other loan terms can be important too. Often, to qualify a borrower when income is tight, the lender recommends or even insists the mortgage be an adjustable rate mortgage (ARM). The payments on an ARM are always lower than on their fixed-rate cousins, making qualifying easier. While the ARM may solve your short-term problem of not otherwise being able to do the deal, an ARM may not be the best thing for the long-term. So long as interest rates are stable or falling, an ARM makes sense. If interest rates are rising, a fixed rate is clearly better.

Once you have stabilized the property and have raised rents, you may be able to qualify for a fixed-rate mortgage. If you have an ARM, you should think about refinancing for just this reason alone, even if the fixed rate would be higher than your current rate. The only exception would be if you are certain you will be selling the property soon, in which case you should leave your ARM alone.

Another occasion when you may want to refinance is to eliminate the requirement to pay private mortgage insurance (PMI). Even if a lower rate isn't available and you don't need any additional funds, it may be to your benefit to refinance. If you have improved the property to the point where your equity is now 20 percent of fair market value or more, you should be able to refinance and eliminate this requirement from your loan.

When seeking a refinance just to remove the PMI requirement, start with your present lender. The lender may be willing to waive the PMI if a new appraisal is obtained proving the increased value, saving you the added expenses of a full blown refinance.

Author's Advice

Whether seeking financing for an initial purchase or for a refinance, do not seek a fixed rate of interest locked beyond your expected holding period. If you are anticipating a five-year hold, you don't need a thirty-year mortgage.

Refinancing Second Mortgages

Second mortgages can be wonderful. A second mortgage can make the difference between being able to buy versus not being able to buy for the cash-strapped investor. The seller will be the holder of the majority of second mortgages that you encounter. That means that the rates and terms of the second mortgage are wide open to negotiation. However, most sellers, who may have preferred to get paid all in cash to start with, are probably anxious to collect the second mortgage as quickly as possible. That can often mean that in order to induce the seller into holding the second mortgage, the buyer had to agree to a more aggressive amortization schedule or balloon payments, or both.

If the property you bought has a second mortgage with these features, you may want to refinance the entire debt on the property, rolling the old first and second mortgages into one new larger first mortgage. In fact, if your second mortgage has balloon payments, you should have a well-thought-out plan for how you are going to meet this obligation.

If you were planning on retiring the first and second mortgage with a new loan, you will need a higher appraisal to qualify for the new loan. An illustration will be helpful:

Initial Purchase Price:	$100,000
Loans - First Mortgage:	$80,000
- Second Mortgage:	$10,000

For the refinance, a new first mortgage of $90,000 will be needed to pay off the two old loans. Let's make the further assumption that lenders are only willing to loan 80% LTV on a refinance of this kind of property. The new loan would require an appraisal of $112,500: $90,000 / 80% = $112,500.

If the property fails to appraise at the higher value, then the loan will not be available. For example, if the property only appraised for $110,000, the borrower would be $2,000 short of the desired goal of raising $90,000 in new financing: $110,000 × 80% LTV = $88,000.

Because of these potential problems, an investor trying to pay off a second mortgage to be able to comply with a balloon payment requirement would be wise to start the refinancing process early, in case anything goes wrong.

When managing your debt, you want to be positioned for the long-term. Unless you have already decided to sell the property, your loan structure should reflect a long-term hold strategy. Short-term financing and balloon payments are loan characteristics that could turn you into a motivated seller. Eliminate these provisions from your loans as soon as you have the opportunity.

Refinancing to Make Improvements

In addition to refinancing to manage your debt, you might also consider refinancing to make improvements to the property. Earlier in this book, you learned about increasing the value of the property by improving it or changing its use. By adding a garage or an additional bedroom, or by changing a residential property to commercial use, you could improve the property's value, increasing the ability to collect more rent.

Some of these improvements might be too costly to pay for them out of the cash flow from the property. Of course, the property cash flow would be higher if the improvements were made. This catch-22 can be resolved by refinancing.

You may have to get permission from local government agencies for certain improvements. Adding a room or a swimming pool would require you first to get a building permit in most municipalities. This may also trigger an upward adjustment of your property taxes.

Buyer Beware

Plan your improvements carefully, and make sure you are in compliance with all local rules, ordinances, and deed restrictions.

Increasingly, some subdivisions are imposing architectural controls and other rules through deed restrictions. These rules and controls can include the exterior building materials used in construction or in subsequent maintenance, controls on parking cars outside garages, storage of motor homes or boats, and so on.

In some ways, refinancing has an added benefit because it imposes fiscal discipline. For example, assume you were thinking about giving a property an extensive facelift, including new siding and new windows. You can afford to pay for these improvements out of your own pocket and you really think the property would look much nicer with the upgrades.

Should you proceed? The answer might actually be easier to find if you did not have the money to make the repairs. Then you would have to borrow the money, and you would not want to borrow the money unless you could increase rent enough to offset the added costs of the extra debt.

Buyer Beware

When you refinance to make improvements, make sure the decision is grounded in good economic thinking. The changes should increase income or cut expenses enough to justify the added cost of the debt. Your cash flow should at least stay the same or hopefully go up, never down, as a result of your improvement program.

Here are some other things to consider when refinancing a property to make improvements:

- Consider a second mortgage, especially if your first mortgage is favorable.
- Consider borrowing against your home instead. You could borrow against your home by applying for a home equity line of credit or by refinancing your home. A home equity line or a home refinance is the easiest financing to get and the rates and terms are better than those typically available on non-owner occupied rental properties. Remember, you are risking your primary residence if for some reason you can't make your payments.
- Shop for lenders. With a refinance, you have much better leverage with the lending community than you may have had when you bought the property.
- Consider getting an ARM if you are planning on selling shortly after making the improvements.
- Pulling cash out is possible with the loan type. Sometimes, it is cheaper with a "subject-to" mortgage, where you provide a list of renovations. The lender holds the contractor's fees in reserve or escrow, paying them once the bills are presented after the work is completed. Other possibilities are a combo refinance—with a first and second mortgage.

You may be able to use a refinance to pay for changes to a property that completely reposition it, adding enormous value. Refinancing can speed you on your way to achieving your wealth goals.

Refinancing to Buy Other Properties

Another reason why you might want to refinance your investment property is to pull cash out so you can use the equity to buy another property. This is a routine transaction among real estate investors. Using the cash, you are using one property to buy another. This alleviates you from having to use your own cash to buy the next investment property.

When employing this strategy, it is important to not get overextended. For example, suppose the property you are refinancing has been a reliable cash cow for you for a number of years. Now a deal has come along that is just too good to pass up. This new property is a real mess, but with your Midas touch, it could become something special.

So you refinance your cash cow to buy an old dog, that property with all the potential. Of course, the new property can only reach that potential if lots of repairs are made. Until that time, it's a black hole of a money sponge. In the meantime, your old cash cow property is no longer producing milk like it used to. With the new mortgage and higher payment, the property still holds its own, but cash flow is much less than it was.

You can begin to see how an investor in this situation can get squeezed. It has happened to some of the sharpest names in real estate like Donald Trump, and it could happen to you. Remember that shaping that old dog up into a winning breed can take twice as long and cost twice as much as you thought.

When refinancing for a new acquisition, it may be better to pull the maximum out that you can, rather than pull out a little now and a little later. Refinancing is too expensive to repeat every time you need a few dollars. For example, if you could pull out $20,000 now, take it all, even if you need only $10,000 to make your next transaction work. Save the other $10,000 for the next possible deal.

Refinancing Strategies to Live Better Than You Ever Dreamed

Imagine receiving for the rest of your life $80,000 in cash, each year. And let's make this dream more enticing: let's make the cash tax-free.

It's too good to believe, right? An impossible dream? Not at all.

One investor (we'll call him Jack) started a retirement plan that beats all. Here's what he did. Jack acquired 11 multifamily buildings. (When he started as a real estate investor, he bought only single-family residences. After several years, he moved to the multifamily type properties.) Jack always paid an extra $100 per month on his mortgage payment.

That extra $100—which came from his tenant's rent payments—and was $100 he could live without, went to the principal of his loan. Just $1,200 a year.

Consider this loan scenario:

$300,000 property
$240,000 Mortgage (LTV = 80%), 360 months/30 loan
Monthly payment at 7% = $1,596.73
At the end of 5 years = $226,193.08 balance of loan due
At the end of 10 years = $212,686.58 balance of loan due

Jack modified the payoff with his extra $100 per month payment. By always paying the extra $100 each month, this is what his loan looked at the end of 5 and 10 years:

At the end of 5 years = $218,756.53 balance of loan due
At the end of 10 years = $188,641.24 balance of loan due

Jack's simple approach assured him $50,000 of equity available at the end of each 10-year cycle. He always planned to take $50,000 out of each property on a refinancing plan. He never planned to own any of his rental properties free of debt.

Jack also enjoyed the benefits of appreciation, something he never counted on when he first started investing for his retirement. Although he admitted that he felt his properties would appreciate, it was not part of his overall plan. He maintained his properties, and on the first round of refinancing, he was always able to pull about $20,000 more out of each property as part of the appreciation.

Now he is "retired" and no longer buying more properties. He is just collecting rents, managing his properties, and making mortgage payments. Jack just financed one of his 11 multifamily units and received $81,588. (Remember that's tax-free.) Jack does not want his name used in this book, but he did tell the authors that he is averaging about $1,400 positive cash flow on each of his 11 properties. (That's $15,400 a month, or $184,800 a year. He does pay taxes on that money.) He said in a couple years, he might cut back on the number of properties he owns, or he might turn over the management to a property-management company. In the meantime, he just enjoys his lifestyle. He takes three cruises a year (just got back from an Alaskan cruise, he reported) and plays golf almost daily.

Jack's strategy can work for you, too. Consider the power of refinancing. When you pull cash out, it is tax-free. If you are retired, what would you do with an extra $50,000 (or more) of tax-free money every year?

Consider modifying Jack's plan. Look at the difference of payoffs with more or less than $100 extra paid on your mortgage each month.

Leslie rented her single-family home with an unusual provision. Her tenant pays rent every other week. Her tenant receives her paycheck every other week, and it was easier for her to pay that way. Leslie takes every other check, and sends a mortgage payment. At the end of the year, she realized that she was in a position to make an extra payment, so she did. If the pattern keeps up, she will shave 8 years of payments from her 30-year mortgage. If she chose to refinance, she has that much more equity to withdraw. For her, it made more sense to keep the bookkeeping intact and just make the extra payment each year.

Refinancing Pitfalls

It may sound simple and obvious, but the greatest pitfall to refinancing is that you have to pay the money back. You already read where refinancing can lead to getting overextended. Further, refinancing postpones the date when your property would be debt-free. Paying off the debt is a sure way to guarantee strong cash flow. Refinancing frustrates that goal.

Refinancing can be expensive. Consider again the earlier case where an investor wanted to obtain a new $90,000 first mortgage to pay off the existing first mortgage of $80,000 and a second mortgage of $10,000. To get the new mortgage, a new appraisal will be required, in addition to a title insurance update and all of the other costs of obtaining a mortgage.

Let's assume that our borrower is particularly savvy and is able to limit the closing costs to just 1 percent of the new loan, or $900. What has really happened here? The borrower has raised $10,000 of new cash on the first mortgage—at a cost of $900. When the cost of the new loan is expressed in terms of the amount of the new money available, then this is an expensive way to raise money indeed. Nine percent of the new money is lost to transactions costs. And remember, this borrower got an extraordinarily good deal on the borrowing costs.

Refinancing can lead to awkward tax consequences, as the following example illustrates:

Assume that an investor has owned a property for a long time. When he bought the property, it cost $200,000. The land value was $30,000 and the remaining $170,000 was subject to depreciation. Fifteen years later, the property is worth $500,000, but the depreciable basis has decreased $92,700 from 15 years of depreciation. Therefore the basis is now $107,300 ($200,000 – $92,700 = $107,300).

One year ago, this investor refinanced the property to build a beautiful new home for himself. The new loan has a current balance of $400,000. Today the investor finds himself with a health emergency and wanting to sell. What happens if he sells the property for $500,000?

Assuming there are no closing costs, the investor would net $100,000 from the sale after paying off the $400,000 mortgage. The investor has a gain of $100,000. But that's not how the tax man views the transaction.

Remember the basis in the property is only $107,300. For capital gains tax purposes, the gain is actually $500,000 – $107,300 = $392,700. Assuming a total federal and state combined effective long-term capital gains tax rate of 25%, the investor would owe $98,172 in taxes. The investor's equity has disappeared!

Refinancing isn't always clear-cut. When comparing mortgages, don't forget to include the extra fees you must pay for the new mortgage.

Real Deal

You may be able to get some fees waived if you are able to refinance with your current mortgage holder. Always check with your current lender first.

Remember that you should be in the driver's seat when refinancing a property. As long as you have maintained the property and made your payments on time, there is no reason why you should not be approved. Take the time to find the loan you want.

Don't be rushed. Keep the goals of your refinancing in mind as you seek a loan. Don't be enticed into a loan that does not meet all your goals.

The Least You Need to Know

- Mortgage interest is the highest expense of owning a property; manage your debt wisely.
- Refinancing to pay for improvements should only be done if net income can be increased to cover the added debt.

- Don't get overextended when refinancing to acquire more properties.
- At least check with your present lender on a refinance before you go elsewhere.

Chapter 23

Investing in Commercial Real Estate

In This Chapter

- Advantages of investing in commercial properties
- Problems of investing in commercial properties
- Types of commercial properties to consider
- Getting started in commercial real estate

Almost the entire thrust of this book has been to educate you in the many facets of residential real estate investing. Having come this far, you are well prepared to begin your investment career. As you evolve from beginner to expert, you may find yourself considering alternative kinds of investment properties beyond residential real estate. There is an additional world of opportunities in commercial real estate investing, and this chapter will give you a brief overview.

Differences in Investing in Commercial and Residential Properties

Previously, we defined commercial properties to include even an apartment building five units or larger. However, commercial properties also include retail properties, offices, and industrial real estate. From manufacturing plants to motels, the nearest fast food restaurant to the mobile home park, all are examples of commercial real estate.

All commercial properties have some characteristics in common. Those characteristics would include a larger price, more restricted financing, and the property potentially being harder to sell.

Pricing Issues

Commercial real estate is more expensive relative to residential real estate. The smallest real estate investment available is typically a single-family rental home. Commercial properties may not always be physically larger, but they will almost always cost more. This cost is driven by location.

The single-family home may be tucked away on a quiet subdivision cul-de-sac. The commercial properties are going on busy commercial corridors. Often, commercial land value exceeds the value of the improvements. In residential real estate, the opposite is almost always the case.

Financing Issues

By far, the greatest real estate lending transaction volume takes place with single-family homes. An entire industry has sprung up around this activity, an industry with its own state and federal regulations and even a secondary market for reselling the mortgages. Most loans are created for resale in the secondary market. This secondary market injects tremendous liquidity while diversifying default risks.

Owing to the volume of transactions, a wide range of loan programs have sprung up to serve various segments of the residential market. Some of these programs are government sanctioned, such as FHA and VA loans. Other loan programs are dreamed up by private financial institutions trying to carve out a niche in the lending industry. Many of these opportunities were outlined in Chapter 12.

These lending conditions and programs simply do not exist for larger commercial properties. The loans on these investments almost never fit the parameters required for sale on the secondary market. Instead, these loans are nearly always held by the maker. Such lenders are lending to hold the resulting note in their own portfolio. These lenders are often called portfolio lenders. A portfolio lender may elect to sell one or more of these loans, but a ready secondary market does not exist.

Accordingly, there are fewer institutions willing to make loans on commercial properties. These circumstances have given rise to mortgage brokers and commercial real estate departments in larger financial institutions that specialize in making these loans. So the lenders are available, they are just harder to find.

They may be harder to please as well. High leverage, creative financing techniques are less likely to work here, particularly in a brisk real estate market. You'd be surprised by the number of investors with millions of dollars available for making enormous down payments on these types of properties. It isn't unusual for affluent investors to buy multimillion dollar properties with no mortgage.

Risk Issues

Commercial property is inherently more risky than residential investment property. People must have a place to live, even when they are unemployed. However a business that isn't making money is eventually going to vacate the office, store, or industrial facility that they have been renting. Those same business owners may stay in their homes as they close their business. A man's home is his castle, but business is business. If you can't turn a profit, then you do what you have to do, which often includes shutting the doors and vacating the property.

It is much easier to replace a residential tenant than a commercial tenant. A residential tenant may be found by placing a classified advertisement in the local paper. Finding a commercial tenant may require the time and expertise of a *commercial leasing broker*.

def•i•ni•tion

A **commercial leasing broker** is a real estate agent who specializes in renting commercial real estate. These agents may further specialize by engaging in renting just office, retail, or industrial space.

Commercial Lease Issues

In residential properties, you can probably develop one lease and use it all the time. The typical rental lease rarely exceeds one year in duration. The lease is drafted by the landlord and the tenant typically accepts the lease without modification.

Commercial leases are dramatically different. A commercial lease may be for twenty years or longer. Often, large corporations with their own real estate departments have a boilerplate lease that landlords must accept. Frequently, these leases are subject to lengthy negotiations between landlord and tenant and the attorneys representing them. Each lease may be unique in character.

Commercial space may sit vacant for months or even years before the investor finds a tenant. Once the new tenant is identified, expensive tenant improvements may be required to customize the space to meet the new tenant's needs. Such improvements can include moving walls, complete redecorating, bringing in new plumbing facilities, and more. In a strong commercial market, landlords can often require tenants to pay for their own improvements. In a weaker market, the landlord may have to pay for these improvements. The commercial real estate investor simply must have deeper pockets to weather these potential storms.

Commercial real estate also does not have the tax shelter benefit typical of residential properties. First, under current tax law, the depreciable life of most commercial real estate is computed on a straight-line basis over 40 years. Residential rental real estate is assumed to have a 27.5-year life. Second, remember that land can't be depreciated. In residential real estate, it isn't uncommon to find the value of the land representing only 10 to 20 percent of the total value of the investment. In commercial properties, the value of the land is usually much higher. Therefore, in commercial real estate, the investor can only depreciate a smaller fraction of the total purchase price over a longer period of years. The result is a lower tax shelter benefit for commercial investment property than residential investment property.

Advantages of Commercial Properties

With all of the additional risks and complications of owning commercial real estate, you may be wondering why anyone would be interested in investing in it. However, there are many advantages.

The greatest advantage to commercial real estate is that it is less management intensive. In residential real estate, the tenants may or may not take good care of their homes. In commercial real estate, the real estate is a place of business. The tenant has a vested interest in keeping the property in tip-top condition, or the tenant may lose business.

The tenant not only has a vested interest in maintaining the property, but he or she may also be contractually obligated to do so. The tenant may be under what is called a triple-net (NNN) lease. NNN leases transfer almost all the responsibilities of real estate ownership to the tenant. Under a NNN lease, the tenant is responsible for the payment of property taxes, utilities, and insurance. The tenant is responsible for maintaining the property, including lawn and snow care, any repairs, and even repair or replacement of major mechanical systems such as the roof or the heating and air conditioning systems. The tenant's vested interest and contractual obligation to maintain the property are often sufficiently strong enough that some investors own NNN leased properties all over the country that they rarely visit. The landlord is confident the tenants will take care of the property on their own.

Author's Advice

A NNN lease property can give the investor all the benefits of owning real estate with almost none of the responsibilities of owning real estate.

Although commercial properties can have inherent additional risks, when the commercial real estate is under lease, some of those risks might be mitigated. Sometimes the tenant is one of the largest corporations in the world. Even smaller local commercial properties may have leases backed by highly successful, strong credit tenants. The length of the lease might be several years, even 20 years, or longer. While the property is under lease, even if the business fails, the tenant is still responsible for paying the rent. It isn't unusual for large corporations or even smaller credit-worthy local businesspeople to continue to pay rent on vacated commercial real estate even after the business that occupied that space closes.

Risk also presents opportunity to the savvy investor. Because the risks associated with commercial properties are greater, the opportunities may be greater as well.

Types of Commercial Properties to Consider

Commercial properties have various uses and come in multiple kinds, shapes, and sizes. However, commercial properties can be loosely grouped into four categories, office, retail, industrial, and larger apartment properties.

Office Real Estate

Office real estate includes everything from small neighborhood offices to medical buildings to larger office structures in office parks and the huge skyscrapers in the largest cities. Areas of concern to office tenants include window space, accessibility to transportation, ingress and egress, parking, and signage, among others.

Offices will accommodate up to thousands of workers during the business day, so access to transportation and parking is vital. Ingress and egress issues can also be critical. Ingress and egress are terms describing direct access to the property. The concern here is that automobile traffic be able to easily enter and exit the site. Any difficulties in accessibility can be disastrous for an otherwise well-located site.

Theoretically, office tenants are less demanding and easier to manage than residential tenants. There are less likely to be weekend or late night emergency repairs. However, when repairs do become necessary, office tenants will be less patient and instead expect more immediate service.

One important aspect of office property management is the *janitorial service*.

> **def•i•ni•tion**
>
> **Janitorial service** is sometimes called "char" service when used in reference to office buildings. The term is an old English word more often used by real estate old-timers.

In a well-run office building, the common areas and public restrooms must be cleaned nightly. This service also extends to the individual office suites themselves, to include emptying of trash, occasional light dusting, and vacuuming.

Office leases come in three general types: gross leases, modified gross leases, and net leases. In a gross lease, the tenant has no other expense associated with occupying the space, except for such services as telephone services and Internet connections. All utilities are included in the rent. In a modified gross lease, the tenant has additional expenses associated with occupancy beyond just the rent payment. Those additional expenses usually include utilities, and may include other expenses as negotiated between the landlord and tenant.

In a net lease, all expenses associated with the building operation are charged back to the tenants based on a prorated share of the amount of space that each tenant occupies. The expenses charged to the tenants would include utilities, property taxes, casualty insurance, char service, repairs, grounds keeping, snow removal, and more. Tenants in a net lease aren't charged for any costs of finding new tenants such as leasing commissions or advertising.

Office buildings featuring net leased space aren't quite the same as a NNN lease. The landlord is still responsible for maintaining the property. He or she just has the opportunity to bill back the associated cost to all the tenants. Sometimes, a single tenant office building can have a NNN lease.

Retail Real Estate

Retail real estate is any real estate where the tenant engages in retail commerce. The varieties are endless, and would at least include neighborhood strip malls, large enclosed shopping malls, big-box *category-killer* stores, and specialty retailers like gas stations, fast food restaurants, and banks.

One of the characteristics of all commercial real estate is that the financial strength of the tenant backing the lease can impact the value of the real estate. This phenomenon is even more prevalent in retail real estate. For example, consider two freestanding retail stores of the same size that command the same amount of rent. Each is rented to a tenant operating a drugstore. One of the tenants is a Ma and Pa operation. The owners have operated a successful business for years, but this is their only store. There is a ten-year lease on this property that has seven years remaining.

def•i•ni•tion

A **category killer** is typically a large retail store featuring a depth of inventory in one specialized area, such as pet supplies, furniture, office supplies, or electronics.

The other tenant operating the other drug store is a huge corporation. The corporation stock is traded on the New York Stock Exchange. The corporation has an investment grade rating, which is to say that professional rating services recognize this corporation to be well managed and in sound financial condition. The corporate tenant also has seven years remaining on a long-term lease.

Given these two alternatives, most investors would view the corporate-tenant-occupied store as being less risky. Therefore, investors would be willing to pay more for the same building. In fact, the nature of the lease and the quality of the tenant can have a huge impact on value on retail real estate.

The impact of a long-term retail lease changes over the life of the lease. As the end of the lease terms approaches, the risk of the tenant vacating increases. There is additional uncertainty. Accordingly, the property's liquidity goes down (a fancy way of saying the property will be harder to sell) and the value may decline with it.

Buyer Beware

Real estate committed to a long-term lease may decline in liquidity and value in the waning years of the lease.

Retail real estate can be among the easiest properties to manage. If the real estate is a gas station, fast-food restaurant, free-standing full-service restaurant, or free-standing single retail store, then there is probably just one tenant occupying the space and the tenant may be under a NNN lease. Therefore, the tenant may be almost entirely accountable for all the costs and responsibilities ordinarily associated with ownership. The disadvantage is that one vacancy can mean 100 percent vacancy.

Retail tenants in a strip center or other multitenant retail sites will have gross leases, modified gross leases, or net leases similar in character to the office leases discussed earlier.

Industrial Real Estate

Industrial real estate includes warehouses and light to heavy manufacturing sites. Industrial real estate can be found in modern lavishly landscaped industrial parks to gritty older industrial districts in some central city locations.

The tenants that occupy these buildings can range in size and quality from fledgling local businesses to well-established brand-name corporations. Industrial properties include single and multitenant buildings. Typically, the management of these buildings is among the least management intensive of any kind of real estate. Only NNN-leased retail stores would require less owner involvement.

Industrial leases include the gross, modified gross, and net leases discussed earlier. Single tenant industrial properties can also be NNN-leased.

Industrial buildings have unique features that may be unfamiliar to some investors. Some of the characteristics that an astute investor needs to be informed about include truck doors, truck docks, ceiling heights, floor loads, utility capacity, and even railroad sidings.

Industrial building may include overhead garage-type doors with higher clearances to allow for larger, taller trucks to drive into the building. This allows these vehicles to be loaded or serviced in a controlled environment. Another feature is a truck dock. A truck dock is a door at an elevation equal to the floor of the typical trailer of a tractor-trailer truck. This arrangement is designed to facilitate loading the trailer without having to lift the items being loaded. Truck docks are constructed by either elevating the floor of the facility or by excavating an approach for the tractor-trailer.

Ceiling heights in an industrial facility can be critical. Some manufacturing processes involve overhead cranes. Buildings with low ceiling heights can be obsolete.

Industrial buildings may need to house heavy manufacturing equipment or be subjected to other stresses mandating greater floor load-bearing capability. Industrial tenants can also be voracious users of electric power or other energy sources. Modern industrial buildings need to be able to accommodate these unique needs.

Older retail, office, and residential properties can feature the charm of a by-gone era. That's rarely the case with industrial properties. Obsolescence can be a death sentence in industrial real estate. The most obvious example is the older, vertical factory building. These properties may live on if converted to loft condominiums, but their usefulness to industrial tenants has been over for a long time.

Further, these properties can have hidden or not so hidden environmental contamination. Sometimes, the cost of cleaning up some of these sites exceeds the value of the real estate! These old, contaminated industrial sites are often called brownfields.

Before getting involved in any kind of older industrial building, you would minimally want a Phase One environmental study performed on the property.

A Phase One environmental study is an inquiry into land use in an effort to determine whether the site might be subject to contamination. No soil borings are taken. Instead, the contractor studies various records to determine the historical use of the site.

If the history shows that the site was undeveloped land before becoming farmland before becoming a home site, then the probability of contamination is remote. The study will also consider known contaminated sites that may be in proximity to the subject site to determine if the site was contaminated indirectly.

Contamination may be direct or indirect. An example of direct contamination would be a site that used to be a gasoline station that had underground storage tanks that leaked. An instance of indirect contamination would be the home near the gas station that suffered contamination because it was downstream in the flow of ground water from the gas station.

Lenders may require a Phase One study if they are concerned about the environmental integrity of a site they are financing. Therefore, these institutions are a great source of qualified contractors.

Alternatively, you can consult the yellow pages of your local phone book under Environmental and Ecological Services or comparable headings.

The minimum cost of a Phase One study is probably at least $1,000 and it goes up from there, depending on circumstances.

Author's Advice

Obtaining a Phase One study is a wise move for the acquisition of any type of commercial property. The cost of an environmental cleanup can exceed the value of the real estate!

If contamination is suspected as a result of the study, then you would proceed to a Phase Two study, where actual soil borings are taken and analyzed in a lab.

Larger Apartment Buildings

Larger apartment buildings are properties containing five residential units or more. It is appropriate to include these investments in commercial real estate even though the buildings obviously contain residences. The reasoning is the lending parameters for larger apartment houses have more in common with other commercial properties than with one to four unit residential properties. For example, the loan made on these larger apartment properties is typically a portfolio loan held by the lender and not sold on the secondary market.

Five-unit and larger apartment buildings obviously have much in common with their smaller cousins, but there are some important differences.

The American dream is to own a single-family home. If that dream is out of reach, the next best alternative is to rent one. But single-family homes represent the most expensive rental option in most markets. Therefore, the prospective tenant may have to make further compromises, perhaps renting one half of a duplex. Larger apartment buildings are further removed from the American dream, but they are also usually cheaper in rent.

With smaller rentals, the landlord may be able to delegate snow removal, lawn care, and all utilities to the tenant. In larger apartment buildings, tenants typically do not participate in any lawn care or snow removal. In many larger buildings, the water and sewer utility is included in the rent. Heat and hot water may also be part of the rent as well.

This situation presents both advantages and disadvantages. Obviously, the landlord has more work to do and more bills to pay with larger apartments. However, being released from these obligations can be an appealing benefit to tenants. Some apartment complexes are lavishly landscaped, allowing the residents to enjoy a park-like setting without any gardening responsibility.

For the growing landlord, consolidating a number of smaller 1- to 4-unit rentals into one or two larger apartment buildings may make management responsibilities much easier. Most investors who continue to acquire more and more residential investment real estate eventually purchase larger apartment buildings.

Bigger Isn't Always Better

It is easy to be intimidated by commercial real estate. Residential real estate is familiar. Everyone lives in some. However, commercial real estate does not need to be off-limits for the small investor.

Smaller commercial buildings can take on some of the characteristics of residential real estate while still maintaining some of the ease of management associated with commercial real estate. Smaller buildings mean smaller tenants, tenants who can be found more quickly without employing or paying a leasing broker.

These tenants will tend to be less demanding and more willing to take the space "as is" or with minimal improvements. Many of these tenants may be new businesses or one-person operations without much track record. Accordingly, these tenants may also be prone to higher failure, delinquency, and collection problems.

Other Important Factors

Commercial properties can be the end game of a successful real estate investing career. Moving into commercial real estate can be the management remedy for the investor wishing to enjoy the fruits of success by curtailing his or her management responsibilities.

Getting Started in Commercial Real Estate

Although owning commercial properties can be the final stages of a successful real estate career, you don't have to wait until that day to get started. Acquiring commercial properties may not be the most prudent first step for most beginning investors, but once you have a little experience, it could be right for you. If you understand the extra risks involved, don't hesitate to take advantage of opportunities in commercial properties.

The best place to start is with larger apartment buildings. You have already learned about some of the unique characteristics of these commercial properties. However, these buildings are still residences, an experienced area for you.

Although buying commercial apartment buildings is a good step, some investors will be attracted to the easier management profile of office, retail, or industrial real estate. A neighborhood office building, small strip center, or industrial building might look attractive to these investors.

An investor considering any kind of office, retail, or industrial space should give careful consideration to the leases. You want to study the leases' expirations. You should know the kind of notice required for any tenant to vacate. Sometimes retail tenants can have a clause in their lease allowing them to vacate if the *anchor tenant* in a strip mall goes *dark*.

def•i•ni•tion

The **anchor tenant** is the main tenant or largest tenant in a property. In retail real estate, the anchor tenant could be a grocery store or a large department store. Referring to space as being **dark** means that it is vacant.

The investor should also study the tenant history for any commercial space. Tenants in smaller commercial buildings may not be committed to long-term leases. However, reviewing the history of these tenancies may reveal that these tenants have been at the location for a long time, faithfully renewing their leases again and again.

Think about how your commercial tenants conduct their business. If the tenant regularly has customers coming to his or her place of business, then that tenant has more invested in the present location. Moving risks losing customers, so the tenant is less likely to vacate. A successful restaurant is a classic example. A plumbing contractor leasing industrial space is a tenant who could more easily move.

Real Estate Partnerships

One way to overcome the higher down payments that may be required in commercial real estate is to form a partnership. Years ago, four doctors contributed $25,000 each to be able to invest $100,000. They borrowed an additional $200,000, and built convenience stores to lease out to a local dairy. The doctors were able to duplicate the formula repeatedly.

Partnerships can be great or grating. A business partnership is much like a marriage and should only be entered into with care. Partnerships inject added complexities and diminish your control. Prudent safeguards are warranted.

Think of why you are forming the partnership. It may be great that you and your partner are good friends, but each member of the partnership should add something to the union that makes the whole greater than the sum of the parts. A good illustration is the partnership where one partner has the financial strength and the other partner provides real estate expertise. The more the partners need each other, the better off the partnership will be.

Each of the partners' duties should be different and clearly defined. Perhaps one partner is the deal-maker and the other handles the day-to-day management. Include each partner's duties in a written partnership agreement.

Your partnership agreement should also include dissolution language in the event of disability or death of a partner or disagreement between the partners. In the event of disagreement, require the matter to be resolved through binding arbitration. Otherwise, you may find yourself mired in litigation for years.

Some other things you should consider before getting started in commercial real estate investing are the following:

- Financing is structured differently than it is for residential properties. Rates, terms, and down payments are different. Usually the interest rate is higher, the term is shorter, and the down payment is greater.
- Residential lenders do not regularly lend money for commercial property.
- Insuring a commercial property is underwritten differently, and generally costs more. Before entering into a purchase contract, be sure to speak with your insurance agent, and understand any complications in insuring your risk in the building. Increased liability insurance is often required.
- Real estate investors buying commercial property to hold for cash flow should prepare for long droughts of reduced monthly income in the event a major tenant vacates.
- Small commercial properties are often great investments for real estate investors. Small businesses need office and retail space. Locations along major commercial routes and in or near other established commercial districts are ideal for this type of investment.
- There are many different types of commercial property opportunities for investors.
- It isn't unusual to ask for, and receive, partial seller financing on a commercial property.
- Commercial properties can attract quality tenants, such as lawyers, accountants, medical providers, and other professionals. These types of tenants can provide steady cash flow to the owner of the commercial property.
- Zoning is often a factor in determining the value of commercial property. Because zoning will define how a property is used, a change in zoning to a better use can result in an increase in value.

By expanding your horizons to include commercial properties, now the entire real estate marketplace presents a profit opportunity for you. Depending on your financial ability, management experience, and investment preferences, you may find commercial real estate the perfect fit.

The Least You Need to Know

- You may find that commercial properties are more difficult to finance.
- Commercial properties are riskier that residential, but can be easier to manage.
- Larger apartment buildings are often the next logical step for the small investor.
- Study the leases and the occupancy history for any commercial property.

Appendix A

Glossary

1003 The form used by lenders to create an application for a mortgage.

acre An area of land consisting of 43,560 square feet.

adjustable rate mortgage A mortgage, commonly called an ARM, where the interest rate adjusts at predetermined times. The interest rate can go up or down, based on an agreed standard, at specific intervals. The change is usually subject to a limit, or cap, and cannot exceed that amount.

amenity A feature of the home or property that serves as a benefit. It can be a natural feature, such as a lake or waterfall, or a man-made feature, such as a swimming pool or hot tub.

amortization The repayment of a loan through regularly scheduled payments of interest and principal.

annual percentage rate A calculated formula to determine and show the actual cost of the loan, always expressed in a percentage rate. The annual percentage rate (APR) includes the interest, points, mortgage insurance, and other costs associated with the loan.

application The formal request for a loan from a lender.

appraisal The document that expresses the fair market value (FMV) of the property. Lenders require an appraisal to ascertain that the property value is in line with the loan requested.

appraiser The licensed professional experienced and trained to render an appraisal of a property. The lender hires the appraiser, but the borrower usually pays the appraiser's fee.

appreciation Changes in market conditions or improvements in the property that increase the value of the property.

assessed value The value of real estate as determined by a government entity for the purpose of taxation. This is often less than the fair market value.

assessor The government official who determines the assessed value of a property. That value is then used by a taxing authority to collect property taxes.

association fee *See* Homeowners' Association.

assumable mortgage A mortgage that can be transferred from the seller to the buyer.

back-end ratio The borrower's other debts, included in the debt-to-income ratio to determine if the borrower can make loan payments. The other debts are the monthly minimum required amount that must be paid on such things as car loans, court-ordered child support, and credit card payments.

balloon mortgage A mortgage that requires a large payoff at a specific time. Initially, the monthly payments are lower, but on a specific date (commonly 3 to 7 years), the entire final payment is due.

bankruptcy Controlled by Federal law, when a person can no longer pay their monthly obligations, they turn their assets over to a trustee, which in turn pays off outstanding debts. A federal judge then discharges any remaining debt, allowing the person a fresh start.

basic policy A basic homeowner's insurance policy that covers specific perils or hazards such as fire or wind damage. Also frequently called an HO-1.

basis points A finance term, it is one percent of one percent (.001 or .1%). For example, 75 basis points is .75 or .75%. If a loan of 6% were increased by 75 basis points, the new rate would be 6.75%.

borrower The person who borrows money from a lender.

broker A licensed real estate professional who has been authorized to open and run his or her own agency. All real estate offices have one principal broker, sometimes called the broker of record.

budget The detailed record of expenditures and income.

building code A set of ordinances, rules, regulations, or laws that determines the standards of design, materials, construction, and workmanship in a building.

buyer's agent A real estate agent hired by a buyer to help him or her find and negotiate the purchase of the home. The buyer's agent works for the best interests of the buyer, and not the seller of the property.

buyer's market The condition when sellers significantly outnumber buyers, driving prices down.

cap A limit, such as the maximum interest rate or increase of a monthly payment used in an adjustable rate mortgage.

cash reserves A sum of money to be held in reserve for a specific purpose.

cash-out refinance During the refinancing of a loan secured by real estate, a borrower may seek a loan at a higher amount than the current loan balance. When this occurs, the borrower is seeking a "cash-out" loan by pulling out money for personal use.

certificate of title Issued by a title company or title insurer, it certifies that the title of the property is clear from any liens or claims of others.

clear title A title to real estate that is free of any liens or legal questions as to ownership of the property.

closing Sometimes called settlement, this is the time when the property is formally sold and transferred from the seller to the buyer, with all costs paid and settled. The buyer assumes the loan obligation, the seller receives all money due, and the property is titled to the buyer.

closing costs The costs associated with purchasing and transferring real estate from the seller to the buyer.

collateral Property pledged as security of a loan.

commission The amount paid by a seller to a real estate agent for negotiating the sale of the property. The fee is usually a percentage of the selling price.

commitment letter Formal correspondence from the lender offering a loan to the borrower. The letter states the terms under which the loan is offered by the lender.

common areas Sometimes also called common grounds, it is an area of a multiunit complex that is available for use by all the owners of the housing units.

comparable market analysis A report created by a real estate agent that surveys the comparable homes recently sold and currently offered for sale in the market area.

comps Recently sold properties that are comparable to the subject property. Comps or comparables are used to establish the fair market value.

condominium A form of ownership where individuals purchase and own a unit of housing in a multiunit complex. The owners also share in the financial responsibility of the common areas.

contingency A provision included in a purchase offer stating that certain events or conditions must occur before the contract is valid.

conventional loan A loan that was created by the private sector, and does not include any government-backed guarantee against the borrower's default.

cooperative A corporation is formed to purchase a multiunit building, and ownership of each unit is purchased by buying a share of the corporation. Cooperatives are often called co-ops.

counteroffer An offer made by either the buyer or seller to the other that changes the previous offer of the other.

covenants and restrictions Rules or regulations that control the types of changes and additions that can be made to a property or condominium within a community. Sometimes called CCRs (community covenants and restrictions).

credit bureaus The large corporations that gather credit history and sell the information as a credit report.

credit history The history of an individual's past credit performance. This record is used by lenders to determine if the person is capable of repaying the loan. The history is maintained by credit bureaus.

credit report A record of an individual's credit history, obtained from Equifax, Experian, and TransUnion, the three major credit bureaus.

credit score A number representing the creditworthiness of an individual. The higher the number better, a score of 720 and above is considered good.

debt-to-income ratio The comparison of gross monthly income to the amount of debt being undertaken by a borrower. The standard is 28%/36%, which means that the total housing payment cannot exceed 28% of the borrower's gross income, and the proposed housing payment plus all other debt cannot exceed 36% of the total gross income. These percentages can vary slightly from lender to lender.

deed The document that establishes ownership of real estate.

deed in lieu of foreclosure Rather than undergo the expense of foreclosure, the borrower turns over the deed of the property to the lender, and surrenders possession.

deed of trust A deed of trust is similar to a mortgage. Rather than recording a mortgage, some jurisdictions record a deed of trust.

default The failure to comply with the terms of the loan by not making monthly payments or meeting other obligations, such as maintaining adequate property insurance.

delinquency The failure to make timely payments by the borrower to the lender.

depreciation The decline of the value of the property because of poor maintenance, declining neighborhood, or other factors. The opposite of appreciation.

developer A person or company that acquires real estate, improves it (often by building new houses), and sells it.

discount point A payment made at closing to reduce the amount of the loan's interest rate.

down payment The amount of the purchase price paid with the borrower's funds and not financed.

earnest money The money put up front by a buyer when presenting an offer to the seller.

easement A right granted by the property owner to another to use the property. For example, the telephone company may have an easement to access a telephone pole on the property.

effective age An appraiser's estimate of the physical condition of a building, or how long it may be expected to be useful. The actual age of a building may be shorter or longer.

eminent domain The right of government to take private property for public use after payment of its fair market value to the property owner.

encroachment An improvement to one property that intrudes unlawfully onto another property.

encumbrance Anything that affects or limits the fee simple title to real estate, such as a mortgage, leases, easements, or restrictions.

Equal Credit Opportunity Act A federal law, the Equal Credit Opportunity Act (ECOA) requires lenders and other creditors to make credit equally available without discrimination based on race, color, religion, national origin, age, sex, marital status, or receipt of income from public assistance programs.

equity The owner's financial interest in the property. It is determined by subtracting any outstanding loans from the fair market value of the property.

escrow account A separate trust account established to pay specific items. For example, a lender establishes an escrow account for a borrower, and each month, the borrower pays 1⁄12 of the property taxes. When the tax bill is received, funds from the escrow account are used to pay the taxes owed.

Fair Housing Act A federal law that prohibits discrimination in all facets of the home-buying process on the basis of race, color, national origin, religion, sex, familial status, or disability.

fair market value A hypothetical price that a willing buyer and seller would agree upon when they are acting freely, carefully, and with complete knowledge of the conditions of the property.

Fannie Mae The nickname used for the Federal National Mortgage Association (FNMA), which is a government-chartered, nonbank, financial services corporation. It is the nation's largest source of financing mortgages.

fee simple The greatest possible interest or strongest possible ownership position a person can have in real estate. This term is often used with deeds, such as a fee simple deed.

FHA The Federal Housing Authority that guarantees home loans. Only 3% down payment is required for an FHA home loan.

FICO score A computer-generated number from the Fair, Isaacs Co. between 300 and 800 that lenders use to determine your creditworthiness. The higher the number, the more creditworthy you are.

first mortgage The mortgage that is in first place among any loans recorded against a property.

fixed-rate mortgage A mortgage where the interest rate remains unchanged throughout the term of the loan.

Fizz-bo *See* FSBO.

flood insurance Insurance that offers coverage for damage caused by rising water. It is required in federally-designated flood areas. Regular homeowner insurance policies do not provide flood insurance coverage.

FmHA The Farmer's Home Loan Administration, which offers guaranteed loans in rural areas. FmHA is a part of the U.S. Department of Agriculture.

foreclosure The legal process in which the lender seizes the property because the borrower defaulted on the loan.

Freddie Mac The nickname used for the Federal Home Loan Mortgage Corp. (FHLMC), which is a government-chartered, nonbank corporation that buys pools of mortgages from lenders and sells securities backed by those mortgages.

front-end ratio The ratio of the borrower's monthly housing payment. It is the percentage of the monthly housing payment in comparison to the borrower's monthly income.

FSBO An abbreviation that means For Sale By Owner. It describes when a property owner chooses to sell a property without the services of a real estate agent.

gated community A private community where you must pass through a security gate for access.

gift letter A letter presented to you by someone giving you funds for the purchase of real estate. A copy of this letter must be provided to the lender as part of your application.

Ginnie Mae The nickname of the Government National Mortgage Association (GNMA), a government-owned corporation overseen by the U.S. Department of Housing and Urban Development. Ginnie Mae pools FHA-insured and VA-guaranteed loans to back securities for private investment.

good faith estimate An estimate of all closing fees, including prepaid and escrow items as well as the lender charges. This estimate must be presented to the borrower within three days after submission of a loan application.

government loan A mortgage guaranteed by FHA, FmHA, or VA.

grantee The person to whom an interest in real property is conveyed.

grantor The person conveying an interest in real property.

hazard insurance Insurance coverage for physical damage to property caused by accident.

HELOC An abbreviation for Home Equity Line of Credit.

home inspection An examination of the structure and mechanical systems to determine a home's safety and condition. The inspection allows a potential home-buyer to become aware of any repairs that may be needed.

Homeowners' Association A nonprofit association that manages the common areas of a planned unit development (PUD) or condominium project. Unit owners pay a monthly fee to the association to maintain common areas such as a pool and for services such as landscaping and utilities.

homeowner's insurance An insurance policy that combines protection against damage to a dwelling and its contents with protection against claims of negligence.

home warranty A contract that offers protection for mechanical systems and attached appliances against unexpected repairs.

housing counseling agency An agency that provides counseling and assistance to individuals on a variety of issues, including loan default, fair housing, and home buying.

housing ratio The ratio of the housing payment (principal, interest, taxes, and insurance) to the gross monthly income. It is also called the *front-end ratio.*

HUD The U.S. Department of Housing and Urban Development. It works to create a decent home and suitable living environment for all Americans by addressing housing needs, improving and developing American communities, and enforcing fair housing laws.

HUD-1 Statement Used at the time of closing, it is also known as the settlement sheet. This is a standard form used to itemize all closing costs. It must be given to the borrower at closing.

HVAC An abbreviation for Heating, Ventilation, and Air Conditioning. It is sometimes used to describe a home's heating and cooling system.

index An economic indicator used to establish the rate of an adjustable rate mortgage.

inspection *See* home inspection.

insurance The protection of risk from specific loss is transferred to another by the payment of a premium.

interest A fee charged for the use of money.

interest rate The percentage a lender charges for borrowing money.

investment property Real estate acquired for the purpose of producing monthly rental income or to resell for more than its purchase price.

investor A person who buys real estate for investments.

judgment A legal decision requiring debt repayment.

joint tenancy An equal and undivided ownership in a property by two or more individuals.

jumbo mortgage A mortgage greater than the amount of the limit set by Fannie Mae or Freddie Mac. Jumbo mortgages carry a higher interest rate than conventional mortgages.

lease A written agreement between the property owner and a tenant that stipulates the payment and conditions under which the tenant may occupy and use the real estate for a specific period of time.

lease purchase An alternative financing option that allows a buyer to lease a home with an option to buy.

legal description A property description, recognized by law, that is sufficient to locate and identify the property.

lender A term that refers to the institution or individual making the loan.

liabilities A person's financial obligations.

liability insurance Insurance coverage that offers protection against claims alleging negligence resulting in bodily injury or property damage to another.

lien A legal claim against a property that must be paid off when the property is sold. A mortgage is a lien.

life cap Used with an adjustable rate mortgage, this is the limit on the amount that the interest rate can increase over the life of the mortgage.

line of credit An agreement by a lender to extend credit up to a certain amount for a certain time to a specified borrower.

loan The sum of borrowed money that is repaid with interest.

loan officer The representative of the lender. Often referred to by other names, such as loan representative, the loan officer solicits loans.

loan origination fee A fee charged by the lender. It is usually 1 percent.

loan servicing After closing the loan, the borrower makes payments as directed by the lender. The company that receives the payments is providing loan servicing. Loan servicing includes the processing of payments, sending statements, managing the escrow accounts, etc.

loan-to-value ratio A formula to determine how much you have financed as opposed to the fair market value of the property, it is often called LTV. It is expressed as a percentage, and shows how much you have financed. If you have financed 75 percent of the value of the property, you have a 75 percent LTV.

lock-in The guarantee of a certain interest rate for a specific period of time.

LTV *See* loan-to-value ratio.

maintenance fee A fee charged by a Homeowners' Association for the upkeep of the common areas of the property.

MLS *See* multiple listing service.

mortgage A legal document that pledges your real estate as security for a loan. The property is the collateral for the amount you borrowed.

mortgage broker An intermediary who arranges a loan for a borrower with a lender for a fee.

mortgage insurance Insurance that covers the lender against some of the losses incurred as a result of a default on a home loan. It is sometimes called PMI, meaning private mortgage insurance. Mortgage insurance is sometimes issued by the government with its guaranteed loan programs, or is available from private companies.

mortgage insurance premium The amount paid by the borrower for mortgage insurance.

mortgagee The lender.

mortgagor The borrower.

multiple listing service A computerized listing service for the homes for sale listed with a Realtor. It is often called MLS. Real estate agents are granted access to the MLS and can use it to locate homes for sale.

negative amortization A type of loan situation where the monthly payment does not cover the principal and interest. The loan balance grows larger instead of smaller.

net income The amount of income earned after expenses.

no-cash-out refinance A refinance loan that does not put cash in the hand of the borrower. The new loan is calculated to cover the balance due on the current loan and any costs associated with obtaining the new mortgage.

no-cost loan Some lenders offer loans at "no cost." The lender pays all costs, but these loans usually are available at a higher interest rate.

note A legal document obligating a borrower to repay a loan at a stated interest rate during a specified period of time.

note rate The interest rate stated on a note.

nothing down *See* zero-down-payment mortgage.

notice of default A formal written notice to a borrower that a default has occurred and that legal action may be taken.

offer A written document submitted by the buyer to the seller offering to purchase their property. After both parties agree, it becomes a legally binding contract. Sometimes called a purchase agreement or sales agreement.

owner financing A purchase transaction in which the property seller provides all or part of the financing to the buyer.

PITI An abbreviation (pronounced pity) that stands for principal, interest, taxes, and insurance.

planned unit development A type of property ownership where individuals actually own the building or unit they live in, but common areas are owned jointly with the other members of the development or association.

PMI An abbreviation for private mortgage insurance. *See* mortgage insurance.

point A point is one percent (1%) of the amount of the mortgage.

preapproved The process of meeting with a lender and providing all financial information to obtain a preliminary financing commitment prior to making an offer to purchase.

prequalified Informally discussing with a lender your ability to borrow, and learning the range of a loan you are likely able to obtain.

principal The amount of money borrowed from a lender to purchase real estate.

property inspection *See* home inspection.

punch list The things that need to be fixed by the contractor or seller before the buyer takes possession.

purchase agreement *See* offer.

qualifying ratio The percentages a lender uses to determine whether you are qualified for a loan.

quitclaim deed A formal legal document that denies a claim to a certain property. It is used to clear problems with a title, and is commonly used in divorce settlements.

radon A radioactive gas found in some homes that, if occurring in strong enough concentrations, can cause health problems.

rate *See* interest rate.

rate lock *See* lock-in.

real estate agent An individual who is licensed to negotiate and arrange the sales of real estate. A real estate agent works for a real estate broker.

real estate broker *See* broker.

real estate investor *See* investor.

Realtor® A real estate agent or broker who is a member of the National Association of Realtors. Realtor is a registered trademark of the Association.

recorder The public official who keeps records of transactions that affect real property in the county. Sometimes also called the "Registrar of Deeds" or "County Clerk."

refinance To obtain a new loan in order to pay off the existing mortgage.

REIT An abbreviation for Real Estate Investment Trust. A REIT invests primarily in real estate and mortgages and passes income, losses, and other tax items to its investors.

RESPA An abbreviation for the Real Estate Settlement Procedures Act. It is a law protecting consumers from abuses during the residential real estate purchase and loan process by requiring lenders to disclose all settlement costs, practices, and relationships.

Rural Home Loan *See* FmHA.

sales agreement *See* offer.

second mortgage A type of mortgage on a property that already has a lien on it in the form of a first mortgage.

seller disclosure A form required by most states that must be completed by the seller that discloses any known defects of the property.

seller's market The condition when buyers significantly outnumber sellers, driving prices up.

settlement sheet *See* HUD-1 Statement.

starter home A house that is relatively small and inexpensive, and is bought as a first home.

subdivision A piece of land divided into plots for building lots for homes.

subprime mortgage A mortgage granted to a borrower who is considered less than perfect. Often the borrower has less than perfect credit, or is unable to easily document income (self-employed). Lenders usually charge a higher interest rate for subprime loans.

survey The examination of a property's boundaries.

sweat equity Using labor to build or improve a property as part of the down payment.

term The length of the loan.

title The right of property ownership.

title insurance Insurance that protects the lender and buyer against any losses from disputes over the title of a property.

title search The process of searching court records to make sure no liens or claims are outstanding against a property.

treasury index An index used to set interest rate changes for adjustable rate mortgages.

Truth-in-Lending A federal law obligating a lender to give full written disclosure of all fees, terms, and conditions associated with the loan's initial period and then adjusts to another rate that lasts for the term of the loan.

underwriting The process of evaluating a loan application to determine whether the loan is a good risk.

VA Department of Veterans Affairs; a federal agency that guarantees the home loans made to veterans. The program offered by the VA is similar to mortgage insurance. The loan guarantee protects lenders against losses that may result if a borrower defaults.

VA loan A home loan issued by the VA.

walk-through A buyer's final inspection of a property, usually on the day of closing or the day before.

wraparound mortgage A new mortgage that includes the remaining balance on an old mortgage, plus the new amount.

zero-down-payment mortgage A mortgage in which the buyer does not make a down payment and borrows the entire purchase price.

zoning Local laws and ordinances that establish or restrict the use of properties and what codes must be followed for new buildings.

Appendix B

Important Forms

This appendix includes the basic forms that you will need to get started in real estate investing. Included are a sample purchase agreement, residential lease agreement, and rental application. Please note that these forms are intended for educational purposes only. Because real estate laws vary by state, it would be impossible to produce a form that would be suitable for use everywhere. You should approach your local apartment association or a real estate attorney about obtaining the proper forms and contracts for your actual use.

PURCHASE AGREEMENT

Date: ______________________

PARTIES:

Buyer: ____

Seller: ____

PROPERTY:

Street Address: ________________________________

Legal Description: ______________________________

____

Included Personal Property: ________________________

____

Excluded Property: ______________________________

PRICE:

________________________________ ($)

FINANCIAL STRUCTURE:

Earnest Money	$__________
Cash to Seller at Closing	$__________
Assumption of Existing Loans/Liens	$__________
New Financing	$__________
New Loan to Seller at Closing	$__________
The sum of the above items should equal the Purchase Price	$__________

The purchase price to be paid as follows:

1. **EARNEST MONEY.** Earnest money shall be deposited with a licensed title company or a mutually agreeable attorney within 72 hours of acceptance by Seller.

2. **FINANCING.** The Buyer shall (obtain new financing) (assume existing financing) (strike one) as described below:

Loan Amount: $ ____________
Interest Rate: ______________%
Amortization: ______________ years
Term: ______________ years
Payment: ______________ monthly

Buyer to obtain a written financing commitment within _____ days of acceptance. The interest rate shall be locked for an initial period of ____ months, at which time the interest rate may be adjusted by not more than _____% per year. The maximum interest rate shall not exceed _____%.

Buyer shall pay all costs associated with obtaining this financing, including any loan origination fee not to exceed _____% of the loan amount.

Cash to Seller at closing shall be adjusted as necessary for any understatement or overstatement of the balance of any financing assumed by the Buyer.

3. **LOAN TO SELLER.** The Seller shall hold a note secured by a second mortgage on the subject property as described below:

Loan Amount: $ ____________
Interest Rate: ______________%
Amortization: ______________ years
Term: ______________ years
Payment: ______________ monthly

The interest rate shall be locked for an initial period of ____ months, at which time the interest rate may be adjusted by not more than _____% per year. The maximum interest rate shall not exceed _____%.

OTHER CONTRACT TERMS

1. **ACCEPTANCE:** This offer is binding only if an accepted copy of this offer is delivered to the Buyer by ______________________________.

2. **PRORATIONS AND SECURITY DEPOSITS:** Loan interest, property taxes, property owner's association assessments, insurance, rents, utilities, and fuel shall be prorated as of the date of closing. All security deposits shall be transferred to buyer at closing.

3. **PROPERTY CONDITION**: Seller warrants and represents to Buyer that Seller has no notice or knowledge of any conditions adversely affecting the Property or this Transaction, including:
   a. Public Improvements. Improvements planned or commenced which may result in a special assessment or may otherwise materially affect the Property or its present use.
   b. Repair Orders. Repair orders issued by government agencies or court order.
   c. Reassessment. Pending or contemplated reassessment of the Property for property tax purposes.
   d. Land Divisions. Any land divisions of the subject property for which required approvals had not been obtained.
   e. Adverse Conditions. Conditions adversely affecting the cost of building on the subject property including, but not limited to, unstable fill, subsurface foundations, rock or low load bearing capacity, disposal or dumping on the Property of toxic or hazardous materials, or high water table.
   f. Storage Tanks. Underground storage tanks (USTs) or aboveground storage tanks (ASTs) on the Property for storage of flammable or combustible liquids or materials including but not limited to gasoline, heating oil or similar substances which are currently or which were previously located on the subject property.
   g. Use. Violation of any laws regarding or regulating the use of the Property.
   h. Environmental laws. Violation of any environmental laws regarding the Property.
   i. Systems Not Serving the Property. Septic tanks, cisterns, 100 KV or higher high voltage electric, steel natural gas lines, or similar systems on the Property that do not service the Property.
   j. Flood Plain, Shoreland, or Wetland. Any portion of the subject property being in a shoreland zoning area, wetland, or 100 year floodplain, according to any government laws.
   k. Appliances and Mechanical Systems. Appliances or mechanical systems not in good working order.
   l. Other Adverse Conditions. Any other adverse condition constituting a health or safety hazard at the Property which would materially and adversely impact the value of the subject property to a reasonable person with knowledge of the kind and type of the condition or circumstance.

4. **INSPECTIONS:** This offer is subject to the following inspections:

a. Environmental Inspection. This offer is contingent upon Buyer obtaining a satisfactory expert opinion disclosing no defects regarding the environmental integrity of the Property.
b. Property Inspection. This offer is contingent upon Buyer obtaining a satisfactory expert opinion(s) disclosing no defects regarding the Property.

This contingency shall be deemed satisfied unless Buyer within _____ days of acceptance files a written notice objecting to any conditions or defects discovered during the inspections.

5. **CLOSING:** This transaction shall close on or before _______________, 20___. Closing will be held at ___________________________________.

6. **TITLE:** Seller(s) agrees to provide marketable title free and clear of all encumbrances except as outlined in this agreement and pay any required transfer taxes to record the deed and mortgage. Seller agrees to furnish title insurance in the amount of the purchase price, showing no encumbrances or exceptions other than those outlined in this agreement.

7. **LEAD PAINT:** Property built before 1978 may contain lead based paint. Buyer and Seller should enter into a separate Lead Base Paint disclosure agreement and Seller should provide Buyer with a copy of the government pamphlet *Protecting Your Family From Lead In Your Home* if the Property was built prior to 1978.

8. **PROPERTY MAINTENANCE / DAMAGE:** Seller shall maintain the Property until closing in materially the same condition as of the date of acceptance, excepting ordinary wear and tear. If the Property is damaged before closing in an amount less than 5% of the purchase price, Seller shall restore the Property and return it to materially the same condition that it was on the date of acceptance. If the damage exceeds 5% of the purchase price, Seller shall notify Buyer in writing of the damage and this Offer may be withdrawn by the Buyer. If withdrawn as described herein, all earnest money paid by the Buyer shall be refunded to the Buyer. Should Buyer elect to proceed with the purchase despite damage exceeding 5% of the purchase price, the Seller shall either: (1) return the subject property to the same material condition existing prior to the date of acceptance of this offer, excepting ordinary wear and tear OR (2) The Buyer shall be the beneficiary of any insurance proceeds awarded relating to the property damage, in addition to a credit at closing in the amount of the deductible on the Seller's insurance policy.

9. **DEFAULT**: If the Buyer defaults under this contract, all monies deposited by the Buyer(s) shall be retained by the Seller as full liquidated damages. If the Seller defaults, the Buyer may pursue all remedies allowed by law and Seller agrees to be responsible for all costs incurred by Buyer as a result of Seller's default.

10. **SUCCESSORS AND ASSIGNEES**: The terms and conditions of this agreement shall bind all successors, assignees, heirs, administrators, trustees, and executors of the respective parties.

11. **ADDITIONAL CONDITIONS AND TERMS**:
    ____
    ____

12. **NOTICES**: All notices of any kind as described in this Offer shall be in writing and shall be delivered to the parties by facsimile, by hand, or by United States Mail with postage pre-paid, or by any other recognized commercial carrier. Such notices shall be deemed to have been served on the date faxed or mailed, delivery charges or postage pre-paid. All such notices shall be addressed as follows:

To the Seller:	To the Buyer:
Name: ____________________	Name: ____________________
Address: ____________________	Address: ____________________
____________________	____________________
Phone: (____) _____-__________	Phone: (____) _____-__________
Fax: (____) _____-__________	Fax: (____) _____-__________

The undersigned have read the above information, understand it and verify that it is correct.

BUYER:	SELLER:
Name: ____________________	Name: ____________________
Print Name: ____________________	Print Name: ____________________
Date: ____________________	Date: ____________________

BUYER:	SELLER:
Name: ____________________	Name: ____________________
Print Name: ____________________	Print Name: ____________________
Date: ____________________	Date: ____________________

RESIDENTIAL LEASE AGREEMENT

EQUAL HOUSING OPPORTUNITY

SECURITY DEPOSIT	MONTHLY RENT	LEASE TERM: (check one)
$________	$________	☐ One Year ☐ Month to Month Start Date: 4 pm __________ End Date: 10 am __________

Lessor ________ DBA ________ Address ________ ________ Phone ________ Fax ________ E-mail ________	Lessee(s) ________ ________ Jointly & Severally Leased Premises Address: ________ ________
Lessor's Agent for collection of rent and other payments, agent for service of legal process, maintaining and other notices and demands; and Lessor's on-site Manager(s): Phone ________ Name(s) ________ Address ________ ________	Members of Lessee(s) family authorized to live in the leased premises: ________ ________ ________ ________ Total Number of Occupants: ________

Application	Material inaccuracy(s) in the rental application shall render this lease voidable at the Lessor's option.
Assignment Sublet	Lessor and Lessee(s) agree the premises are to be used for residential purposes only. Occupancy is limited to the persons named on this lease agreement. There shall be no Lessee assignment or sublet without prior written consent of the Lessor. Lessee shall remain liable under any assignment or sublet granted by Lessor.

Rent	Lessee(s) shall pay to Lessor all amounts due for rent and any other fees or charges, including any sales tax if applicable, on or before the first day of each month for the term of this lease.
Payments	Payments shall be made payable to: ______________________ and mailed to the Lessor's address above. Notices and other correspondence to Lessor shall be sent to the same address or other such address as Lessor may designate in writing. Payments may be made in the form of cashier's check, personal check, or money order. No cash payments are acceptable. Monthly rent is due the first day of each month during the lease term.
Late fee	Any installment of rent or other charges received later than five days after the first of the month is subject to a late fee of $5 per day with such late fees not to exceed $25 in any one month. Time is of the essence with respect to all payments. Payments are applied first to fees, second to any previous balance, last to current rental due. Any amount due shall not be deemed to be paid until the check clears the bank upon which it is drawn.
NSF	Lessee(s) payments by check that fail to clear the bank for any reason shall be subject to a service charge of $25 in addition to any late charges referred to in the lease. After the second Lessee NSF payment, Lessee will be required to make future payments by cashier's check or money order only. Lessor's acceptance of a partial payment shall not constitute an accord and satisfaction nor shall Lessor forfeit the right to collect any balance due on the account, despite any endorsement, stipulation, or other statement on any check. Lessor may accept partial payment with any conditional endorsement without prejudice to Lessor's right to recover the balance remaining due or may pursue any other remedy available under this lease or by law.
Heat & Utilities	___________ shall be responsible for the heat at their expense. If Lessee(s) is responsible for furnishing heat, Lessee(s) agree to maintain a temperature sufficient to prevent damage to plumbing or any other damage. Should any such damage occur because of Lessee failure to provide adequate heat, Lessee shall be held responsible for any damage. Lessee is responsible for his own gas and electric bills.

	____________ shall pay for the sewer and water utility. In the event Lessee fails to pay any utility charges when due, Lessor, at Lessor's option, may pay the past due utility charges and seek reimbursement from Lessee. Lessee shall pay all charges for telephone and television services. If Lessee(s) vacates prior to the end of this term, Lessee(s) is responsible for the utilities not provided by Lessor to the end of the lease term. Lessee may not withhold rent or terminate this lease due to an interruption in utility service that is the responsibility of the third party utility service provider. Refuse collection shall be paid by __________ and __________ shall provide the containers. Containers shall be stored in the garage until pick-up day.
Delayed Occupancy	If occupancy of leased premises is delayed due to construction or the holding over of a prior Lessee, Lessor shall be liable to Lessee only as follows: This lease shall remain in full force and effect; however, (1) the rent shall be abated on a daily basis during the delay, and (2) in the event that such delay continues for three or more days, Lessee may terminate this lease by giving notice in writing to Lessor no later than the fifth day of such delay, whereupon Lessee shall be entitled only to a refund of the refundable portion of Lessee security deposit, and the refundable portion of any prepaid rent. The above terms do not apply to minor repairs which may appear on a Tenant Inspection Report.
Entry	Lessee agrees advance notice is not required for health, safety or emergency repair situations to preserve and protect the premises or occupants from damage. Lessee(s) agree to allow Lessor and service personnel to enter premises at reasonable times with 12 hours advance notice, with or without Lessee(s) permission, to inspect, make repairs or improvements, show to prospective purchasers or renters, or to comply with any applicable law, regulation, health or safety need. Lessee(s) is deemed to have consented to entry of service personnel upon making request for maintenance services.
Snow & Lawn	________shall be responsible for snow removal. Inclement weather may require Lessee(s) to apply additional salt on walkways as necessary. _________ shall be responsible for grounds keeping, including lawn cutting, weeding and trimming.

Security Deposit	The security deposit is intended for securing this lease and insuring the return of the premises in proper move out condition. Lessee will not substitute this deposit for any part of rental payments, fees or NSF charges. The deposit may be commingled with Lessor's operating funds and Lessee waives any rights to interest payments on the security deposit or prepaid rent. Lessee is responsible for completing and returning to Lessor a Tenant Inspection Report within 7 days of occupancy; Any damages not referenced on the Tenant Inspection Report may be deducted from the deposit. Upon vacating, the premises must be left in a clean, undamaged condition ready for the next occupant. This means the better of: (1) the condition of premises when turned over to Lessee (normal wear and tear excepted) or (2) The condition of premises following the completion of any work preformed to improve the premises (normal wear and tear excepted). Lessee(s) agrees to the assignment of the deposit to a new Owner in the event that the property is sold. All sums due under this lease may be deducted from the deposit, as will the cost of restoring the premises to a clean and rentable condition.
Guests	Temporary guests are limited to one two-week stay every six months, provided their presence does not interfere with the quiet enjoyment of other occupants, and if the number of guests is not excessive for the size of the premises. Lessee(s) is liable for all charges caused by the acts of any guests.
Conduct	Lessee(s), guests, invitees and all occupants will respect the quiet enjoyment of the community at all times.
Pets	Pets are not allowed anytime or anywhere on the premises or grounds, unless Lessor approves such pet in writing and Lessee(s) provide all applicable documents and deposits required.
Liability Loss	Lessee(s) is responsible for insuring Lessee(s) personal property and expressly waives any claims against Lessor for loss or damage thereto by reason of fire, theft, and act of God or other causes other than active negligence of Lessor. Lessor is not liable for injuries to any person unless caused by negligent acts of Lessor. Fish tanks and waterbeds require a liability endorsement form satisfactory to Lessor.

False Alarm	Any false alarm resulting in fines or costs to pay contractors to reset or restore equipment shall be charged to the Lessee(s).
Security Devices	Any security device or service provided by Lessor or others is provided strictly at the option of the Lessor. Lessor is not responsible for any losses to Lessee(s), which may result from failure, disrepair or discontinuance of such systems. This lease creates no contract for or an obligation to provide a security service. Any agreement to provide such service shall be made by Lessee(s) and an independent contractor not associated with Lessor. Lessee(s) hereby indemnifies and holds harmless the Lessor from any claim, losses, liabilities, or demands arising out of or in any way pertaining to security services provided by another. Any locked lobby is not a security system.
Casualty Loss	In the event the leased premise suffers casualty loss or damage as a result of fire or other casualty, and in the event that as a result of such loss or damage the premises are rendered uninhabitable, and in the event the premises may be restored or damages repaired to a condition comparable to their prior condition, then this lease and the liability for rent shall continue, except that liability for rent shall be abated during any period of repair or reconstruction. In the event that the premise cannot be repaired within sixty days from the happening of such injury, than this lease shall cease and terminate from the date of such injury. Liability for rent, damages, and waste, etc. shall not abate if damages are caused by negligence of Lessee(s) their guests, invitees, or occupants.
Hazardous Material	Lessee(s) shall not use or keep any flammable or hazardous material in the premises. Hazardous material shall be understood to mean any material defined as hazardous by any government agency.
Breach of Lease	Lessee(s) shall be liable for all acts of negligence or breaches of this lease by the Lessee(s), Lessee(s) occupants, guests and invitees. If this lease is for a term of one year or less, and should Lessee(s) neglect or fail to perform any of the terms of this lease, Lessor shall give Lessee(s) written notice of such breach requiring Lessee(s) to remedy the breach or vacate the premises on or before a date of at least five days after delivery of such notice. If Lessee(s) fails to comply with such notice

	Lessor may declare this tenancy terminated and institute action to expel Lessee(s) from the premises without limiting the liability of the Lessee(s) for the rent due or to become due under this lease. If Lessee(s) have been given such notice and have remedied the breach or have been permitted to remain in the premises, and within one year of such previous breach, Lessee(s) commits a similar breach, this lease may be terminated if, before such breach is remedied, Lessor give Lessee(s) notice to vacate on or before a date of at least 14 days after delivery of such notice. In the event either party defaults on any requirements of this lease and the other party fails to act on account of that default, the failure to act shall not constitute an amendment of this lease or an indication that later defaults shall result in similar failure to act. All Lessee(s) are jointly and severally liable for the terms and payments under this lease.
Renewal	Renewal of this lease is not automatic. Lessee(s) must give the Lessor and Lessor must receive written notice of termination of tenancy at least sixty (60) days prior to the last day of the Lessee(s) final month of tenancy or this lease shall continue as a month-to-month tenancy. Month-to-month tenancies are also required to submit a sixty (60) day notice.
Sixty (60) Day Notice to Vacate	If Lessee(s) fails to give proper written notice to Lessor, Lessee(s) will be held responsible for rent until the premises begin producing revenue. Vacating notices can only be given for the last day of the month.
Abandonment	If Lessee(s) is absent from the premises for seven (7) consecutive days without notifying the Lessor in writing of such absence, and rent is due on the premises, Lessor will deem the premises abandoned. If Lessee(s) shall leave any property on the premises after vacating or abandoning the premises, the property shall be deemed abandoned and Lessor shall have the right to dispose of said property as provided by law at Lessee(s) expense. If Lessee(s) abandons the premises before the expiration of the lease term, the Lessor shall make a reasonable effort to re-lease the premises, and shall apply any rent received, less the costs of re-leasing, to the rent due or to become due under the terms of this lease. Lessee(s) shall remain liable for any deficiency. Lessee(s) is obligated for the rent and utilities until the apartment begins producing

	revenuer or until the term of the lease expires, whichever comes first. Lessor is not required to mitigate Lessee(s) damages at Lessors expense.
Holding Over	Continuing to occupy the premises after 10:00 am on the last day of the lease term is holding over and may result in a hold over charge. If Lessee(s) retain possession of any part of the leased premises after the termination of this lease or upon termination of Lessee(s) tenancy, whether terminated by lapse of time or otherwise, then in addition to other rights and remedies provided by law, Lessor may treat such retention of possession as constituting a renewal of this lease and so bind Lessee(s) on a month-to–month basis on the same terms and conditions herein, except that the monthly rent will automatically increase to twice the rent in effect for the term immediately preceding the commencement of the holding over. Provisions of this paragraph do not exclude Lessor's rights of re-entry or any right or remedies allowed by law.
Rules & Reg's.	Lessee(s) shall observe and comply with the Rules and Regulations, Additional Lease Provisions, any addendums or notices established by Lessor. Lessor reserves the right to amend any rules and regulations or other documents at any time upon a fourteen-day written notice to Lessee(s). Any violation of the rules and regulations, addendums, or non-standard lease provisions shall be deemed a breach of this lease agreement.
Lead Paint	Premise is / is not housing built prior to 1978. Housing built prior to 1978 may contain lead-based paint. Lead from paint, paint chips or dust can pose health hazards. Lead exposure is especially harmful to young children and pregnant women. Before renting pre-1978 housing, the Lessor must disclose the presence of known lead-based paint hazards in the dwelling. Lessee(s) must receive a federally approved pamphlet on lead poising prevention, "Protect Your Family From Lead in Your Home."
Code Violation	The leased premises are not subject to any code violations.
Rendered Void	Should any part of this lease or any addendums be found unenforceable under any laws or be rendered void by

	government body, only that part of the lease shall be stricken and the remaining portion of all documents shall remain in full force and effect.
Received Copies	Lesee(s) have received a copy of the ____ Additional Lease Terms, ____ Rules and Regulations, ____ Pet Addendum (if applicable), and ____Lead Base Paint booklet and Addendum.
Read All	Lessee(s) have read and understand the terms of this Lease and acknowledge receipt of a copy with all addendums and attachments.
Signature	LESSOR: ______________________________ DATE: ______________________________ LESSEE: ______________________________ DATE: ______________________________ LESSEE: ______________________________ DATE: ______________________________ LESSEE: ______________________________ DATE: ______________________________
Guaranty	Guarantors of Lessee(s): The undersigned guarantee(s) the payment of all amounts due under this Lease and the performance of all Lease terms by Lessee(s). Guarantor: ______________________________ Guarantor: ______________________________ Date: ______________________________

ADDITIONAL LEASE PROVISIONS

EQUAL HOUSING OPPORTUNITY

The following provisions may obligate the Lessee(s) to pay additional sums or result in deductions from the security deposit. These Additional Lease Provisions shall be incorporated into the Lease.

Utilities	Prior to occupying the premises, Lessee(s) shall contact the appropriate utility providers to have services transferred to Lessee(s) name. Failure to transfer services prior to and at the end of the lease term will result in a $25 fee per occurrence. Unpaid utility charges may be deducted from the security deposit. Lessor does not furnish additional connections or line services for television or telephone. Lessee(s) shall contract for such services at Lessee(s) expense. Lessor shall approve any changes in writing in advance.
Filters	Lessee(s) will clean & replace the furnace and air conditioner filters as needed. Failure to keep these filters clean may result in damage to the equipment. Lessor may charge $10 per replacement of each filter.
Pets	If Lessee(s) do not have a pet addendum and Lessee(s) are found to have an unauthorized pet the Lessee(s) will be assessed a fee equal to one months rent, and Lessee(s) will be in breach of their lease. Lessee(s) shall also be liable for any damages.
Repairs / Neglect	Charges resulting from Lessee neglect shall be billed at $25.00 per hour per person if Lessor or Lessor's employee makes the repair. Repairs by contractors shall be billed at cost.
Windows & Window Treatments	Lessee(s) will close all windows during rain and the heating season. Lessee shall be responsible for any damage that should result from a failure to close windows. Failure to close windows may result in a $5.00 charge per window left open. Window treatments and windows will be cleaned both inside and outside upon vacating. Window treatments must appear white from the exterior.
Refuse	Lessee(s) will comply with all government recycling regulations. Failure to comply may result in damage charges billed to Lessee(s). Charges may result from not placing

	refuse in the proper containers, leaving refuse outside of the containers, or not breaking down cardboard. Lessee(s) must take batteries, oil, chemicals, tires and other hazardous wastes to an appropriate disposal site. Trash must not accumulate and must be routinely removed from the premises.
Flooring	With proper care, carpet and vinyl flooring surfaces have an expected life of not less than seven years. Normal wear and tear excludes but is not limited to stains, cuts and tears. Charges against the security deposit for replacement will be based on the depreciated life of the carpet and/or vinyl. Partial replacements or repairs will be completed when possible.
Transfers	Intra-Community transfers shall be subject to a charge of $75.00.
Watering	Water used for landscaping or vehicle washing is not permitted when Lessor provides the water and sewer services.
Special Charges	Potential Additional Charges: $ 30.00 Per hour for any cleaning beyond one hour upon vacating. $ 30.00 Per hour for removal of personal property. $ 25.00 Basement cleaning or other storage areas. $ 25.00 Lock out fee, regaining entry into an apartment or building. $ 12.00 Per cleaning of window tracks, $6.00 per window cleaning. $ 50.00 For any requested lock change of if keys are not returned upon vacating. $ 120.00 Garbage disposal replacement. $ 45.00 Shower and or tub cleaning, each $ 25.00 Toilet cleaning inside and outside. $ 4.00 Per light fixture and switch plate cleaning. $ 35.00 Cleaning louvered bi-fold doors. $ 5.00 For any key replacement. $ 45.00 Range cleaning interior and exterior. $ 10.00 Range hood cleaning. $ 4.00 Per range drip plan replacement. $ 45.00 Refrigerator cleaning inside and out. $ 4.00 Per each cabinet cleaning (doors, shelves, drawers)

Additional Damages	Additional cleaning and damage costs not listed will be assessed as they occur. Costs may be subject to a 15% administrative charge.
Appliances	Appliance repair or replacement made necessary from other than normal wear and tear will be the responsibility of the Lessee(s). Lessee(s) will not install any washer, dryer, dishwasher or air conditioner without prior written permission from Lessor.
Other Occupants	Lessee(s) will be assessed a fee equal to one months rent, and Lessee(s) will be in breach of their lease agreement for any unauthorized persons found occupying the premises.
Specials & Concessions	Any rent special or other concession tendered to Lessee as an inducement to enter into a specific lease term will be immediately refunded to Lessor in full if Lessee(s) do not fulfill the term of the lease in full. Repayment is due at time of notice to vacate. The special for this lease is ____________________________________ ____________________________________
Signatures	LESSOR: ________________________ DATE: ________________________ LESSEE: ________________________ DATE: ________________________ LESSEE: ________________________ DATE: ________________________ LESSEE: ________________________ DATE: ________________________
Guarantor	*Guarantors of Lessee(s): The undersigned guarantee(s) the payment of all amounts due under this Lease and the performance of all Lease terms by Lessee(s).* Guarantor: ________________________ Date: ________________________

RULES & REGULATIONS

These Rules & Regulations are an additional inclusion for the Lease Agreement and may be amended by the Lessor as necessary.

1. Personal Property. Personal property left in common areas may be disposed of by Lessor without further notice.

2. Play Areas. Skating, skateboarding and chalk use is not permitted anywhere on the premises.

3. Neighbors. Lessee(s) are responsible for the conduct of their guests in all areas of the premises. The sound level from TV's, and other audio equipment must not be objectionable to other residents. Minors are to be supervised at all times. Playing in interior common areas is prohibited.

4. Parking Rules. No vehicle storage is allowed. Park only in designated resident and guest parking areas. All vehicles must display current license plates and be moved on a regular basis. No commercial vehicles, recreational vehicles, or trailers are permitted in the parking lots.

5. Fire Lane. Vehicles or bicycles are not permitted in any fire-lane or entry walkways at any time.

6. Security Deposits. Lessee(s) are responsible for the exchange of any security deposits between one or more Lessee if the premise remains occupied.

7. Alterations. Any alterations to premises, including but are not limited to, painting, stenciling, wallpapering, shelf papering, hooks and hangers, anchors, adhesive hangers, non-slip tub decals, stickers, tape and large nails are not permitted without prior written permission from Lessor. Nothing may be attached to the exterior of a building or any interior woodwork or laminated surfaces. Lessor shall without further notice remove any items at Lessee(s) expense if prior written approval was not obtained. All improvements are to inure to the benefit of Lessor unless otherwise stated in writing. Lessee(s) will not alter, change, or install any item that may affect the insurance coverage, create a safety hazard or building code violation, or endanger the premise in any way. Lighting will only have the proper wattage bulbs placed in them.

8. Wiring Changes. Any additional wiring or other connections to the premise must have prior written consent of Lessor. Alterations will be made

according to Lessor instructions for the benefit of the Lessor at the Lessee(s) expense, including maintenance and operation. Lessee(s) will not interfere with any part of the building or any mechanical or electrical system. Lessor shall remove, at Lessee(s) expense, any item attached or installed without prior written consent of Lessor. Installations will become the property of Lessor upon vacating unless otherwise provided. Lessor may require that the building be restored to the original condition at Lessee(s) expense. Lessee(s) will not allow any liens to be attached to the property

9. Patios / Balconies / Decks. Only patio furniture in good condition will be allowed on patios and balconies and no other items. Wind chimes and bird feeders are not permitted.

10. Quiet Hours. Quiet hours are from 9:00 PM to 9:00 AM daily.

11. Vehicles. Vehicle leaks or damage to any surface from a vehicle shall be the Lessee(s) liability. Improperly parked vehicles will be towed at the owner's expense with or without notice to the owner. Vehicle maintenance is not permitted in any parking lots.

12. Smoke Detectors. Lessee will maintain smoke detector batteries in operating condition at all times.

13. Condition. Lessee will keep premises in a clean and tenantable condition and in as good a repair as at the beginning of the lease term, excepting normal wear and tear. Smoke stains, burns and odors are not ordinary wear and tear.

14. Notification. Lessee(s) will inform Lessor in writing of any changes in vehicles, home phone, cell phone, employer and work phone, or emergency contacts.

15. Locks. Neither party shall add or change locks without prior written permission from both parties and must provide the other party with keys to the premises. Denial of access is a breach of the lease.

16. Satellite Dishes. Satellite dishes cannot be attached to the building, and wires will not be bored through the premises without written notice from Lessor prior to any installation.

17. Entry doors. Entry doors and all other doors will remain closed when not in use. Do not slam any door.

18. Laundry room. Remove laundry from the equipment in a timely manner. Clean the lint trap after each use of the dryer. Clean up any spilled laundry detergent or other mess. Smoking or loud music is not permitted. Do not overload the equipment or the user may be held liable for any damages.

19. Insurance. Lessor's insurance policy does not provide coverage for any Lessee(s) personal property. Lessee(s) should obtain rental insurance coverage.

20. Additional Rules. In order to insure the ongoing quiet enjoyment of the premises, Lessor shall maintain the right to make other reasonable rules and regulations as Lessor may deem necessary. Upon notice of such rules, these additional rules shall have the same effect as if originally a part of this Lease.

21. Mail and Packages. If available, as a courtesy, the on site manager may accept packages from US Mail or other commercial carriers for residents who are not at home. No promise is made to be present to accept packages. Lessor is not responsible for any missing or damaged packages.

22. Combustible materials. Combustible materials shall not to be stored anywhere on the premises

23. Identification. Lessor reserves the right to demand Resident identification at any time while on the premises.

24. Garage Sales. Lessee shall not conduct garage, rummage or yard sales of any kind on any part of the premises at any time.

Lessee has read the rules and agrees to abide by the Rules and Regulations listed above.

LESSOR: ______________________________
DATE: ______________________________

LESSEE: ______________________________
DATE: ______________________________

LESSEE: ______________________________
DATE: ______________________________

LESSEE: ______________________________
DATE: ______________________________

PET ADDENDUM

DATE: ______________________________

LESSOR: ______________________________

LESSEE: ______________________________

LESSEE: ______________________________

LESSEE: ______________________________

Apartment/Unit address: ___________________________________

Additional Security Deposit: $ ___________ ________________
refundable / nonrefundable (circle one)

Additional Monthly Pet Rent: $ ____________________________

This Pet Addendum is attached to and made a part of
the Lease dated __________.

Lessee(s) agrees to the following terms and conditions:

1. Only the pet(s) listed and described below are authorized to be kept in the premises.

2. Pet(s) will not cause danger, damage, nuisance, noise, health hazard, or soil the apartment and premises, grounds, common areas, walks, parking areas, landscaping or gardens. Lessee(s) agrees to clean up after the pet(s) and agrees to accept full responsibility and liability for any damage injury, or actions arising from or caused by his/her pet(s).

3. Lessee(s) agrees to not leave food or water for the pet or any other animal outside the dwelling.

4. Lessee(s) agrees to register, license and immunize the pet(s) in accordance with local laws and requirements.

5. Lessee(s) warrants that the pet(s) is housebroken and has no history of causing physical harm to persons or property, and that the pet(s) has no vicious history or tendencies.

6. Lessee's potential liability under this Addendum is not limited to any additional rent or security deposit paid.

7. Lessor's remedy in the event of Lessee's failure to meet Lessee's obligations in this Addendum includes requiring the Lessee to remove the pet(s) from the premises.

8. Dogs and cats must be controlled at all times. Dogs and cats must be kept on a short leash while in common areas or on the grounds.

9. Lessee(s) will properly dispose cat litter on a frequent basis such that there shall be no odors arising from the cat litter.

10. Birds will be properly caged. Seeds and droppings will be cleaned up frequently to prevent accumulation and/or damage to carpeting/floors.

11. Pet(s) description:

Kind	Type or Breed	Color	Name	Age	Weight
______	____________________	______	______	______	______
______	____________________	______	______	______	______

Signatures:

LESSOR: ______________________________
DATE: ______________________________

LESSEE: ______________________________
DATE: ______________________________

LESSEE: ______________________________
DATE: ______________________________

LESSEE: ______________________________
DATE: ______________________________

RENTAL APPLICATION

EQUAL HOUSING OPPORTUNITY

Phone (555) 555-5555 Phone (555) 555-5555 Fax (555) 555-5555

EACH ADULT APPLYING MUST COMPLETE A SEPARATE APPLICATION

Applicant Last Name ______ M.I. ______ Applicant First Name ______ Birthdate ______

Home Phone ______ Work Phone ______ Social Security No. ______

Present Address ______ Apt # ____ Rent: $____ Dates From: ________
City______ State ______ Zip______ To: ______
Landlord's Name ______ Phone: (____) _____ - ______
Previous Address ______ Apt # ____ Rent: $____ Dates From: ________
City______ State ______ Zip______ To: ______
Landlord's Name ______ Phone: (____) _____ - ______
Applicant Employer ______ Dates
Employer Address ______ From: ______
City______ State ______ Zip______ To: ______
Position ______ Supervisor ______
Gross Monthly Wage: $ ______ Supervisor Phone & Extension (____) _____ - ______ X ______
Previous Employer ______ Dates
Employer Address ______ From: ______
City______ State ______ Zip______ To: ______
Position ______ Supervisor ______
Gross Monthly Wage: $ ______ Supervisor Phone & Extension (____) _____ - ______ X ______
Additional Monthly Income $______ Additional Monthly Income $______
Source: ______ Source: ______
Phone: (____) _____ - ______ Phone: (____) _____ - ______
How were you referred to this apartment?
____ Referred by current resident - Resident's name: ______
____ Newspaper Classified Advertisement - Newspaper name: ______
____ Yard sign/banner ____ Rental magazine ____ Other: ______

Applicant: Have you ever been convicted of a felony? Y N

Others sharing occupancy:
Name: ______ Relationship: ______ Age:______
Name: ______ Relationship: ______ Age:______

Applicant's Parent or Relative:
Name: _______________ Relationship: _______________
Address: _______________ Phone: (____) _____ - _______
City: _________________ State: ______ Zip: _________
Automobile Information:
Make of Automobile: ____
Year: __________ License Plate: __________________ State: ______________
Make of Automobile: ____
Year: __________ License Plate: __________________ State: ______________

APARTMENT INFORMATION

(To be completed by Landlord or Manager)

Address of apartment to be rented Apt. # No. of Occupants

_________________________________ ______________ ____________

City ___________________________ State ________________ Zip________
Move in date: _______________________ Rent: $______________________
Lease term: _________________ Days of notice required to vacate: ________
Heat included with rent? __________ Pets: Y N Pet fee: $_____________

The undersigned applicant(s) acknowledge and agree to the following:

1. This application cannot be processed without an application fee. The applicant(s) has tendered an application fee of $___________.
2. If the application is accepted, then the entire application fee shall be applied toward the security deposit of $________. If the application is not accepted, the entire application fee will be refunded by mail to the applicant(s) at the applicant's address as shown on this application.
3. If this application is accepted and applicant(s) fail to occupy the rental premises for any reason, applicant(s) must give written notice to the Landlord or Manager within 48 hours of the date of this application. FAILURE TO GIVE NOTICE WILL RESULT IN FORFEITURE OF THE APPLICATION FEE.
4. By signing below, the applicant(s) grants the Landlord the authority to verify all information given, to access police and other related files, and to obtain a copy of the applicant(s) credit report.
5. The undersigned applicant(s) certify all the information provided is true and accurate. Also that the information and terms of this application become a part of the lease for the rental premises, and any misrepresentations or incomplete applications shall be grounds for rejecting this application or for terminating the lease at the Landlord's option.

I certify that I have read, understand, and agree to all the above terms and conditions.

__________ ______________________ ______________________

Date Applicant Landlord or Manager

Appendix C

Real Estate Websites

This appendix catalogues various places on the Web where you can find property management software, TIC Companies, real estate forms, real estate information, real estate for sale, and foreclosures for sale.

Property Management Software

Realty Software
www.propertymanagementsoftware.cc
$125
Offers free trial
Management Software for all types of rental or leased property including houses, apartments, commercial, industrial, condo, and vacation rentals.
435-649-6149

TenantPro7
www.tenantpro.com
$565.25
Offers free trial
Fully integrated property management software with an accounting system.
Property Automation Software Corporation
1100 Centennial Boulevard, Suite 230
Richardson, TX 75081
1-800-964-2792

Realty Automation Residential & Commercial Property Management Software
www.fullhousesoftware.com
$295
Complete tenant management and accounting software for all types of properties, including single family, multifamily, office, retail, self storage, and condominiums.
1-800-653-8428

Rent Tracker
www.renttracker.com
Free property management software for up to three units
Rent Tracker 10 $49 for up to ten units
Rent Tracker Pro $99 unlimited units
No phone number

TIC (Tenants In Common) Companies

TIC Properties, LLC
www.ticproperties.com
TIC Properties
500 East North St, Suite F
Greenville, SC 29601
864-672-4842

For 1031 LLC
http://hr.for1031.com
For 1031 LLC
12426 Explorer Drive, Suite 220
Boise, ID 83713
1-888-866-1031

Legacy Real Estate & Investments, Inc.
http://legacy1031.com/TIC.htm
Legacy Real Estate & Investments, Inc.
5550 Bates St
Seminole, FL 33772-7149
1-866-891-1031

Real Estate Forms

Rent to Own Lease Addendum
http://reiclub.com/forms/rtoaddendum.pdf
Move in Condition Report
www.totalrealestatesolutions.com/realestateforms/html/RentalMoveInOutChkLst1.html

Real Estate Industry Information websites:

Free Real Estate Forms
www.reiclub.com/real-estate-legal-forms.php

Free Real Estate Forms
www.totalrealestatesolutions.com/realestateforms/index.cfm

IRS Forms
www.irs.gov/formspubs

Real Estate Information

Census Bureau
www.census.gov

Aptresearch.com
Apartment market summaries, employment statistics, building permits
www.aptresearch.com/cgi-bin/searchEngine.cgi?mode=1&randDir=6104-28347-0901104

Urban Land Institute
Multi-family trends
www.uli.org/AM/Template.cfm?Section=Current_Issue2&Template=/TaggedPage/TaggedPageDisplay.cfm&TPLID=54&ContentID=7598

NMHC – National Multi Housing Council
Industry information
www.nmhc.org

Inman News
Industry news
http://inman.com/default.aspx

The Center for Commercial Real Estate
www.1031exchange-tic.com/glossary.htm
Commercial real estate definitions and glossary of real estate terms

Department of Housing and Urban Affairs (HUD)
www.hud.gov

Properties for Sale

Loopnet
Commercial Properties for sale
www.loopnet.com

Realtor.com
Houses and apartments and some commercial properties for sale
www.realtor.com

Foreclosures

HUD foreclosures
www.hud.gov/homes/homesforsale.cfm
Includes links to properties for sale through the IRS, FDIC, VA, SBA, GSA (general service administration) Freddie Mac, and others.
Best single free foreclosure site. Includes links to all others.

Index

Numbers

A

B

C

D

E

J–K

L

O

P

Q–R

S

T

U

V

W-X-Y-Z

Go commercial and reap the rewards!

1-59257-468-8 • $19.95

The Complete Idiot's Guide® to Commercial Real Estate Investing, Third Edition, shows you exactly how to approach the marketplace and determine the type of property that will be your best value.

Available at your favorite booksellers or online retailers

www.idiotsguides.com